IN SEARCH OF ENGLAND

A paean of praise for all the fascinating variety of England's places and people.

Within England's borders life changes mile on mile. Industrial towns give way to moorland, high forests run down to wide estuaries and Morris men perform their ancient dances in the civic centres of new towns. Roy Hattersley celebrates crumbling churches and serene Victorian architecture, magnificent hills and coasts, our music, theatre and local customs. He travels through the literary landscapes of Shakespeare, George Eliot and John Clare and reflects on Larkin and the poetry of Hull, discovers bell ringers in Somerset and truth-seekers on Glastonbury Tor, and salutes the hardy English seaside resort, before returning to his beloved Peak District.

IN SEARCH OF ENGLAND

by

Roy Hattersley

Magna Large Print Books
Long Preston, North Yorkshire,
BD23 4ND, England.

British Library Cataloguing in Publication Data.

Hattersley, Roy
    In search of England.

    A catalogue record of this book is
    available from the British Library

    ISBN   978-0-7505-3279-2

First published in Great Britain in 2009 by Little, Brown

Copyright © This Collection Roy Hattersley 2009

Cover illustration of the Lake District by Andrew Davidson,
originally commissioned by Cumbria Tourism

Published in Large Print 2010 by arrangement with
Little, Brown Book Group Limited

Magna Large Print is an imprint of Library Magna Books Ltd.

Printed and bound in Great Britain by
T.J. (International) Ltd., Cornwall, PL28 8RW

To Buster,
who travelled most of the way with me

CONTENTS

AUTHOR'S NOTE

Most of the articles and essays which follow were first published in newspapers and magazines between the autumn of 1965 and the summer of 2008. The only exceptions are extracts from *Goodbye to Yorkshire*, *A Yorkshire Boyhood* and *Who Goes Home?*, which were published during the same period. The articles are reproduced more or less in their original form – including the (occasionally execrable) headlines. Origin and date of first publication are identified at the end of each piece. In theory the articles have been grouped together according to subject matter. Often the association is vague. Sometimes it is tenuous. Once or twice it is non-existent. 'From the Original Story' has been added to the pieces on English literature because I so enjoyed writing it and in order to demonstrate that even that sacred subject should not be treated too seriously.

Three of the regular columns which I wrote during those forty-three years – 'Listening to England' for the *Guardian*, 'In Search of England' for the *Daily Mail* and 'Letter from Arcadia' for the *Spectator* – were overt and unashamed expressions of affection. Rereading other articles from the same period – columns for the *Spectator*, the *Listener*, *Punch* and the *Guardian* and occasional pieces for *The Times* and *Observer* – I realised that many of them were, subconsciously, variations on the same theme. My only excuse is that they represent my genuine feelings about the England that was, is and yet may be.

INTRODUCTION

I freely admit to being a strange sort of patriot. I have never believed in the unique virtue of the Anglo-Saxon race and I cannot bring myself to rejoice in the thought that once upon a time the sun never set on the British Empire. Nor – even during my wartime school-days – did I glory in the myth that 'soldiers of the queen ... had always won'. Long before I had heard of Isandhlwana and Majuba Hill, I found it impossible to cele-brate the superiority of the Maxim gun over the spear. Even my exposure to the patriotic muse did not make me a juvenile John Bull. I preferred 'laughter learned of friends and gentleness under an English heaven' to 'let dusky Indians whine and kneel, an English lad must die'. I still do. When a clamour arose for Saint George's Day to be made an official holiday, I suggested (in *The Times*) that the proper English reaction to such a suggestion was embarrassment.

I am an Englishman. My passport was issued by the United Kingdom of Great Britain and Northern Ireland and it describes me as a British citizen. But English is what I feel and, therefore, English is what I am. I have never believed that my nationality made me superior to 'lesser breeds without the law' or that, thanks to an accident of birth, I possessed elevated views on liberty, democracy and tolerance which are denied to other races. My allegiance is cultural (which means William Shakespeare and cricket) and geographical (which means the Peak District and the Pennines) and usually I do not make a fuss about it.

Indeed not making a fuss about being English seems to me an essential ingredient of Englishness. If we possess a national characteristic which should be (in Shakespeare's ungrammatical words) 'the envy of less happier lands', it is our emotional reticence – the 'modest stillness' which Henry V regarded as the proper response to peace and security. American school children swear an oath of allegiance to the flag which they fly on their public buildings because the United States is a new country which is unsure of its identity. Italian city squares are decorated with statues of the heroes of the Risorgimento because Italy was only 'unified' a hundred and fifty years ago. The Scots and Welsh proclaim that Scotland and Wales are nations in their own right because – very reasonably in my view – they want their countries to be neither treated nor regarded as an adjunct to England. We English do not need to behave in those flamboyant ways and we lose something that is essentially English if we start to copy the behaviour of less secure nationalities.

When Gordon Brown wrote about 'common values' which bind the Union together he was really describing the virtues which should inform any civilised society and I very much doubt if Jack Straw, who soon sets off on a journey of exploration, will return with a definition of citizenship which is exclusive to Britain (and Northern Ireland) as a whole – unless he comes to the Victorian conclusion that only we were given divine dominion over palm and pine. But there is one characteristic which at least distinguishes the English from equally admirable races. And I will gladly give his peripatetic researchers suitably diffident evidence on the subject. We pride ourselves on not boasting about being English.

When G.K. Chesterton wrote of 'the people of England, that never have spoken yet', he did not mean to suggest that we had nothing to say for ourselves – merely that while other nationalities 'talked of freedom, England talked of ale'. We chose that subject because, being free, we did not need to assert the importance of liberty and because we would have been embarrassed to proclaim our love of what we knew to be our birthright. If we abandon that natural reserve and replace it with oaths, flags, national days and long-winded statements of the civic virtues to which we should all aspire, we may do something to create a feeling of 'Britishness'. But an essential part of what it means to be English will be destroyed.

Men who wear roses in their button holes on 23 April will be offended to learn that I explain my affection for England with an analogy from farm-yard psychology. But it does reflect my honest position. Chickens are infatuated by the first bird that they see after they have cracked their way out of the egg. I saw England. In consequence, it is the only place in which I want to live – the only wing under which I wish to shelter.

During half a century of serious, or at least national, journalism, I was conscious that were I to put together a book about England – part hymn book and part gazetteer – I would be making a dangerous journey in the footprints of giants. In the *Guardian*, back in 1983, I paid tribute to two of the most famous travellers along the winding English road.

Fifty years ago this autumn J. B. Priestley set off on his *English Journey*. He was just thirty-nine and with *The Good Companions* already on the bookshop shelves his reputation as a popular but serious novelist was already secure.

His inconsequential essays had begun to add distinction to the foot of several newspapers' pages. Soon he was to write the meticulously constructed plays with the intriguingly ingenious plots. But the Postscripts which followed the Nine O'Clock News and made him a welcome visitor in a million wartime homes were still five peacetime years away.

Yet despite the success which he had already enjoyed and the fame which still lay ahead, the story that began on a motor coach driving to Southampton is incomparably the greatest achievement of his 89 years.

It is a miracle of straightforward English. Armed with 'the minimum of clothes, a portable typewriter, the usual paraphernalia of pipes, notebooks, rubbers, paper fasteners, razor blades, pencils, Muirhead's *Blue Guide to England*, Stamp and Beavers' *Geographic and Economic Survey* and, for reading in bed, the tiny thin paper edition of the *Oxford Book of English Prose*', he began to write about England as no one had written about it since Cobbett. Indeed, he wrote about this tight little, right little sceptred isle with an unselfconscious simplicity that Cobbett could not match.

When Cobbett rode through Hampshire he wrote about the changing pattern of commercial life. 'Between Southampton and Western Grove we cross a bridge over the Itchen River.' The countryside was littered with grand houses and 'just at the back' of the grandest of them all was 'another paddock place inhabited by a man who was a coachmaker in the East Indies and whose father or uncle kept a turnpike in Chelsea a few years ago. See the effects of industry and enterprise!' Cobbett found it easier to grieve at other men's misfortunes rather than to rejoice at their success.

Priestley's vignette of the social and commercial condition of Southern England is so subtle that at first the reader does not realise that it is a commentary on how we lived then. There are no booming explanation marks or didactic asides. The story is told by a 'thinnish fellow, somewhere in his forties' who had 'a sharp nose, a neat moustache, rimless eyeglasses and one of those enormous foreheads – roomy enough for an Einstein – that so often do not seem to mean anything'.

The thinnish stranger wanted to talk and made an excuse to move across the coach's gangway. 'He was the kind of man who comes into a few hundred pounds in his early twenties and begins to lose money steadily ... there are a few thousand like him up and down the country, especially in growing towns and new suburbs. At the end of one venture they begin another passionate search for an opening.'

The twentieth-century reincarnation of Messrs Micawber and Polly began his commercial critique in Surrey with gloomy news about the profitability of tearooms. By the time that the travellers had reached Hampshire, emigration to South Africa was on the agenda. The prospects for raincoats and waterproof hats, cheap furs, the shoe trade and wireless maintenance were all thoroughly discussed on the journey south.

I am far too much in awe of J.B. Priestley to allow myself the cynical suspicion that the man with the domed forehead and a flair for bankruptcy never existed. I prefer to think that in this, as in other encounters, Mr Priestley was fortunate in attracting into his company characters of unusual interest and humorous habits. I suppose that he sifted through three months of conversation and wrote down just the home-made aphorisms that kept the journey bounding joyfully along.

I have a vision of the red and round-faced Mr Priestley attracting a moving army of casual acquaintances. Not for nothing was he called 'Jolly Jack' – most often by people who had never met him. He looked approachably avuncular.

And what he wrote about England confirms his good temper as well as his excellent judgement.

Other travellers through England – especially those who have set out during the last decade – have found much that displeased their eye, offended their sensitive susceptibilities and infuriated their passions for innovation and improvement. J.B. Priestley found much in England of which he disapproved. But he always travelled hopefully.

He 'thought about patriotism' and wished that he 'had been born early enough to be called a Little Englander ... that *little* sounds the right note of affection. It is little England that I love ... I dislike Big Englanders. I wish their patriotism began at home so they would say – as I believe most of them would if they only took the trouble to go and look – "Bad Show!" to Jarrow and Hebburn.'

I am not sure whether or not William Cobbett loved England, or if the England of October 1826 through which he made his way to Southampton was less lovable than the England of autumn 1933. But I am sure that without the sort of fondness that J.B. Priestley feels it is impossible properly to describe what life is like in this slightly tarnished golden jewel set in an increasingly polluted silver sea.

Affection is not the easiest emotion to express in print. It too easily turns embarrassingly mawkish. But Priestley's expressions of territorial infatuation never raise a blush. For he seems to be writing about a plain man's passion. 'I would rather spend a holiday in Tuscany than in the

Black Country' he confesses. 'But if I were compelled to choose between living in West Bromwich or Florence, I should make straight for West Bromwich.'

I include that ancient Endpiece in my introduction to this anthology because the final quotation from J.B. Priestley – West Bromwich versus Tuscany – seems particularly appropriate to the circumstances in which the book is being put together. I am on the west coast of Italy. The sun is shining, the sea is blue and I am enjoying myself immensely. But, when the time comes for my holiday to end, I shall return to England with the joy of knowing that I am going home.

Living at This Hour

Comparing Shakespeare with other poets and playwrights is usually an unrewarding exercise. His genius is literally incomparable. But in one respect – particularly important in this anthology – contrast between him and other writers is possible. Eliot, Hardy, Tennyson, Browning – were, in part, made by England. But England – at least the England of our imagination – was made by Shakespeare. He, more than any other man or woman, created the idea of martial England on which our patriotism is based. We think of it as the sceptred isle of which John of Gaunt spoke – regretting the temporary passing of the 'fortress built by nature'. It is also Shakespeare who takes credit or blame for the Arcadian delusion which portrays England's story as a rural idyll.

Only second-rate writers – an essay on Anthony Trollope, the politicians' favourite novelist, follows – can be described as *exclusively* English. For it is neither subject matter nor place of birth which determines where and to whom a book belongs. E.M. Forster wrote that to say that *The Seven Pillars of Wisdom* was about the war in the desert was like saying that *Moby-Dick* is about catching a whale. He meant that T.E. Lawrence used the Arab Revolt as a vehicle for an exploration of hope and fear, love and hate, loyalty and betrayal. *Middlemarch* describes the life of a market town in Victorian England. But it is *about* life.

With the exception of Trollope – the frustrated politician – I admired and envied all the writers about whom, over the years, I wrote. I knew only one of them well. Philip Larkin was the librarian at my university. Indeed we first met immediately after he fell off his bicycle outside the gates of the main building. Our relationship is best illustrated by a suggestion made to me, some years later, by Andrew Motion, Larkin's biographer. A couple of days before I was due to open an exhibition of Larkin's letters, Motion telephoned with an offer. The letters which were particularly offensive about me could be covered during the ceremony.

Larkin and I last met in the, now closed, French Club in Saint James's. We were eating at separate tables but – as he left – he came over to me, took me by the hand and led me into the kitchen. It was filthy. 'There,' he said. 'You will never want to have lunch here again.' I remain astonished that a man of such joyous malevolence could write poems of such sublime sensitivity as 'Dockery and Son' and 'The Arundel Tomb'. There may be something peculiarly English about his perversity – or my forbearance.

Ministering Angles

'We get men into the House now who are clever and all that sort of thing and who force their way up, but who can't be made to understand that everybody should not want to be Prime Minister.'

That is not Lord Shinwell's icy judgement on Parliament's new generation. Nor is it faint Salisbury praise, damning the 'too clever by half' young Tories who entered the House of Commons in the early Fifties. It is Mr Barrington Erle, the 'good party man' of Trollope's six political novels. In 1874 those 'views had been familiar for the last forty years'. No doubt in another forty today's thrusting young men will preach the virtues of humility to their successors. For Trollope captured the timeless trivia of politics more than any other English writer.

Phineas Finn, the Irish Member; Mr Bonteen; Plantagenet Palliser, Duke of Omnium and Prime Minister of England, are divided from the modern Member of Parliament by a hundred years of social revolution. Yet to the credit of Trollope (or perhaps to the discredit of Parliament) much of what was said about them then could be said about us now.

Parliament's procedures have changed over the last hundred years, but the essential characteristics abide. Mr Turnbull, who always caught the Speaker's eye, and, being an orator, was 'not

25

called upon either to study detail or to master ... facts' could easily find a place in the Parliament of 1970. It is still possible that 'the most unpopular man in the House may make himself liked by owning freely that he has done something that he ought to be ashamed of'. The uninitiated are still surprised to discover that 'despite his assumed fury the gentleman was not irate. He intended to communicate that look of anger to the newspapers ... and knew from experience that he could succeed in that.'

It is these glimpses of real political attitudes – assiduously collected in the public gallery of the House of Commons and during Reform Club conversations – that bring Trollope nearer than any other English writer to the creation of a credible political novel. Often his judgement about politics and politicians is wrong. But that is unimportant. His errors are the errors real people made about real politicians a hundred years ago – and are still making today.

Aspirants to office succeed, young Phineas Finn was told, 'by making themselves uncommonly unpleasant to those in power, thus being taken to the Treasury bench, not that they may hit others, but that they may cease to hit those who are there'. Two books and six years later Lord Brentford says the same. 'Most men rise now by making themselves thoroughly disagreeable.' In the real world it was no more true than it is now, when Mr Enoch Powell sits on the back benches to prove Lord Brentford wrong. But it is not a difference between fact and fiction. The difference is between what happens and what is popularly supposed to

26

happen. Even a hundred years ago it was widely believed that politics had deteriorated and politicians fallen from grace.

St Paul's Magazine contained the first instalment of *Phineas Finn* in the year of the second Great Reform Bill. *Phineas Redux* was published in 1874 as Mr Gladstone's first Administration fell. *The Prime Minister* was planned while Disraeli was buying shares in the Suez Canal.

That is now said to be the golden age of English politics. Yet in these three novels Trollope wrote 'loyalty in politics was simply a devotion to the side which a man ... cannot leave without danger to himself'; 'there is nothing of loyalty left in politics' and 'had some unscrutable decree of fate ordained ... that no candidate could be returned to Parliament who would not assert the earth to be triangular, then would arise immediately a clamorous assertion of triangularity amongst political candidates'.

And these are not presented as the deviant views of some dispossessed and disenchanted Adullamite. They are offered as the opinions of Liberal elder statesmen, ambitious Government Whips and the Prime Minister himself. They are clearly Trollope's own beliefs – beliefs common in England even when giants canvassed the land. A great political novel would reveal the truth about politics rather than repeat the common prejudice, but that is not within Trollope's power. What he had seen he could report brilliantly. But his understanding came from observation not participation, and in politics the onlooker misses the best part of the game.

Politics is about issues, and they are the one thing that political fiction cannot provide. Even in those of the novels which are genuinely concerned with politics the great issues of the time make only fleeting appearances. Ireland is mentioned in passing. Woman's suffrage appears as anathema to elderly peers and the preoccupation of 'progressive' young women. The disestablishment of the Church – the whole Anglican Communion, not just the Church of England in Wales – dominates parts of *Phineas Redux*, but by then Trollope has turned unashamedly from fiction to a caricature of fact. Mr Daubeny *is* Disraeli – 'by many accounted a statesman, whereas to me, he has always been a political Cagliostro'. And when we begin to believe in Disraeli, Daubeny becomes incredible. We know it was Disraeli who hung on to office for six months after his majority had gone, sustained only by moral flexibility and verbal flair. We know too that after Disraeli's eventual defeat, the new President of the Board of Trade was not murdered by a bigamous Armenian Jew turned Christian clergyman. That happened in Daubeny's world. When the issues are real, the characters are not. When the characters are made to live, there are no real issues in their political lives.

The illusion of political reality is easy to create for an author who leant for so long over the Stranger's Gallery railing. At the height of his glory, Phineas Finn, First Lord of the Admiralty, went to sea in the Admiralty Board yacht. As no doubt did Mr Childers, the First Lord in Mr Gladstone's government. For a moment it is all real. For the silver from that yacht still stands in the office of the Minister of Defence. But real First Lords – as well as arguing about the cost of new ships, a perpetual preoccupation of Navy Ministers in which Finn takes part – were bombarding Alexandria or changing the fleet from sail to steam. These are things that Phineas Finn can never be allowed to do. Even the Duke of Omnium must live through seven Parliaments and six thousand pages fired only by a patrician vocation to public service and a devotion to his Decimal Currency Bill. The great issues we know belong to real Prime Ministers. The Duke must govern without a programme.

So we are left with the glimpses of how life was, and is, in Westminster. The Duke of Omnium, having become Chancellor of the Exchequer, 'could afford to put up with the small everyday calamity of having a wife who loved another man better than she loved him'. Quintus Slide is that well known sort of journalist who claims 'if it is true I have every right to publish it. If it is not true I have the right to ask the question.'

Today neither the professional ethics of one, nor the personal sorrow of the other would be thought the stuff of which popular novels are made. Politicians were no more admired a hundred years ago than they are today, but they did seem a good deal more romantic. Trollope is now left to those who love Parliament and who spend their lives there – and expect to feel in their retirement the emotions that the Duke and Duchess of Omnium felt in theirs. 'They sighed to be back amongst the trumpets. They had suffered much amongst the trumpets, yet they longed to return.'

Guardian 26 June 1971

How I Came to Casterbridge by Way of Reykjavik

A month ago Hampshire meant nothing more to me than the marvellous myth of Upper Wessex and the absurd reality of Regatta Week at Cowes. Now I at least know what part of that county looks like. The New Forest between Brockenhurst and Beaulieu is what South Yorkshire would become if God stamped His foot on the hills between Bradfield and Bolsterstone and flattened them into a gentle undulation of bracken, gorse and grass. An immortal soul remorselessly crushing the people as well as levelling the land is probably the way that Thomas Hardy country was created. I spent the first day of the year reading the *Wessex Tales* and waiting for fate to strike again at the imaginative woman, the distracted preacher, the three strangers and me.

Thomas Hardy's path first crossed mine thirty-five years ago at the old Sheffield City Grammar School. I was struggling to get my Yorkshire accent round 'when the Present has latched its postern behind my tremulous stay' when my agony was interrupted by an intense child with spectacles and a high-quality gabardine and gymslip. She asked about *Tess of the D'Urbervilles.*

Miss Dickens, our elderly English teacher, described Tess as 'a silly girl in a white dress who got herself into trouble and caused everyone a great deal of unnecessary inconvenience'. John Fowles will be disappointed to discover that, long before he wrote *The French Lieutenant's Woman,* an old lady with hair curled into a bun was measuring nineteenth-century dilemmas against twentieth-century values. Three years later, Hardy came into my life again at the Sheffield Little Theatre, a cultural institution that gloried in its ability to overcome the problems of a six-foot stage. It actually produced *The Dynasts* behind two pairs of flickering footlights without cutting out a single coronation or peace conference.

My disbelief hung willingly suspended well into the third hour. Then the six actors who had been The Russian Infantry at the Battle of Borodino and the Grande Armée at Austerlitz turned into three Prussians under Blücher who joined with Wellington's three Grenadier Guards at Waterloo. I squeezed into the chip shop just before the notice on the steam-streaked window was turned to 'closed'. Hardy was forgotten for another two years.

When I read *Tess* and *Far from the Madding Crowd* the heroine from both books took advantage of my adolescent ignorance and convinced me that the Vale of Blackmore and The Chase were the green and pleasant lands in which we ought to build the New Jerusalem. Sheffield – despite the Peak District and the moors that run from city boundary to distant skyline – was the

31

dark satanic mills.

Tess and Bathsheba inhabited an Arcadia of high meadow grass speckled with buttercups, fat, well-groomed sheep that would have died of shame as well as exposure on the Pennine foothills, and hay making under cloudless skies. The related story about the sailor selling his wife and daughter at a Saturday market I chose to ignore. That happened at Weydon Priors. I must have passed the town on my way to Upper Wessex. These days, I think it is called Andover.

Since I was sixteen, my vision of England has changed. But I still have a sentimental attachment to the idea of old men in leather gaiters and cotton smocks discussing the price of corn – though I never think of them as 'gaffers'. In Sheffield that term means the boss, a group of men sometimes denied the respect accorded to the 'elderly rustics' of the Oxford dictionary. And even that incident at Weydon Priors and the awful fate that later befell The Mayor of Casterbridge never quite destroyed the notion that Hardy is the novelist of England, Home and Beauty.

Indeed one night in Reykjavik, whilst commanding Her Majesty's forces in the cod war to end all cod wars, I turned to Mayor Henchard for consolation and solace. It was a cold night because the supply of volcanically heated water that normally circulated round the Embassy radiators had mysteriously been cut off. A blizzard and sixty thousand tons of disputed fish separated me from home and there was no schoolboy conveniently available to rally the ranks with cries of 'play up, play up, and play the game'.

But in the bookcase in my chilly bedroom I found the *Oxford Book of English Verse*. So, sitting up in bed, I tried to improve my morale by singing 'Summertime on Bredon' at the top of my voice. After I had urged the noisy bells to be dumb half a dozen times, the Housman Therapy lost its effect. In desperation I turned to 'one evening of late summer before the nineteenth century had reached one-third of its span'. I reached 'a general drama of pain' – the last words of The Mayor of Casterbridge – by morning.

The 'drama of pain' taking place in the Icelandic Foreign Ministry ended a couple of days later. Back home in England, I read (shamefully for the first time) *Jude the Obscure*. After that, I explored no more Thomas Hardys until the final week of last December. Then, armed with a venerable volume of the *Wessex Tales*, I made my way to Lymington.

Perhaps 'The Withered Arm' is not ideal holiday reading. Miss Dickens would have described it as the story of a Holmstoke housewife who foolishly believed that touching the corpse of a hanged man would cure her infirmity. But, in spite of the Gothic absurdity, it aroused memories of the England that once existed, at least in my imagination. Hardy believed that in old England 'an unmaliced and unimpassioned nescient will' ground down the people without even realising their suffering. Between Brockenhurst and Beaulieu He ground down the countryside as well. In South Yorkshire the hills still point hopefully to heaven.

Guardian 23 January 1982

Who Cares?

Last Sunday was open day at Bovington Camp. I was not there. I suspect that, with the New Challenger battle tank on view, my absence was barely noticed. Indeed, as the Royal Armoured Corps had omitted to send me an invitation to 'Open Day 83' it may well be that no one expected me to be present. So I do not use this column like the Court and Social pages of *The Times* to explain – as if I were a dowager duchess oppressed by age and arthritis – why I have failed to discharge my social obligations.

I fear that there is more than a touch of the N.F. Simpsons in my concern about my whereabouts on the afternoon of Bovington's exposure to the tank-loving public. Mr Simpson (elderly and literate readers will recall) is the author of an anti-logic play called *One-Way Pendulum*, in which an aggressive barrister cross-examines a harassed defendant with the classic question, 'When you might have absented yourself from anywhere in Britain why, on that particular afternoon, did you choose to absent yourself from Norwich?'

Before elderly, literate and didactic readers reach for their pens and paper to expose the inaccuracy of the quotation, let me confess more serious guilt. My interest in my failure to visit Bovington is almost as irrational as the N.F. Simpson question. For when I saw *The Times*

34

photograph of the new battle tank, I could not believe that anyone within travelling distance of the Armoured Corps depot would actually choose to go there.

For Bovington is on the southern tip of Wessex. Ten miles due east of Casterbridge. In the real world, I have spent many hours driving across the moorland which surrounds it and cursing the great wounds that tank tracks have cut into the good Dorset earth. At least, I think that it was in the real world. For I was looking for Clouds Hill.

To do Bovington Camp justice, Clouds Hill would not have called me if the tank training ground had never existed. For Private Shaw (alias 352087 Aircraftsman Ross, T.E. Lawrence and, worst of all, Lawrence of Arabia) would not have used the cottage as a retreat and refuge for himself and the other squaddies who bashed out their basic training on the Bovington square. Colonel Lawrence (retired), not surprisingly, did not enjoy his basic training. During the war in the desert, slow march in review order had played very little part in either strategy or tactics. And he had been through it all before, during the desperate days when he had attempted to lose himself in the RAF.

Lawrence sold a gold dagger, given him in Mecca in 1918, to replace the roof and ceiling of Clouds Hill. And, during his agonised years in the army, whatever he wrote was produced simply to finance cottage repairs. That such a dispossessed and disenchanted man should feel so deep an attachment to the place is, in itself, a reason for visiting Clouds Hill. So is the vision of its distinguished visitors – Thomas and Mrs

35

Hardy, George Bernard Shaw (who left a copy of *Saint Joan* inscribed 'To Private Shaw from public Shaw'), and E.M. Forster who described the scene for the *Listener* in 1938.

There was no alcohol at Clouds Hill. For Lawrence still maintained his Islamic enthusiasm for coffee and tea. And there was very little food. Lawrence was the masochistic sort of aesthete who just put aside all fleshly pleasures and then acquired an intellectual anorexia nervosa which permanently suppressed his appetite. For the convenience of his friends, he kept a large supply of tinned fish and baked beans. They were eaten at will. I would gladly have visited Clouds Hill just to see where Thomas Hardy wandered the living room, using a pen as a fork as he ate pilchards straight out of their oily can. But the real reason of my visit was to read the words which Lawrence himself carved over the cottage door.

I find much that I know of Colonel Lawrence intensely unattractive (not least the dislike of alcohol and the detachment from food) though in mitigation I remember the way in which he writes. And of those who write well, much is rightly forgiven. It is difficult to imagine a more elegant complaint against happiness than his description of a portly Arab. 'I begin to suspect him of constant cheerfulness. His eyes had a confirmed twinkle and though only thirty-five he was putting on flesh. It might be due to too much laughter.' However, the words which he carved on his lintel were not his own.

They were Greek. The biographers print them in the ancient script and E.M. Forster offers *ou phrontis* as a modern version. Everyone agrees that they translate as 'I don't care' – the culminating and climactic line from a story by Herodotus concerning a young man who, at the banquet to celebrate his betrothal to a princess, disgraced himself and therefore forfeited both bride and dowry. We have no way of knowing if the reckless response to his rejection was genuine. For the suitor was drunk and his riposte was instantaneous.

Lawrence carved 'I don't care' above the door at Clouds Hill when he was stone cold sober. And in spite of his many talents, he was not a sufficiently proficient mason for the work to be done in a few minutes. He must have stood for hours, precarious on a chair or uncertain on a ladder, chipping away at the lintel and conscientiously engraving his cottage and his life with the motto by which he wanted to be remembered.

That is not the action of a man who believed what he carved. Indeed, it is the behaviour of someone who cared very much indeed, but hoped that little acts of bravado would convince the world that he did not care at all. For all its naïveté, that combination of characteristics is profoundly endearing. It makes up – at least in part – for the love of motorcycles, the inclination to be photographed in flowing white robes, even the antipathy to food and drink. For it demonstrates a secret vulnerability. Is it possible that people who could have gone in search of that house and that inscription chose, instead, to look at tanks?

Guardian 9 October 1983

From the Original Story

The successful musical has four good songs and three acts. Boy meets girl. Boy loses girl. Boy and girl are reunited. The formula has intrigued me for years. And, at last, after a whole decade, I have hit upon an idea which – although not original – will pack in the coach parties. True to the classic tradition, my musical has a chorus or narrator. He starts the show with a melodic question:

Who's that tapping at the window?
It happens every evening after dark.
From chimney-pot to basement
There is not a single casement
That has not been smudged and smeared by
   fingermark.
Who's that peeping round the curtain?
It really is a practice I deplore.
For it's desperately unnerving
When a ghastly gaze unswerving
Stares in a window on the second floor.

The narrator soon finds out. And he begins to tell the tale of the ghost and her two lovers. The characters gradually develop. One is a hypochondriac whose feeble constitution contrasts sharply with the muscular savagery of the anti-hero. The valetudinarian explains his wry philosophy:

38

As long as you've got your health
Every day is sunny, every joke is funny, every
  bush a vine;
As long as you've got your health
Every baby's bonny, every goose is swanny,
  every day is fine.
As long as you've got your health...
I wish that I had mine.

At this point (we are by now into the second act)
the plot takes the sudden turn that experienced
dramatists believe to be essential. A conversation is
overheard and misunderstood. As a result the star-
crossed lovers separate and go bitterly on their
different ways. An old family servant, instead of
comforting the distraught suitor, reproves him for
listening to other people's conversations:

Serves you right for listening at keyholes,
Serves you right for crouching outside doors.
For whenever an eavesdropper
Slips and comes a frightful cropper
All decent people join in the applause.

As a second-act finale that takes some beating.
Perhaps Cardinal Newman's lyrics (set to music
by Edward Elgar in a show that never got to
Broadway) match it for moral certainty. Neither
Hart nor Hammerstein (why do all the really great
lyricists have names which begin with H?) could
have produced a wittier quintrain. How, I wonder,
would they have made the second change of mood
and contrived the happy ending which is essential
to the show's success – and still have remained

faithful to the original work on which this smash-eroo is based? I relied on the basic text. Thus the curtain comes down to the author's own words:

> So they all end up together
> On the hills amongst the heather
> And in the quiet earth they'll lie content.
> Round their moorside mausoleum
> We will sing a last Te Deum
> And the harebells chime a soft accompaniment.
>
> CHORUS: All together let us sing
> Death, oh death where is thy sting?
> Grave, thy victory will be pyrrhic –
> Hence, this joyful final lyric.
>
> Now three headstones in a row
> Mark the place where, down below,
> They lie at rest and safe, at last, from harm.
> As the moths go fluttering by
> Across Yorkshire's benign sky
> Their flapping wings will syncopate our psalm:
>
> CHORUS: All together let us sing etc.

Of course, for the show to run and run, it needs a good title. I thought of a single word followed by an exclamation mark in the manner of Lionel Bart. Impresarios making offers should, there-fore, mark their envelope in the top left-hand corner with what will become a legend of the English musical state, *Heathcliff!*

Guardian 22 November 1983

Stamford, by George Eliot

Although he was a mediocre poet, John Betjeman was not a bad judge of stone or brick. He was, however, inclined to go to extremes of admiration and disapproval. His prayers for the obliteration of Slough confirm that he was more an aesthete than a moralist. And although Broomhill was the heavy Victorian home to generations of Sheffield steel-masters, its lilacs and laburnums do not quite make it 'more elegant than any other industrial suburb'. But, when he called Stamford 'England's most attractive town', he was making something very close to a statement of fact. We are attracted to Stamford because the style and shape of its buildings are associated in our imaginations with the lost age of elegance before the railways made us all cosmopolitan and the dark, satanic mills defiled the pastures green.

Stamford is a Georgian town, and is dominated by architecture of the respectably solid school which pre-dated much of the shoddy Regency work that was spread across Brighton and Bath. Many of the streets and squares are much as they were when William Pitt the Elder formed his first ministry. But Stamford has become not so much the place that time forgot as the town that the A1 bypassed. Once upon a time Scotgate, Red Lion Square and St Mary's Hill were part of the Great North Road. Now, even on cattle-market day, there is something like peace in the pedestrianised High Street. Stamford was the perfect backdrop for the BBC's adaptation of *Middlemarch*.

The town has taken the choice seriously. Book-shops enjoy record sales of the Penguin classic. The library is inundated with requests to reserve anything by George Eliot. The curator of the municipal museum, John F.H. Smith, has given two '*Middlemarch* lectures'. One is best described by the fashionable contradiction in terms, 'con-temporary history', aimed to 'recapture some of those heady days when the BBC took over the town'. The other drew fascinating parallels between Stamford's life and George Eliot's art – Reform Bill hustings, fever hospital and muni-cipal scandal. Anticipating a sell-out, Smith moved the lectures from the museum to the local theatre. It was packed both nights.

He claims to have few reservations about being described in the *Observer* as 'Stamford's nearest equivalent to the Reverend Edward Casaubon'. He insists that the desiccated pedant's name must be pronounced with the emphasis on the second syllable, admits to feeling 'some sympathy' for the would-be author of *A Key to All Mythologies*, and believes that 'so did George Eliot'. Under Smith's guidance, the museum has provided a guide to 'set locations' – Mawmsey, the grocer, 25 Mary Street; The Old Infirmary, Brown's Hospital. It is difficult to distinguish between interest in the book and fascination with the filming. But Smith describes the town as 'almost taken over' by *Middlemarch*. Perhaps almost, but not quite.

In the High Street, four students from the college of further education were discussing a compact disc which was decorated with a representation of scarlet lips that turned into a trickle of blood and spelled out the title *Sounds of Kiss* FM. Three of them had never heard of either George Eliot or *Middlemarch*, although one confessed to asking his mother to record the first episode on the family video. The owner of the lurid CD was preparing for A-level English – set books: '*Hamlet, Cat on a Hot Tin Roof* and *Withering Heights*'. No joke was intended. The reputation of Stamford scholarship was redeemed by the arrival of two of their colleagues. 'It is difficult to concentrate on the story,' said one, 'because you keep thinking about which part of town you're watching.' The other thought *Wuthering Heights* 'quite good', but found the 'movements in time ... the flashbacks' distracting.

Perhaps Dorothea Brooke, the authentic heroine of English literature, is wasted on the young. But it was not unreasonable to expect the women of Stamford – who, thanks to television, had followed her career as far as Casaubon's seizure – to admire her wish for self-improvement and her selfless devotion to a husband who was temperamentally (and perhaps physically) incapable of reciprocating her affection. But they persisted in feeling sorry for Casaubon.

The pavement opinion from the narrow cobblestoned footpaths of Stamford was almost unanimous in its refusal to allocate blame. Mary Sandall, who did not think Dorothea 'all that liberated' even for her day and age, excused the cold fish of a husband with the explanation that

43

'artists are like that'. Kim Ford 'supposed that she married him to get an education'. There was a clear implication that, in consequence, she deserved all the trouble that came her way. May Daley was touched by the way in which Dorothea wanted to share her husband's work and life, but doubted 'if she knew enough really to help him'. Those were not the opinions of elderly ladies in felt hats, unfashionable boots and woollen gloves. They were the judgements of young women with children in prams. In Stamford, the Monstrous Regiment does not seem to be on the march.

Susan Southall, polishing the brass knob on the oak front door of number 18 Great George Street, was – during the first episode – actually in favour of Miss Brooke becoming Mrs Casaubon. But she accepts that both her judgement and Dorothea's were woefully mistaken. 'She knows now that she was wrong and that she should leave him. But I can't imagine her going off with anybody else. They didn't in those times, did they?'

Ian Monro, regional director of the National Farmers' Union, thinks Dorothea was 'attractive but naïve'. The television programmes show the *Middlemarch* Quality 'enjoying the land not working it. But in those days those sort of people behaved like that.'

Perhaps it is the quality of the adaptation that allows Stamford viewers to climb into their sets and find themselves in the early nineteenth century. But the town itself is a sort of time machine. Anyone who lives in what is visually pre-Victorian England must find it easy to suspend their feelings of historical disbelief.

44

It was Janet Thompson – accompanying her husband on an expedition to get his computer mended – who talked of Dorothea as 'a woman out of her time. She wants to do so much. She wants to contribute.' Mrs Thompson – the one uninhibited admirer found during a long search – could imagine our heroine 'feeling tempted. But she would not run. She is the sort of woman who stays around and makes the best of things rather than looking elsewhere.' Mrs Thompson – probably expressing her own preference rather than imagining Dorothea's – thought that 'elsewhere' was more likely to be Tertius Lydgate, the dashing doctor, than Will Ladislaw, the penniless painter.

And what about *A Key to All Mythologies?* 'It sounds very important,' said Jack Williams of Grantham. 'I don't know about that sort of thing,' admitted Janis Taylor as she bustled past St George's Church, in which Edward took Dorothea as his wife. 'I suppose he must have been very clever.'

Everyone who had seen the second episode believed that if God and George Eliot had spared Dr Casaubon for just one more Monday, he would have produced a great work of scholarship. The idea that it was all a waste of time had not entered a single Stamford head. Nor was there the slightest suggestion that Relate ought to be called in to advise Dr Casaubon on his uxorious duties.

Thanks to the vox pop of Stamford, I have begun to worry that Dorothea Brooke is no more than a middle-class heroine, a woman who appeals only to bookshop-browsers, concert-goers and season-ticket holders at local repertory

45

theatres. It is the first bad – as distinct from improper – thought that I have had about her in more than forty years. So I console myself with the hope that, as the series progresses, more and more viewers will realise the true nobility of her character and how well she deserves the reward that will be hers after six episodes.

What is certain is that, thanks to the BBC, the story – if not exactly the novel itself – has passed at least temporarily into Stamford's life. If the tales from the bookshop are true, a whole Lincolnshire town is about to enjoy one of the great pleasures of life.

Guardian 29 January 1994

Almost Washed Away on Will's Birthday

The rain changed from drizzle to downpour just as the procession prepared to move off. But, at Stratford-upon-Avon last Saturday morning, our spirits remained effortlessly undampened. We had assembled to celebrate England's greatest miracle – the birth of William Shakespeare. And the quintessentially English weather only added to the quintessential Englishness of the occasion. Holding our posies with the relaxed assurance of accomplished bridesmaids, we splashed through the puddles with as near to abandon as the Anglo-Saxon character allows.

It was a well organised procession, under the

command of a retired brigadier and led by a military band. But it managed – in its English way – never to be quite disciplined. It usually straggled, often dawdled and sometimes stopped altogether. In the High Street, all the flags unfurled at more or less the same time but everyone was surprised that they all flapped together in the cold wind. The crowd looking up at the twenty flagpoles gave two cheers – one for the flags and the other for the unexpected success of their release.

When the head of the column reached Shakespeare's birthplace, the rear ranks huddled together in the damp back garden whilst they waited their turn to walk through the sacred house. The delay had the most English of reasons. One by one the dignitaries who led the parade paused to wipe their shoes before they stepped inside.

Six or seven hundred celebrants walked through the shrine in Henley Street – entering, like tradesmen, through the back door and leaving, like honoured guests, through the front. And did those feet in ancient times walk on the now well-worn flagstones? The reverential thought was disturbed by the sight of the advance guard, leading the way back into the gathering mist. First came a giant beadle – magnificent in scarlet and ready, at the drop of his tricorne hat, to step back into *Oliver Twist*. The mayor of Stratford – appropriately robed and chained – was preceded, as his pomp required, by a mace bearer. The borough's chief executive was dressed as town clerk from the days before local government reorganisation required every aspect of municipal life to be given a new name. The Bishop of Coventry, purple from

47

collar to hem, looked entirely Trollopian. But bishops always do. Two or three yards behind him, the country gentry were represented by men in top hats and women whose headgear cannot be described by a single adjective. But the ranks of the establishment had been infiltrated. Half a dozen scruffs, in anoraks and plastic macs, had insinuated themselves – and, no doubt, been welcomed – between the prince of the Church and the knights of the shires. Order had gladly broken down, confirming that, despite Shakespeare's universal genius, we were celebrating his birth in an entirely English way.

When Garrick revived the birthday celebrations in 1769, the people of Stratford were described as responding to his plans with two emotions – fear and avarice. Not this year. Despite the rain, they lined the route of the procession and properly cheered not the visiting dignitaries but friends and neighbours who had joined the festivities in the costumes of the collected works – Henry V under an umbrella, Lady Macbeth protecting her perm with a rain hat and Falstaff struggling to hold up the cushion which had broken loose from its moorings beneath his doublet and fallen to the place where his cod-piece ought to be. A reporter from local radio gave a running commentary as the pageant passed by. 'These must be the Merry Wives of Windsor. Yes, I've just had it confirmed. They are not, repeat not, members of Princess Katherine's French court. They are definitely the Merry Wives of Windsor.'

Garrick got the idea for his jubilee celebration from a mulberry tree – planted, as a sapling, by

Shakespeare himself and chopped down in its maturity by a clergyman who claimed that it was blocking his light. Part of the Holy Timber was made into a casket which the town council sent to Drury Lane as an expression of Stratford's admiration for the greatest actor of his day. Garrick responded by announcing from the stage that he was going to immortalise what was already immortal. And the rest of the Sacred Lumber was made into tawdry souvenirs which were sold at unreasonable prices during the festivities. In a week, enterprising citizens marketed more goblets and medals than could have been made from the whole of Burnham Wood. On Saturday, the best relic on offer was a sprig of rosemary which – I was assured – was taken from a bush which had grown from a cutting which had itself been pruned from a sprig planted personally by Anne Hathaway. And it was free. Even now, it is in a glass of water, waiting for its roots so that it can glorify my garden.

The higher minds of eighteenth-century England – Johnson and Walpole amongst them – stayed ostentatiously away from Garrick's 1769 extravaganza, fearing vulgarity, frivolity and, worst of all, self-advertisement. E.M. Forster wrote that the act of clear intention was 'to place the bard's fame and his own upon a permanent and mutual basis'. And the scope of the playwright's genius certainly offers almost irresistible temptation to exploit his work on behalf of all sorts of unlikely causes. At the birthday lunch of 1993, Sir Edward Heath demonstrated entirely to his own satisfaction that Shakespeare was an enthusiastic supporter of the single European currency.

I make no complaint about that. Though last Saturday I did not reveal the research of my textual study which confirmed, beyond all academic doubt, that Shakespeare wanted to rewrite the Labour Party constitution. As Othello almost said, 'It is the Clause. It is the Clause. It is the Clause, my soul.' But had I chosen to make that scholastic and uncontroversial point I would have done no more than illustrate the central fact of this year's Stratford celebration. Treated sensibly, Shakespeare can provide whatever sort of pleasure we choose. He is the sacred and the profane, the vulgar and the refined, the erudite and the ignorant combined into one glorious whole. Long may the citizens of Stratford celebrate his existence in every sort of way and every sort of weather. We were doubly blessed last Saturday. We only got soaked. In 1769, Garrick's less Shakespearean celebrations were completely washed away.

Guardian 24 April 1995

A Bard for the World But Not for the Globe

After weeks of agonising indecision, I have firmly decided that I am unequivocally ambivalent about the Globe Theatre. Dull would he be of soul who failed to be excited about Sam Wanamaker's dream. And the way in which determination turned hope into reality was even more heroic than the original romantic idea. But although I feel the hair rise on the back of my neck every time that I think of Shakespeare's plays being performed in exactly the same place, and in almost exactly the same way, as they were performed in Shakespeare's time, I know in my head (if not in my heart) that the contrivance is certainly dangerous and probably wrong.

I was convinced of the danger and error by the boyhood memories that mention of the Globe brings to mind. It does not bring to mind Donald Wolfit's touring company bringing *King Lear* to Sheffield or the local rep putting on *Hamlet* to inspire A-level English students. I remember visiting the City Museum at York and being told, as we walked down the perfect replica of a Victorian street, that we were reliving the past. That is not where Shakespeare belongs.

Shakespeare, as well as Milton, should be living at this hour – not treated as if he is part of our quaint and almost forgotten past. The Globe is an enchanting building and its magic is increased by the knowledge that all of the design, and most of the materials, which gave the concept shape and form are faithful to the theatres which were built in Shakespeare's England. But that makes it dangerously like the centrepiece of an Elizabethan theme park. What Shakespeare has to teach us is as relevant today as it was four hundred years ago.

Let us take a single example from the several thousand which prove my point. 'I have no spur to prick the sides of my intent, but only vaulting ambition' confessed Macbeth. He went on to say that it 'o'er-leaps itself and falls on the other'. If in the years since 1606 anyone has written a better warning to politicians with a lust for power but a lack of principle, I have yet to read it. I do not want that sort of essentially contemporary genius to be kept on display under glass.

Enthusiasts for the Globe will certainly argue that they are bringing Shakespeare to the people. And I understand the attraction of recreating the spirit of Elizabethan England before A.C. Bradley discovered aspects of the tragedies that the author himself had failed to notice. But I do not believe that the talk of oranges on sale in the bear pit and fighting amongst the paying public will make even the more raucous of the comedies come alive. Admittedly most of the silly talk about duels and strolling players did not come from the management, but it is the inevitable result of a building which looks as if it is part of The Shakespeare Experience.

Ten years ago, I would have been unthinkingly on the side of the Globe. Shakespeare, I believed in my ignorance, ought to be reproduced in the way which I imagined that Shakespeare intended. I thought that actors, dressed in ruffs and tights, should stand at the centre of the stage, look straight into the audience and speak the lines in the measured diction which allowed the playgoers to understand the poetry. In this paper, I denounced a *Troilus and Cressida* set in the Crimean War, *The Winter's Tale* enlivened by a jazz orchestra and a *Comedy of Errors* with sets of twins which were so spectacularly dissimilar that, although each confusion was a good joke, no confusion was credibly possible.

I justified my objection with the example of *Joe Macbeth* – a Hollywood adaptation of the Scottish play which made the Thane of Cawdor a Chicago hoodlum with ambitions to take over the rackets for the whole town. The film was a flop. Shakespeare, I used to say, cannot be improved upon. Play him straight. Play him original. My delight at seeing the Globe musicians in their original costumes, playing original music on original instruments would have been unconfined.

Then Stanley Wells – during one of those glorious birthday celebrations which they hold at Stratford every year – put me right. Mr Wells is one of the world's great authorities on Shakespeare, and with Gary Taylor, of America, has co-edited the new, massive and most authoritative Oxford edition of the Complete Works. Shakespeare, Wells told me, expected his plays to be adapted to the circumstances of time or place. They were not intended for publication, or meant to be the basis of questions in the GCSE examination. They were a framework within which a good night out could be built.

Shakespeare was meant to make us glad – not as a museum piece but as part of our everyday lives. Paradoxically, keeping true to the spirit of his work requires us to make changes in costume and stage direction from the way it would have been done in his time. That confirms him as part of here and now.

Despite all that, I was absolutely honest in what I said about my firm ambivalence. When I think of the Globe, a frisson of pleasure runs through my apprehension about its consequences. Perhaps all

I ask is that it be kept in proper perspective. The Globe is a Shakespeare museum, and it is wonderful that we can see the way in which his plays were once produced. But when the school parties have giggled at the boy with the placard which announces 'Another part of the forest', they ought to be taken off to a more modern representation of Arden. Then they will know that what Shakespeare wrote was about them and their daily lives. Shakespeare is the playwright of eternity.

Guardian 2 June 1997

Genius Helps, But Love Is All You Need

Robert Browning would not have been at all surprised by his wife's success. The ignoramus who spoke on behalf of BBC Education may have been 'gobsmacked by the popularity of a Victorian woman who is so forgotten that her work has been dropped from the *Oxford Dictionary of Quotations*'. But the poet's husband – who regarded her verse as 'the finest sonnets composed in any language since Shakespeare's' – knew that her attraction would not fade.

His assessment of her place in the pantheon of English literature may have been slightly biased by the fact that he was not married to Milton, Shelley, Keats or Wordsworth. But 'since Shakespeare' there have been few better *love* poems than 'How Do I Love Thee?' – the winner of last week's television popularity poll. If Matthew Arnold's 'Dover Beach' is too sombre, and Yeats's 'When You Are Old and Grey and Full of Sleep' is too sad, number VIIL of the *Sonnets from the Portuguese* has only one rival. That too was written by Elizabeth Barrett Browning. It begins: 'If thou must love me, let it be for naught'.

Robert always challenged head-on any doubts about either the quality or the appeal of his wife's work. The *Collected Letters*, put together sixty years ago, include a note to the Rev Hugh Reginald Haweis, which might have been composed to confound last week's Philistines. It opens with complaints about classic misprints. Quotations from Browning – included in a book by the scholar-clergyman – appeared as 'Fair, like my peers' instead of 'Fare like my peers', and 'with his human hair' rather than 'human air'. But the serious reproof comes in the final paragraph. 'On one point you are totally misinformed. You will be glad to know that, instead of the poetry of EBB being "almost forgotten", it is more remembered – or at least called for in order to be remembered – than it ever was.'

In a letter to Dr F. J. Furnival, he responded to the suggestion that Elizabeth's work needed to be popularised by the publication of a brief anthology of shorter poems, with an author's ultimate act of abnegation. He concluded a page of praise for the longer poems with the assurance that 'these, I rejoice with all my heart to know and say, are in no need of any assistance. Their popularity keeps ever far in advance of mine.'

He was writing of the enthusiasm for his wife's

work in late Victorian England. In Italy, she was held in even higher esteem. The plaque on the wall of Casa Guidi in Florence – where they both lived and she died – commemorates a great English poetess. No mention is made of her husband.

Honesty requires the admission that in Tuscany, Elizabeth Barrett Browning is admired more for her support of Italian Unity than for her iambic pentameter. And it must be similarly conceded that Robert was prudent to confine the comparison of his wife's achievements to poetry published after 1609. Any love sonnet which is matched against Shakespeare's is bound to be seen as a poor reflection of pure genius. But even to make the fatal contrast is a tribute to Elizabeth Barrett Browning's talent. Nobody ever bothers to waste words by saying that the playwrights of her period failed to produce anything as good as *Hamlet* or *King Lear*. And it is possible to talk about the two sets of sonnets in the same breath.

Love comes in many different shapes and sizes. Shakespeare (who wrote 154 sonnets) and Barrett Browning (who wrote forty-four) covered most aspects of the subject, from the negligent suitor's cynical explanation that he is testing his sweetheart's constancy to the sentimental hope that anyone immortalised in fourteen lines of verse need not fear age or infirmity. From time to time, both poets deal with the same subject. Putting the alternative treatment side by side, it becomes absolutely clear that the *Sonnets from the Portuguese* are, in the words of the coffee commercial, good but not that good.

In Sonnet CXVI, Shakespeare asserts that:

'Love is not love which alters when it alteration finds'. In her Sonnet XIV, Elizabeth is not quite so certain. She fears that even true love may – if it is built on a smile, a look, a way of speaking gently or a trick of thought – disappear with the disappearance of the endearing characteristic.

For these thing in themselves, Beloved, may
Be changed or change for thee – and love so
   wrought
May be unwrought so.

So she implores: 'If thou must love me, let it be for naught'.
Shakespeare shows more confidence in the human instinct for fidelity.

Love's not Time's fool, though rosy lips and
   cheeks
Within his bending sickle's compass come;
Love alters not with his brief hours and weeks...

As a result, he admits no impediment to the marriage of true minds. Shakespeare's unambiguous self-confidence is more than male certainty, and Barrett Browning's timidity is less than female reticence. It is the difference between a very good and a great poet. But Elizabeth is entitled at least to breathe the same immortal air. Up there on Mount Helicon, she will not be unduly worried by the idiocy of an ignorant spokesperson from the BBC.

Guardian 13 October 1997

Ferry across the Humber
to the Land I Love

The sun must have shone on some of the happy days that I spent in Hull and, surely, once or twice during those four enchanting years, the sky was a cloudless blue. But looking back, all my memories are in shades of grey. I blame the Humber. Other rivers shine like silver. But the estuary into which the Hull meanders and upon which Kingston stands, glints like steel. And it dominates the landward approach to the city.

Last week, I travelled along the line that Philip Larkin took on the day of *The Whitsun Weddings*. Larkin was leaving for the west, so it was not until he had passed 'the backs of houses and crossed a street of blazing windscreens' that 'the river's drifting breadth began, where sky and Lincolnshire and water meets'. For me, travelling in the opposite direction, what Andrew Marvell called 'the tide of Humber' suddenly appeared, broad and still beyond the southern carriage window. As always, the thought that came into my mind was: 'Forget about Sabrina Fair under the glassy cool translucent wave.' The Humber is the river which inspires the modern muse.

It was long after I had left Hull when I realised that something in its air encourages poetry. When I first sailed on the New Holland ferry – half steaming and half swept along from bank to bank

58

in a lazy arc – I only smelt the fish dock and heard the sound of the night trains which carried the fresh catch to London. Poets, I thought, should only write about 'Where the remote Bermudas ride / In th' ocean's bosom unespied'. Marvell (writing 'To His Coy Mistress') had, I assumed, thrown in the reference to the Humber in the hope of ingratiating himself with the city he wanted to represent in Parliament. At eighteen, I had a foolishly dramatic view of literature and a properly low opinion of politicians – even though I intended to desert one in order to become the other.

I cannot say that it was Larkin – appointed to run the university library the year after I registered – who educated me. Back in 1952, I simply thought of him as a man in a tweed hat, who sent me notes of complaint when my borrowed books were overdue for return. He did, however, seem an improvement on Miss Cummings, his predecessor – an ancient bluestocking who wore button boots when they were unfashionable and skirts which almost swept the library floor.

Now, at the mention of her name, I feel only gratitude. It was at her memorial service that Larkin, desperate for alcohol, visited the dean of his old college and talked about 'Dockery and Son'. What he wrote about that meeting is perhaps the saddest poem in the English language, and I can never understand why I – pathologically happy – like it so much. I take the same perverse pleasure in 'The Arundel Tomb'. What Larkin bitterly dismisses as an untruth seems to me a great redeeming fact of all our lives. 'What will survive of us is love.' When I saw the Humber again last week, I thought about Philip Larkin and, as soon as I got home, I read 'The Arundel Tomb'.

Then I looked for Douglas Dunn's Terry Street poems. When I lived in Hull, I lodged round the corner from that unfashionable address, and if anyone had told me that it would become the subject of a 27-piece anthology, I would have assumed that they had spent the night in the nearby bonded warehouse.

But years after I first saw the real Men of Terry Street – 'they come at night, leave in the early morning with ticking of bicycle chains, sudden blasts of motorcycles and whimpering of vans' – I began to understand that poetry, like life, can be both prosaic and beautiful. At its absolute best, both qualities are combined with sympathy and affection which is wholly free of sentimentality. That is what makes the last lines of 'A Removal from Terry Street' so wonderful. The whistling youths in 'surplus US army jackets' removing their sisters' few belongings on a squealing cart are followed by a man 'pushing of all things, a lawn-mower'.

There is no grass in Terry Street. The worms
Come up cracks in concrete yards at midnight.
That man, I wish him well. I wish him grass.

Last week, as the grey rain beat on the grey pavements, I wondered if it was Hull's unrelieved ordinariness that encouraged poets to understand that ordinary things also reveal the ways of God to man. Geography put the city at the end of the line and made it impossible to visit on the

60

way to anywhere else. When I first spilt out of Paragon Station, it also looked like the end of the world, balanced so near to the rim of the flat earth that to travel further east would be to risk falling into eternity. It must have stretched the poet's imagination in a way which was never necessary in Rome or Florence.

I feel far too affectionate towards Hull even to speculate that Hull poetry is a reaction to the city's essentially unpoetic character. In any case, when I was there in the Fifties, it had the charm of an East Riding Salford, *Love on the Dole*, 'Dirty Old Town', *This Sporting Life*, that sort of thing. And its romantic place in English history was secured when John Hotham, by closing the gates to the Duke of York and King Charles's demand for ship money, started the Great Civil War. In those days, it lived by the sea. But by the time I arrived, its tide had gone out.

Perhaps whatever there was in the air that stimulated poets was nature's compensation for its slow decline. I rejoice at the change of circumstance – the new factories, the marina stuffed with millionaires' yachts and the waterfront development that puts London's dockland in the shade. But I hope the poetry survives the prosperity.

Guardian 24 November 1997

This Contest Was Won
Four Centuries Ago

As the November evenings draw in, it will become increasingly important to remember that the BBC's search for the greatest Briton has little to do with real interest in the rival merits of the candidates. If something serious were intended, Anne Robinson would not be presenting the series, William Ewart Gladstone, George Eliot and John Milton would have been included in the slate of nominees from which the viewing public made its initial choice and Diana, Princess of Wales, would not be on the final shortlist.

To be fair to the BBC, once somebody had the bright idea of stimulating weak-minded interest by pretending that there was a competition, a sensible programme was impossible. The genuine contest was over before it began.

The title was won four centuries ago and has been retained ever since by the man who makes Britain in general, and England in particular, different from the rest of the world. Whatever our other failures and failings, we remain special and superior because we alone have William Shakespeare. His champion status cannot be changed by the sort of vote that the BBC organises to determine the sports personality of the year.

Shakespeare would walk away with the title if he were no more than the greatest poet and dramatist the world has ever known. But that is only the beginning of his claim to be England's Englishman. What he wrote defines what we are. England made him but he, in turn, helped to make the England of our imagination. On the day after British troops were evacuated from Dunkirk, the pupils of my primary school all chanted in unison: 'Come the four corners of the world in arms and we shall shock them.'

Our notion of national identity – distinct from the culture and customs of our continental cousins – is enshrined in Shakespeare's histories. Henry V, proposing to Princess Katherine, typifies our relationship with France 403 years after the scene was written. Affection combines with self-interest to encourage a closer alliance. But the language is a problem.

The poet of England always exhibits an admirable English realism about his native land. He searched for Arcadia in the Forest of Arden. And, to guarantee the continued support of his royal patrons, he chronicled the reigns of successive Henrys and Richards in a way that owes more to Tudor prejudices and propaganda than to objective history. But Shakespeare avoids the mawkish sentimentality that characterises so many self-styled patriots.

John of Gaunt's regularly misunderstood hymn of praise to the 'royal throne of kings' ends with the complaint 'That England, that was wont to conquer others, hath made a shameful conquest of itself.' England had made mistakes and might make mistakes again.

Shakespeare has become part of our language.

Some of the aphorisms are so vivid that they have turned into clichés. But few of us pass a day without using or hearing a dozen phrases which we would find in a book of Shakespearean quotations. Years ago I asked Senator Pat Moynihan – a surviving member of John F. Kennedy's New Frontier – if he had really responded to the news of the President's death with an expression of fear that he would never feel young again. Not quite, he told me. His first thought was, 'Our revels now are ended' (*The Tempest*, Act IV Scene 1 line 148).

No other dramatist has possessed Shakespeare's ability to analyse the fundamental human emotions. The world's greatest plays about love, ambition, jealousy and grief were all written by him. Each one of them – *Hamlet, Macbeth, Othello* and *King Lear* – teaches perceptive readers something new about themselves. Add to that the political lessons inherent in *Coriolanus* and *Julius Caesar* and it is easy to forget Shakespeare's real purpose. Shakespeare was meant to make us glad. Last summer, I saw *Pericles* at Stratford, a play that some critics think not good enough to be the Bard's own work. It was pure delight and I staggered out of the theatre thinking that if this is the worst he ever did, the best must be a series of miracles.

The canon is thirty-seven miracles long – each one as relevant to the year 2002 as it was to 1600. Forget the togas, the doublet and hose and the various androgynous costumes in which Shakespeare is often performed today. What Shakespeare has to say about love and hate, hope and despair, triumph and failure means as much now as it did when it was written. Enobarbus exaggerated the splendour of Cleopatra's progress along the river Cydnus because he wanted to be associated with a sensation. Which of us has not done something similar in the hope of impressing our friends? Shakespeare speaks for us all at our worst and best. That is why Ben Jonson called him 'Not of an age, but for all time.' BBC please note.

Guardian 4 November 2002

The Poet of the Countryside

John Clare was the poet of the English countryside – not alone in his devotion to this green and pleasant land but unique in his attachment to the soil. He began his working life as a Northamptonshire farm labourer and hedge setter and those early years – perhaps the happiest of his life – inform all his work. The titles he gave to his books of poems are, in themselves, enough to confirm his devotion. He was The Village Minstrel and The Rural Muse. But the collection that most eloquently proclaims his love of rural England is *The Shepherd's Calendar*. It celebrates the months of the year. March was a time of migration.

He hears the wild geese gabble o'er his head
And pleased wi' fancies in his musings bred

He marks the figured forms in which they fly
And pausing follows wi' a wandering eye.

Birds were not the only symbols of wind and weather with which he illustrated his calendar. One of his stories described drinking and seduction at the Helpston autumn festival and was regarded by his publisher as too improper for publication. Helpston was Clare's village and the cottage in which he lived is now restored and dedicated to his memory. The row of five tenements was converted, long ago, into a single house, but the old fireplaces and an ancient staircase remain. Next door is the Blue Bell where Clare worked as a potman, groom to the landlord's horse and drover to his cattle. Clare was a man of multiple talents and innumerable occupations.

For a brief spell he was a soldier – or at least a militiaman called temporarily to the colours in order to repel the anticipated French invasion. He was not a successful or conscientious recruit. During one drill, believing that he was being picked out for humiliation, he assaulted a corporal. Clare did not fit easily into alien surroundings. The one benefit he seems to have gained from his service for King George was the acquisition of a second-hand copy of Milton's *Paradise Lost* and a copy of Shakespeare's *Tempest* with half a dozen pages missing. They were important acquisitions for a man whose family was so poor that, when the enclosures denied them use of the common land, it bargained for the ownership of an apple tree so that the profit from the sale of its fruit could pay their rent.

66

The trees still blossom at the edge of the garden in which Clare walked two hundred years ago. But the dovecote between the cottage and the public house is silent. In Clare's time it was the home to a thousand birds – each one living in its separate niche. They were bred to eat – the delicacy of the rich, which potmen and plough-boys never tasted.

Clare was not totally without schooling. Village life in early nineteenth-century England usually included a one-room school in which the children of the poor were taught to read a little, add and subtract, accept the teaching of the Church of England and respect their betters. Clare enjoyed what little formal education he received, but, like all schoolboys in poetry and prose, he loved the end of the school day more.

Harken that happy shout – the schoolhouse
  door
Is open thrown and out the younkers teem
Some run to leapfrog on the rushy moor
And others dabble in the shallow stream

If his verse is to be believed, it was at school that he discovered the genius of his imagination. The strength of his poetry lies in the power to describe what he sees simply and graphically and to record what he feels without embellishment or inhibition. But translating sights and sounds – together with the way they excite the emotions – requires a creative imagination. Clare, it seems, possessed one from an early age.

Our fancies made us great and rich,
No bounds our wealth could fix.
A stool drawn round the room was soon
A splendid coach and six.

Perhaps the imagination got out of hand. There were fantasy conversations with Lord Byron and periods of black depression. Friends attributed his despair to the loss of Mary Joyce, his real love, and his decision to marry Martha Turner in the hope of consolation. At least as disturbing to his troubled mind was a move away from his native Helpston to Northborough, only four miles away, but a place that Clare could never think of as home. He became violent and the illusions about Byron were replaced with bogus claims to have become a prize fighter. It was certainly not failure that drove Clare to madness. His first book of poems was published in 1820 when he was only twenty-seven, and during the early years of his long life he enjoyed the support of wealthy patrons who recognised him as a great vernacular poet. During an age in which 'nature' was worshipped as the fount of art as well as virtue, Clare, the 'natural', seemed to represent the Arcadian dream of a life in a rural idyll.

The madness could not be contained. In 1837 he was certified insane and admitted to Doctor Allen's General Lunatic Asylum in High Beach near Epping. He absconded and walked back to Helpston in the belief that Mary Joyce was waiting for him there. The discovery that the hope of a reunion was vain had a less destructive effect than friends and family feared. His fame had faded. But although out of fashion, he wrote on – even when in 1851 he was again committed to an asylum where he died in 1864.

Much of John Clare's poetry, like his life and death, is sad. It deals with lost love, lost innocence and the slow decline of rural England at the brutal hands of the industrial revolution. But it is, like the English countryside itself, almost always gentle.

I see the sky
Smile on the meanest spot
Giving to all that creep or walk or fly
A calm and cordial lot.

That is an idea of England that is well worth preserving.

RSPB *Birds* Magazine May–July 2008

Consecrated Ground

I inherited my interest in churches from my father. Long after he was dead, when I discovered that he had been a Catholic priest but deserted his calling for love of my mother, I wondered if the need to visit places of worship had survived his apostasy. But during my boyhood – when we would call in every church we walked or cycled past – I assumed that he was inspired by no more than a passion for the past. My father was not an historian. Interpretation and explanation did not interest him. But, like Goldsmith's Mr Hardcastle, he loved all things old. So we spent many happy hours together under the tattered colours of county regiments and alongside the tombs of obscure Knights Templar. And – thanks to his years at the English College in Rome and the Gregorian University – he translated, on sight, the Latin inscriptions on the memorial tablets. I did not realise it at the time but I was absorbing part of England's history through my pores.

Battle honours and coats of arms tell only a small part of the story. The men who built the cathedrals – laying stone on stone – played just as important a part in making England as the gentry whose endowments paid their wages. They are buried outside the churches' walls. I spent many happy days among the graves of 'village Hampdens' long before I read Gray's *Elegy*. The overgrown graveyard of Wadsley parish church was immediately over the wall at the bottom of my boyhood garden and I played soldiers there during the war. I smashed hundreds of slime-encrusted jam jars (pretending they were hand grenades) on weeping angels and broken columns. And sometimes I read the inscriptions on the tombstones. 'Also an infant aged three weeks...' It was the first time that I began to think about the short and simple annals of the poor.

For more than half a century, I have maintained my father's habit of never going into a church when a service is in progress and shared my mother's conviction that funerals are no more than posthumous self-indulgence. Yet I am still fascinated by Gothic arches and Norman fonts and I remain entirely at home in graveyards. Atheist though I am, I know that the Church helped to make me – and not just the Church of England with prayers for 'our Sovereign Lady' and the Royal Coat of Arms over the chancel steps in memory of Charles I, saint and martyr. The course of English religion, and therefore the course of English history, was changed at Whitby Abbey, four hundred years before the Reformation – though a year ago nobody in the fish and chip queue along the quay was willing to believe it.

Amongst all the things I learned from my father and mother was the importance of treating churches – though not religion – with reverence and the absolute necessity of respecting graveyards despite the equal obligation to regard grief and mourning as private emotions. I also learned that there is a lot to be learned about England on consecrated ground.

74

Work and Worship

East of the road that runs from Harrogate to Ripon, agricultural Yorkshire rolls and ripples its way past York and Malton to the sea. In some parts of the county, the horizon is sharp and clear, a precise line drawn by factory roofs and limestone escarpments. But here the fields run endlessly on until soil and sky can no longer be distinguished. In the Pennines, farming is little more than the ownership of dishevelled sheep and the constant reconstruction of dry stone walls. But here, sleek cows graze in meadows separated by hawthorn hedges and exude all the contented confidence of a thousand years of pastoral prosperity.

The view across the Swale and over the Howardian Hills is only a glimpse of the rich farm land that covers over half of Yorkshire. For Yorkshire is a rural county. The factory towns of the south-west and the barren hills that mark the border with Lancashire are the Yorkshire of the music-hall comedian and the north country comedy. But they cover only a few of the broad acres. South of Middlesbrough there is no industry in the North Riding. North of Hull, the East Riding is exclusively agricultural. Certainly the north York moors grow little more than sheep and heather, and the further the farmer gets from the east coast, the more likely he is to be ploughing shallow soil. But even in the west, when the

75

land begins to rise, the dales run rich and fertile up between the fells. Most of Yorkshire is clouded hills and pastures green. The dark Satanic mills are pushed away into the corners of the county.

When Sheffield was a village, Leeds a parish and Halifax and Huddersfield hamlets, if they existed at all, the great sweep of rural Yorkshire flowered and flourished. It was powerful as well as prosperous, wise as well as wealthy; the natural home of the Augustine, Cistercian, Benedictine and Carthusian monks who prayed and proselytised in medieval England. For the contemplative orders who hoped to meditate their way to heaven, far from the world and its temptations, Yorkshire provided a refuge. For the zealots who wanted to plant Christ's flag in every market place, Yorkshire offered a challenge.

Looking back over north-west Yorkshire from the top of Sutton Bank it is easy to believe that the communities which moved into the vales of Wharfe, Aire and Nidd chose security as well as salvation. Behind are the north York moors, too high to be really hospitable. But below is the mirror image of the view from the Harrogate to Ripon Road. The fertile fields are exactly the right setting for merry monks and fat friars – but that is not how it was when the great Abbeys were founded. The twelve monks who left York and St Mary's Benedictine comfort to live a life of Cistercian austerity walked west into a wilderness. Where they settled is now light and green and beautiful – not least because the Brothers of Fountains Abbey laboured to make it so. Fountains Abbey has been a ruin for four hundred years. But

76

it is a ruin as the Acropolis and Baalbek are ruins. It is a memorial to another civilisation – its craftsmanship, its art and above all its persistence.

The best – though historically improper – way to visit Fountains is through Studley Roger and along the consciously prepossessing tree-lined avenue that leads to Studley church. It is a road in the great tradition of planned and planted English roads – designed for eighteenth-century squires to drive along without having to twitch their reins to left or right. At its end the style and the character change. In the abbey grounds, the Lords of the Manor of Studley have built themselves a little Chatsworth Park, not a place for country squires but a haven for the educated aristocracy of the Enlightenment. The landscaped lakes and the cultivated canals are properly precise. The Temple of Piety – ochre behind its colonnade, like a late Habsburg hunting lodge – is clearly the result of meticulous draftsmanship. The Roman wrestlers locked in metal combat, and Hercules labouring against Antaeus, are so clearly the outcome of classical education and conscious good taste that they need protecting from rough people and rude elements by iron railings and polythene sheets. Round the corner, through the wood, Fountains Abbey is open and free to anyone who wants to walk over the close-cropped grass that grows between what is left of its once magnificent walls. Once it was the model of English medieval ecclesiastical architecture. Yet it has no period. In ruins it proclaims virtues that defy time and style.

Years of dogged and detailed devotion were more important than moments of sudden inspiration in the building of Fountains. After every flush of genius there had to follow years of aching muscles and torn hands. Fountains was built in praise of God and keeping going, and during the decades of addition and improvement it changed from a little shrine in the forest huddled against the hill to a city in itself spreading across the flat green valley of the Skell.

The first monks built modestly from local stone. Their successors had greater ambition. They built the nave and the choir, and beyond the choir the Chapel of Nine Altars with its great east windows. They built a chapterhouse and a refectory, and a long cellarium with vaulted roof and centre pillars. They built an infirmary for the monks and another for the lay brothers, a guest house for strangers and all the pantries and kitchens that a community of a thousand souls could reasonably require, complete with tall chimneys that took the smoke, if not to heaven, at least out of the bakeries and above the dormitories. And fifty years before the monasteries were dissolved they built the perfect Perpendicular tower.

The Reformation ended four hundred years of continuous building. It took extraordinary men to dress and lay each piece of stone and labour to add the extra cubit to an abbey that had gradually grown for two or three hundred years. The work could only be done if each humble task was an individual achievement; a proof of crafts-manship and a demonstration of devotion in itself. Every monk and mason knew that the work would never be done. There was always some-thing else to be added for the glory of God and in celebration of human achievement. The monks of Fountains believed that they could work themselves to heaven. Given another four hundred years they would have covered half of Yorkshire with their Gothic arches.

Henry VIII interrupted the work that should have lasted for eternity. The swift, formal Dissolution of the Monasteries and the three hundred years of casual neglect which followed turned much of Fountains Abbey into roofless walls and mounds of earth where altars used to stand. But in ruins the Abbey has a unique magnificence – the suggestion of what once was there as awe-inspiring as the reality of what remains. It is easy to understand why the men who inhabited it heard the clear and constant call of duty.

One of the duties of monastic life was to go forth and collectively multiply. St Mary's begat Fountains. Fountains begat Kirkstall. And, as part of a different line, Embsay begat Bolton in the valley of the Wharfe. The Augustinians at Bolton lasted a year longer than the Cistercians at Fountains. Indeed dissolution came only just in time. Abbot Moore had almost finished his new west tower when the King's messenger arrived. Had the desecration been delayed another year the early English front of the old Abbey would have been covered over and forgotten. Thanks to Anne Boleyn, the Abbey was spared that destructive improvement.

That Bolton was never finished was a blessing. Its beginning was a benefaction. According to Wordsworth, the 'stately Priory was raised' because a greyhound (the sort that tugs at Diana, not the kind that goes with cloth caps and mufflers) pulled the Boy of Egremont into the Strid – a chasm only four feet wide, where the Wharfe runs fast and ten feet deep before it wanders, slow and shallow, past the abbey. His mother founded the priory as his memorial.

Across the river on the Hill of the Standard, Francis Norton, another Wordsworth hero, fell, stabbed 'from behind with treacherous wound' in defence of family, fortune and the north of England. But on a warm Whit Monday evening, there is nothing menacing about the Wharfe at Bolton and the hills that hem it in. Paddling children wobble their way across the pebbles of the river bed. On its banks a dozen cricket matches overlap.

In the Devonshire Arms, the prefabricated gift shop in the car park and the Post Office and general store in its little garden, business is brisk. The neglect of winter is forgotten and the cash registers combine in a continuous carillon. Abbeys are obviously a good investment. When Abbot Moore handed Bolton to the Crown in 1540, its annual income was £390. To a king interested in theft as well as theology, that made it a better prospect than Rievaulx. Although high on the north York moors, Rievaulx at Old Bylands should have been worth more than £351 a year. In 1131 the valley of the Rye was 'a place of Horror and waste solitude'. By 1167, because of hard work and fast building, there were so many monks and lay brothers within its walls that 'the church swarmed with them like a hive of bees'. Originally there had been two Abbeys in the valley. On the right bank Savigniac monks

80

lived on land given them by Roger de Mowbray. On the left bank, Cistercians enjoyed the benefice of Walter l'Espec. The arrangement proved unsatisfactory. Each monastery was confused by the other's bells – 'which was not fitting and could not be endured'. Graciously the Savigniac monks agreed to up altar and move to Stocking. But they still owned the right bank and virtually all the flat floor of the valley. For the Rye ran close against the left-hand slope and all that could be ploughed and planted lay on the Savigniac side. Gradually, by cunning and by contract, the course of the river was changed. Sometimes the bank was moved surreptitiously to the right. Sometimes the river was drained and shifted by agreement. By the end of the thirteenth century, Rievaulx – the monastery which remained – owned all the land from Penny Piece to Ashberry Hill. Its writ still only ran as far as the Rye, so the abbot remained lord of only the left bank. But the river had been pushed hard up against the western slope. All that was fertile now lay on its left. Beyond the right bank was thick forest and steep hill. It had taken the monks several lifetimes to move the river. But they had all the time which the world could provide. Their strength was the willingness to work on until the last trumpet sounded like a factory hooter to signify that man's little working day was over.

The Cistercians of Rievaulx were indomitable in their determination to make the valley worthy of this work and worship. The Savigniacs were indefatigable in their willingness to search the north of England for a home which did justice to

81

their creed and calling. They began at Furness in Lancashire. Roger de Mowbray's gift tempted them across the Pennines and they established a house at Old Bylands on the Rye. Then there was the confusion of bells and conflict of convenience with their brothers across the stream. So they moved on and began to build again at Stocking. They ended their travels on the southern slopes of the Hambledon Hills. It took years to drain the land before the building could begin. To the monks, the moves from place to place were just another part of the service to the Lord. They built and rebuilt. At every stop, they called the infant abbey 'Bylands'. They had come to Yorkshire to build Bylands to the Glory of God. Forty years and three sets of foundations later, neither the name nor the task had changed.

The triumph of work as well as worship was celebrated in every monastery in Yorkshire. At Gisborough the monks pulled down the Norman priory simply for the joy of replacing it in the Decorated style. At Whitby, Caedmon proved that by application a humble ploughman could become a great poet. He was helped by divine revelation and the patronage of St Hilda, but from the dream onwards he was singing the story of the Creation and Redemption fourteen hours a day. The abbey that his patron founded on the windswept site of a Roman signal station was host to the great Synod of 664. There were long days of disputation and competitive logic and conflicting theology. The Synod of Whitby had to choose between the rival merits of the Celtic and Roman rites. In the end St Peter's legion won and the English Church was set in its ways for almost nine hundred years.

The abbey – ravaged by Danes and attacked by Norwegians – survived as long as the Roman Mass. It was dissolved on 14 December 1539. Its estimated value on the day of its confiscation was £437-2-9. Within a month of its surrender to the King's Commissioner, it was leased to Richard Cholmley of Pickering. True to his Yorkshire nature, he bought the freehold at the first opportunity. Whitby was a valuable property, with an annual income second in Yorkshire only to Kirkstall, where the monks had begun the great tradition of Leeds by making a fortune out of wool. Thanks to hard graft, Kirkstall was worth £500 a year.

Deo adjuvante labor proficit is the motto of half the industrial towns in Yorkshire. People who could actually turn the moral into money have always endeared themselves to a county that wanted piety to show a profit. So Yorkshire admired the monks and loved the old religion and when Henry closed and confiscated their monasteries, Yorkshire rose up in the Pilgrimage of Grace.

The dissolution of the monasteries was neither the first nor the most terrible act of ecclesiastical destruction to have been visited on Yorkshire. William of Normandy, 'harrying the North' in revenge for earlier rebellion and determination that the rebels should not rise again, devastated all the land from the Humber to the Tyne. No house was left standing, no horse or human left alive. In the Domesday Book half of north Yorkshire is marked 'wasteland'.

On that wasteland Saxon churches had once stood. From it the great Norman cathedrals grew. Thomas of Bayeux laid the first Norman stones at Ripon. Much of it, commissioned by Archbishop Roger of Pont l'Evêque, still stands – heavy and permanent, determinedly intact in a see of ruined abbeys and dissolved monasteries – looking as if the money ran out just before it was finished according to a grand and complicated design. In fact, it was finished over and over again and became the most constantly and carefully restored church in Yorkshire, with a central tower so changed and improved that it is one style up the northern side and another down the southern. But the east front, without saint or statue, seems made for decoration that the diocese could not afford and the squat west towers create an irresistible impression that they were planned to reach fifty feet nearer to heaven. In fact it was all done according to the dreams and desires of England's 'second oldest city'. If more money had been wanted, devout Yorkshire men would have provided it. They were prepared to live and die for their church, pay for its glory and fight for its continuation.

On Skipworth Moor in 1536 it was fighting and dying that Robert Aske demanded of the men who marched with him to save the monasteries. The Pilgrimage of Grace had no hope of defeating the King and his castles. The price the pilgrims paid for defence of the holy houses was lifelong exile or savage execution.

They captured Pomfret Castle. They besieged Skipton, Whitby and Scarborough, kneeling outside the castle walls in prayer for supernatural

84

reinforcement. The Mayor and Commoners of Doncaster swore an oath of adhesion to their cause. But these were local triumphs, the little victories of an amateur army. When the Duke of Norfolk and his professional soldiers rode north, the pilgrimage disintegrated. But the devotion of Yorkshire to the old Christianity and to the priests and monks who laboured for its great glory had been established for ever. In Yorkshire piety is still respected, determination still admired and hard work still revered. No doubt, in heaven they have similar values. When the monks of Fountains, Rievaulx, Bylands and Bolton arrived, they must have found it just like home.

Goodbye to Yorkshire 1976

A Quick Sparkle of Baroque

According to the local guidebooks, Saint Michael and All Angels, at Great Witley in Worcestershire, is the finest baroque church in England. And those of us who cannot distinguish that excessively ornamental style from the related school of Rococo extravagance ought not to dispute their proud judgement. From a distance it seems overshadowed by what remains of Witley Court – a proper ruin which crumbles before the tourist's eye as a proper ruin should.

Fortunately Witley Court has escaped the ravages of official restoration. So it does not look

85

like a corpse that has been painted and powdered before being immortalised in embalming fluid. In the intimidating shadow of disintegrating magnificence, Saint Michael and All Angels appears reluctant to exhibit the exuberance that the Oxford Dictionary insists is essential to the baroque tradition.

Perhaps baroque is not so much a style of architecture as a school of interior decorating. For, inside Saint Michael and All Angels every flashy feature of the genre is on display. The ceiling illustrates the big events of the New Testament in twenty-three glowing episodes. The walls are embossed gilt scrolls and ormolu laurel leaves. The altar is enlivened with mosaic panels.

However, its general garishness ought not to be exaggerated. Although the patrons of an eighteenth-century playhouse would have thought such vulgarity an undesirable distraction from their elegant entertainment, the manager of a Mecca ballroom might imagine that the opulence added a touch of class to Latin American night.

I was brought up to believe that anyone who squinted sacrilegiously through half-closed eyes during the Lord's Prayer should see only bare stone and unseasoned wood. If our minds wandered during the Magnificat or Nunc Dimittis, it was the classic curve of the arches or the carvings on the pulpit that stole our attention. Oliver Cromwell had whitewashed all the colour from our church walls.

So, Saint Michael and All Angels offended against every principle of ecclesiastical architecture that my low church childhood had taught me was essential to proper piety. Yet as soon as I entered its gilded portals I felt my usual urge to experience a minor religious revelation. I did not hope for a sudden flash of blinding light. But a quick sparkle that caused temporary short-sightedness would have been neither unexpected nor unwelcome.

The same feeling always creeps up on me whenever I enter a church – whatever its shape or size, age or denomination. Unfortunately – at least for the illusions of any religious friends – it always disappears as soon as I return to the daylight beyond font and porch. Even as I stand mid-pew and spiritually unfulfilled, I realise that the immortal longings are only temporary. I want to experience a plausible miracle. Graham Greene's vanishing strawberry marks and resurrected bomb victims are not for me. They are too difficult to explain away at the end of the mystical affair.

I prefer the superficially supernatural. Kneeling by the Brideshead deathbed I would have instantly accepted Lord Marchmain's last convulsion as the sign of grace that guaranteed eternal rest. But I would have recognised it for the muscular spasm that it was, once I returned to the harsh world of Shadow Cabinets, Thursday deadlines and the unfulfilled promise of the Sheffield Wednesday Football Club.

The sudden desire for momentary redemption is the temporary victory of atavism over atheism. Ancestor worship lurks just below the surface of the theologically respectable Established Church. The Anglican Communion is as much concerned with memories of mortal achievements as it is with

87

the hope of moral salvation. The tombs of cross-legged crusaders, the memorials to long-forgotten squires and the shoe-scraped tablets that cover what time has left of last remains remind the visitor of more than the history of England. They bear witness to the centuries of worship and belief. On the top deck of a bus or in the second row of the stalls scepticism is irresistibly easy. In church it is only possible for those who are prepared to tell the ghosts that they all got it wrong.

Saint Michael and All Angels seems designed to demonstrate the continuity of Christian worship. Consecrated in 1735, it appears to have been added to and, theoretically, improved during every subsequent decade. It possesses metal standard lamps that might have been designed for a pre-war provincial production of *Private Lives*.

Its floodlights are a tribute to post-war technology. The automatic burglar-proof postcard dispensers are clearly the product of the ingenious and suspicious Seventies. They were vandalised circa 1981. More important, although the church stands at the end of a mile-long muddy track, the faithful still make the wet pilgrimage on Sunday mornings and sing their holy songs to the accompaniment of an organ which George Frederic Handel once played.

These days I rarely go into a church which is less than a hundred years old. The guidebooks only point me at religious monuments that are sanctified by age and generations of pious parishioners – the sort of people who still spend ninety minutes each week in the concentrated hope of life everlasting. Between the time when the two smallest choirboys emerge from the vestry door and the moment when the final note of the valedictory blessing echoes from some mysterious Gothic or Early English recess, they really believe in the promise of the psalms. Redemption and eternal rest seem as inevitable as the roast beef and Yorkshire pudding that awaits them at home.

Of course such delicacies are special to Sunday. But they have been enjoyed for so long that the aroma hangs permanently in the air. No wonder that spiritually deprived Bisto Kids like me sigh 'ah' for religious certainty when we sniff the odour of sanctity.

Guardian 13 March 1982

Rooted to the Spot

Last week, I went back to the tribal homelands – not the land of my grandfather (which is Sheffield, and still a place of regular pilgrimage) but to the border country from which my mother and her female forebears come. They were born on the little Derbyshire peninsula which juts out between Nottingham in the south and Derbyshire in the north, an inland promontory which comes to a pointed end at Shireoaks where (according to local legend) the trees which grew before the interference of the Boundary Commission could spread their branches into three counties. Halfway along the archipelago of pit villages is Steetley.

89

On most maps, Steetley is not even a dot and the meticulous Ordnance Survey records no more than pithead winding gear, a handful of houses, a sprawling farm and a church which has neither tower nor steeple. The church is really a chapel, but not of the non-Conformist variety. It is a chapel of the elevated sort; a private place of worship created to accommodate the exclusive convenience of a single great family. Gley de Breton built it. The Vavasours inherited it and owned it until the Reformation. Then it passed through the Howards from the Wentworths to the Pelham-Clintons.

During the age of enlightenment, Steetley was neglected and abandoned. The roof fell in and the walls, which bore the marks of Cromwell's artillery, were overgrown with Gothic ivy. In 1880 (the year of my grandmother's birth) the climbers and creepers were cut away and All Saints' Chapel was re-roofed and restored. It now stands, according to local guidebooks, 'the most perfect and elaborate specimen of Norman architecture to be found anywhere in Europe'. I have never quite accepted that whole description – despite the perfect curve of the apse and the exquisite detail of the triple arches.

For Steetley has always seemed to be more specimen than example. Specimen is small whilst elaborate is example. Steetley chapel is only 56 ft long and less than 16 ft across at the widest point of the nave. If, like the great churches of Christendom, its size were to be recorded on the floor of St Peter's in Rome, the brass studs which mark its length would be driven into the sanctified

90

flagstones immediately inside the massive sculptured doors.

Indeed, Steetley chapel is so small that it is not allowed to be a parish church in its own right but exists as a subtenant of Whitwell down the road. But a service is held there each Sunday and the churchyard is kept as pruned and cropped as any burial ground in England. All Saints' is of a size that inspires neatness and tidy respect. On the day of my grandmother's funeral, great uncle Ern smoked his pipe whilst leaning over the cemetery gate so that the tobacco smoke would not pollute the air above the consecrated ground.

Great uncle Ern and the consecrated ground are now one and indivisible. There is no headstone to mark his resting place. For he was the last of the Skinners and the desire to immortalise the family's memory died with him. But Steetley churchyard is half filled with the crosses and broken columns of his friends and relations. His mother and father sleep side by side. And his adopted sisters Jane and Charlotte Hartill – though separated in life by almost twenty years – are united in death by identical memorials. Anne, the Skinners' natural daughter, has a cross of the same pattern and my grandmother, their youngest child, lies in the shade of trees which mark the line where cemetery and pasture meet.

My grandmother was a gardener's daughter and she was born in a tied cottage halfway along the Worksop road. The house belonged to Henry Sweet Hodding of Harness Grove and the squire is buried in a row of graves which runs behind the line of Skinner crosses. The master lies under marble, whilst his man and his man's family slumber beneath nothing better than granite. But whilst masons may discriminate, death never does. At the foot of the Hodding grave there is a memorial to his grandson Harry – lieutenant, the Sherwood Foresters. Lieut. Hodding died of wounds near Cambrai on 8 November 1918, three days before the Armistice was signed.

Churchyards are dangerous places. For once inside them the temptation to philosophise is almost irresistible. Walter Raleigh fell for it with his soliloquy on death the leveller. Thomas Gray made his reputation by musing amongst a collection of tombstones which now lie equidistant between the M40 and the M4. And they did not even have the excuse of standing about their grandmother's bones. In Steetley churchyard, I thought not about death but about the lucky lives of those families who feel rooted in one spot. The Skinners thought that their little piece of the Derbyshire–Nottinghamshire border was the only place to live and die. I envy them their territorial certainty.

When I first saw my grandmother's grave it was an ochre gash cut into the summer clay. Last week the wound had healed and the broken moss-covered cross looked as natural a part of the landscape as the holly bushes and the oak trees. The cycle was over and the circle complete. Having come from Steetley she had returned there and become part of the soil. She was not scattered in the wind or blown out of a crematorium chimney but contributed to the earth, and her grandson, who barely remembered her and got into trouble for grinning during her funeral service, could stand on a patch of damp turf and know exactly where his roots were planted.

There are still people in England who are baptised and married in the same church and expect, one day, to be buried beside the path that they have often walked from lychgate to porch. I do not claim that they possess the heroically humble virtues which Gray attributed to the village Hampdens of Stoke Poges. But they knew where they came from and the direction in which they were going. It must help them rest in peace.

Guardian 29 December 1984

The Gray That Tolled the Knell of Parting Day

At St Giles they have no doubts. The *Oxford Companion to English Literature* may – in its tentative, academic way – write that 'perhaps' the churchyard is Stoke Poges. But the congregation at Sunday morning service knows that Gray's *Elegy* was certainly inspired by, and probably written amongst, the mould'ring heaps in which their rude forefathers lie. They can point to the yew tree which shaded the poet as he composed his hymn to honest joy and useful toil. Last Sunday, visitors sheltering from the rain beneath its branches had their view of the church obscured by a souvenir kiosk.

The kiosk notwithstanding, St Giles might have been created to act as a backdrop to an idyll of rural England. There is hardly a century since the Conquest nor a school of church architecture that is not celebrated in its stone, flint and Elizabethan brick walls. Slough and the motorway are five miles to the east. And Stoke Poges itself epitomises the new Barbourism of gravel drives, double garages and ostentatious orange burglar alarms. But St Giles – hidden at the end of its lane and behind its two lychgates – is part of a more tranquil past which was to fortune and to fame unknown.

Its fame now spreads across the Atlantic. William H. Chadley Junior and William H. Chadley III, splashing along the rose-bordered path that leads between the gravestones, were precise about their reasons for braving the October downpour and risking pneumonia. Elderly father and middle-aged son both learned Gray's *Elegy* by heart during their schooldays outside Philadelphia. Neither was sure if poetry was still an essential part of American education. William Penn's association with Stoke Poges was not, they insisted, a secondary reason for their pilgrimage. But they did have a subsidiary motive. Bernice 'Bonnie' Winterstone, the doyenne of Pennsylvania's literary establishment, called her house 'Stoke Poges'. They looked forward to returning to Villa Nova township with the news that they had seen the real thing.

There were no souvenirs for sale on the morning of the Chadleys' visit. But had they arrived on a weekday – with one of the coach parties that visit Windsor, Eton, Hampton Court and the Thames in rapid succession – the kiosk would have been open with Thomas Gray pencils, paperweights carved from wood which has fallen from the (presumably no longer rugged) elms and assorted glassware engraved with pictures of St Giles on display. The profit is used to augment the work of the voluntary 'reapers' who keep the churchyard so immaculate that it is difficult to believe that, in or about 1751, it was described as a neglected spot.

The glassware on offer includes vases, goblets and bells. Carol Hawkes, spinster of that parish, who is to marry Alistair Barber on 3 December, will give a bell to each of her bridesmaids. 'Is it not,' asked a visitor who was too clever for his own good, 'inappropriate to mark so joyous an occasion with a memento of the curfew that tolled the knell of parting day?' The leaders of the kirk leaped on his ignorance. The world was left to darkness and to Gray with the sound of alien bells ringing in their ears. The peal was probably rung in Windsor for, on a quiet day with the wind blowing in the right direction, the Royal Borough is still in earshot – though it is impossible to recognise even the distant prospect of Eton College. The bells which hang in St Giles tower – from which the ivy mantle has been removed to protect the stone – do not depend on Thomas Gray for their fame.

That is the problem with the parish church of St Giles. It deserves to be judged and enjoyed on its own considerable aesthetic and artistic merits. Yet

95

visitors with even the slightest literary inclination cannot separate it in their minds from the poet who lies alongside his aunt and mother outside the east window of the Hastings Chapel. The *Elegy* has become so much a part of the English subconscious that even in the middle of the day, moping owls are expected to complain to the moon and the herd in the adjoining field looks as if it is about to low before it winds slowly over to The Leas – one of the largest houses in Church Street.

The churchyard does not boast a single storied urn or animated bust – an omission that keeps it true to the spirit of the *Elegy*. For the poem was written in praise of village Hampdens and mute inglorious Miltons whose virtues, being unrecognised, were not immortalised in stone. There is a naval memorial, from which the detachable anchor was stolen, and a row of poignant headstones that commemorate four schoolboys, drowned off Land's End on 8 May 1988. One of them has a football half buried in the earth between the vases. Ironically, it is only Gray himself whose life and work is celebrated by the sort of vainglorious tribute that fails to call the fleeting breath back to its mansion.

The Gray Monument defies the years. It is grand enough to have been conceived in the eighteenth century, ugly enough to have been built in the nineteenth and is apparently – though not actually – made of one of those synthetic materials in which statues of the socialist-realism school were moulded in the twentieth. It was erected nineteen years after the poet's death and must – we can reasonably assume – have been planned, financed and designed several years earlier. It is difficult to imagine the memory of a modern writer being perpetuated by a massive stone sarcophagus balanced on a suitably gargantuan catafalque, barely ten years after his death. These days, we treat poets with less respect. And we have lost the taste for monumental sculptures. Gray can take some of the credit for that.

The monument – sacrilegious in conception and pagan in design – stands suitably outside consecrated ground in a field, which the National Trust preserves to safeguard the churchyard's rural setting. The cenotaph is protected on three sides by a dry moat (that the grazing cattle could, but dare not, cross) and on the fourth by its obscurity. Visitors can walk from the car park and through the graves to the church door without realising that the agoraphobic monstrosity is over their right shoulder. It is also, thanks to merciful trees, virtually invisible from the road. As a result, it is untouched by graffiti and the citizens of Stoke Poges are innocent of its existence.

Indeed a random sample of local inhabitants suggested that most of them are totally untouched by Gray and his *Elegy*. A young lady named Liz, watching her boyfriend play football in the field that faces the Gardens of Remembrance, had no doubt about the reasons for Stoke Poges's notoriety. It has, she told me, an avenue which is exclusively inhabited by television personalities – including Frank Bough. In a filling station on the road to Beaconsfield, a BMW driver immediately identified William Gray as the local Tory MP. And a youth on a bicycle – be-

97

lieving my question to be a request for directions – was sorry that he could not help.

The congregation at Sunday service was different. More than half of those tested could recite the *Elegy*'s opening couplet and almost as many were able to identify the century – and the right half of the century – in which it was written. The vicar produced a lady (by name Jean Porter) who, he claimed, could recite the poem from start to finish. When I discovered that she had made the flawless recording for the cassette which the souvenir shop sells, I disqualified her from my survey. A doctor's teenage daughter, who had been obliged at school to write a modern version of the poem, was chastened but wholly typical of the regular churchgoers' relationship with Gray. They think of him as a parishioner as well as a poet.

It would be impossible for anyone who walks through that churchyard every Sunday not to feel some relationship with Gray. His tomb – although it does not bear his name – is identified by a plaque on the church wall. His family pew is in the church. But, more important, the spirit of England is all around. At Stoke Poges the visitor expects Thomas Tallis to play the organ, Archdeacon Grantley to read the lesson from the eagle lectern in front of a Grinling Gibbons rood screen and Rawdon Crawley to kneel down with difficulty as the Reverend Mr Collins leads the congregation in prayer.

It is one of the most English places in all England and it seems only right that it should be the inspiration of an *Elegy* which – because of the virtues which it extols as much as the scenes which it describes – is perhaps the most English of all England's poems.

Guardian 31 October 1992

Nil Nisi Bonum

In the last year of that Parliament, there was a by-election in Birmingham. Victor Yates – the long-serving Member for Ladywood – died, as he had lived, with absolutely no regard for the convenience of his colleagues. After immense pressure had been put upon me by Denis Howell, my friend and constituency colleague, I agreed to attend the funeral. I travelled up to the Midlands with Brian Walden and Roy Jenkins.

Jenkins announced, before our train reached Watford, that funerals should not be treated with unnecessary solemnity. Walden and I – comparatively young and normally highly impressionable – did not, at first, take him at his word. So we got out of our taxi, at the late Member's front door, wearing our mourning faces. As if to justify our dolorous demeanour, a group of city councillors – acting as mutes and pall-bearers – rushed forward to slot us into the day's careful arrangements.

A cavalcade of limousines stretched along the full length of the road and we were ushered towards the Daimler that was reserved for Members of Parliament who were not Privy Counsellors. It was a hierarchical event so, as we moved up to near the front of the cortège, we passed Austin Princesses and Rover saloons which were designated for use by ex-Lord Mayors, honorary aldermen, councillors and Justices of the Peace. At one point an old man, who walked with the aid of two sticks, asked our escorts which car he could travel in. 'Who are you?' they enquired. He replied that he was 'Nobody. Just an old friend of Victor's.' He was sternly told that there was no car for him. In a way, he was lucky. The church was just around the corner. But we made our distinguished way to its gate via just about every road in the constituency. Traffic lights were turned off and saluting policemen held back the buses and lorries as we made our mournful progress.

Victor Yates's funeral is the one occasion in my life when I have known a lychgate to be used for its proper purpose – rather than a shelter from the rain, a refuge for courting couples or a hideaway for teenage smokers. The coffin was laid to rest under the imitation Elizabethan eaves whilst the bearers prepared to carry it into church. To my surprise, one of the bearers was me. Walden and Jenkins, in a similar state of shock, grasped two of the other brass handles and Denis Howell – whom we blamed for the whole day's arrangements – took up his place as the other member of the quartet and gave us instructions in the stentorian manner of a boat-race cox. Unfortunately, we could not obey them. Victor, a small man in life, was too heavy in death for us to lift. I tried to ignore Brian Walden's suggestion that his money was being buried with him.

Much to my relief, it immediately became obvious that we were not the first four hearty males to fail the coffin-lifting test – no doubt a sign of diminished manhood in primitive societies. For an assistant undertaker rushed forward with a stainless steel contraption that looked like a cross between a hospital trolley and an hors d'oeuvre dispenser from a posh restaurant. The remains of the late Member were placed upon it and we, his grieving colleagues, were told that all we had to do was hold on to the handles and walk down the aisle. The bier would take the weight and most of the mourners would not even realise that we had been forced to rely on artificial aids. We tried our best. But we were barely past the font when it became clear that the dear departed was not lying straight in his last resting place. So it was impossible to steer his Viking funeral ship on anything like the right course. One by one, we were crushed against the side of the pews to grunts from us and little suppressed screams from the congregation. We were rescued by the head undertaker, who pushed the coffin from the back like the man who returns a collection of supermarket trolleys to their proper place.

In my own defence, I must point out that my behaviour during the service was far better than Brian Walden's. I did not giggle when the vicar spoke of Yates as a 'man who would not say a bad word about anyone', or pretend to play 'We Do Like to Be Beside the Seaside' on a theatre organ when the coffin disappeared for incineration behind its velvet curtains. Nor did I offend Doris Fisher. Councillor Fisher hoped to be (and did become) Victor's successor, losing the seat at the by-election but regaining it six months later. In a proprietary sort of way, she stood at the church door repeating the mantra, 'What shall we ever do to replace Victor?' Brian's suggestion that he should have been embalmed and re-nominated was badly received. But it was that sort of day.

The buffet car was open on the southbound train, so we were able to console ourselves with British Rail *vin ordinaire*. Strangely enough, the wine helped to sober us up. I therefore believe that Roy Jenkins was entirely serious when he observed to nobody in particular, 'That was my first all-day funeral since Martin Luther King.'

Who Goes Home? 1995

Grave Thoughts

I spent much of my boyhood in a churchyard. The storied urns and animated busts ran – like the crosses, row on row – right down to our garden wall. So I was familiar with the inscriptions of remembrance long before I read the poetry of death. My father's favourite was 'We shall meet: but we shall miss him.' But I preferred the epitaph of a sergeant farrier which was engraved below crossed hammer and pincers. 'Beneath the portals of his grave, There lies a soldier bold and brave. And when the last great trump doth sound, He is to fettled quarters bound.'

At the time, everything to do with the army fascinated me. My churchyard period lasted roughly from El Alamein to Arnhem and for much of that time I played soldiers among the tombstones. Old jam jars, lined with green slime, smashed with a highly satisfying noise when lobbed, like hand grenades, against broken columns and weeping angels. The verger's grandson was killed crossing the Rhine, but I was too young even to wonder how the old man felt when, on the day after the telegram arrived, he dug somebody else's grave.

Fortunately, David Lean's *Great Expectations* did not arrive in Sheffield until I was old enough to take a shortcut home from the youth club without fearing that Magwitch would jump out at me from behind an ivy-covered obelisk. Anyway, I had begun to find something comforting about the smell of churchyards – rotting chrysanthemums, stagnant water, cats and laurels. It is still reassuringly reminiscent of youth and home and I cannot walk past a tombstone without reading the inscription.

These days, my weekend walks usually begin along the neat path of a country churchyard in which the rude forefathers of our hamlet first slept almost three hundred years ago.

Perhaps there is something special in the White Peak air. For stone after stone marks the grave of an ancient. Every member of the Fiddler family celebrated an eightieth birthday. Constande was ninety-one when she died on 24 February 1810.

Nonagenarians are not a novelty to me. I intend to be the third in direct, if not quick, succession.

What fascinates me about the Fiddlers and their long-lived contemporaries is that they almost certainly spent all their days in half a dozen villages which were an hour's walking distance of each other. No doubt news from the big world outside slowly filtered through their thick limestone walls.

When Constande Fiddler was twenty-four, Charles Edward Stuart's Jacobites passed by on their way from Manchester to Derby. And five years before she died, Nelson fell at Trafalgar. But despite the turbulence beyond the parish boundaries, the Fiddlers enjoyed the tranquillity that comes from a feeling of belonging.

Why, I wonder, did Thomas Gray say that melancholy marked such people for its own? Walking through the churchyard it seems incredible that, forty years ago, I could not wait to leave the part of England in which I was born and begin what I hoped would be a metropolitan life in London. I was neither as snobbish nor avaricious as Pip. After all, I wanted to become a Labour MP – not, in those days, a certain passport to fashionable society and untold wealth. But I did not understand the moral and message of *Great Expectations*. Trees without roots are easily blown over.

It did not take me long to learn the truth. I knew, from the start, that I did not belong in London, and although I identified with Sparkbrook (my little bit of Birmingham) I certainly never felt part of the city as a whole. When I thought about the place from whence I came, my mind filled with second-rate poetry. I had gone south when all the world was young and every goose a swan. But it was not long before I decided that, one day, the men who were boys when I was a boy would sit and drink with me.

At least I am back in the pubs, even though the people are different. Fortunately, they all seem very much the same. Alone in the city with William Wordsworth, everyone that passed by was to me a mystery Now I take it for granted that men and women whom I have never met were at school with me. And I assume that old ladies who nod to me in the street were once my next-door neighbours.

It is called being at home. The lucky Fiddlers never went away.

Guardian 31 May 1999

Listen, You'll Hear a Miracle

At ten minutes to five in the evening, the light, illuminating York Minster through the great north window, is beginning to fade. Tourists – whose five-pound entrance fee helps to preserve England's greatest Gothic cathedral – are being turned away. Earnest worshippers are hurrying to Evensong.

The nave and transept are deserted. The congregation, fifty at most, sit in the heraldic crested seats which, on major feast days, are occupied by the Dean and Chapter. In the organ loft, Philip Moore, Master of the Music, plays a voluntary.

Two girls in red cassocks light the candles on the desks in front of the choir stalls. An extraordinary display of musical virtuosity is about to begin.

Sacred music has been sung in York for more than a thousand years – first by the monks who found a home in the city before the building of the Minster had even begun and then, when it was accepted that laymen could worship as well as watch the priests at prayer, by choirs and congregations. Today, as required by the scriptures, they make a joyful noise.

The choir has changed with the years. It is made up of adult 'Songmen' and pupils from the Minster Choir School. The Songmen are, as is to be expected, enthusiasts for choral music who happily supplement their regular earnings with payment for doing what they enjoy – £9000 a year for most of them and £3500 for the 'choral scholars' who have won a place in the University of York.

But it is the children who are a modern miracle. There are thirty-three: seventeen boys and sixteen girls. They sing together only on exceptional occasions. On most days the genders alternate at Evensong.

Some cathedrals keep the sexes separate because girls in their early teens are inclined to intimidate their male contemporaries. Philip Moore, whose duties include being choirmaster to the boys, says only that their voices are different and that since boys' choirs are 'unique to England' their separate identity should be preserved. The tact is typical. Moore, sometime Eton music master and a composer, is the sort of Englishman who believes courtesy and modesty are major virtues.

The excellence – the result of Moore's respect for church music's great traditions – is not confined to the boys' choir. The girls – singing, with the Songmen, Quem Vidistis Pastores (Whom Did you See, Shepherds) as an Evensong anthem – must have made the angels envy the musical quality of their praise.

Moore says that deciding who can become a chorister is his most difficult job. He looks 'less for exceptional voices than for musical inclination' and a general ability which will guarantee success in the day-to-day work of the classroom.

Only half of the Minster School are choristers. For them, the school day is long and hard. It begins at 8 a.m. with the usual formalities. Then there is almost a full hour of practice, rehearsal and personal coaching before normal lessons begin at 9.10 a.m. At 3.45 p.m. choristers move from school to Minster for a half-hour practice. Then the choir which is to sing at Evensong joins the Songmen in the body of the church and rehearses again for another twenty minutes. Evensong ends after 5.30 p.m., completing a working day which has lasted more than nine hours.

Some of the choristers – eight- to thirteen-year-olds – begin the day with journeys which most adults would find exacting. One travels twenty-one miles from Leeds, another twenty-four miles from Goole in East Yorkshire. Yet somehow they manage to preserve the enthusiasm which is essential to their performance. Charity Mapleton – at thirteen very senior and runner-up last year as Young Chorister of the Year – admits that at first she was not sure if she could survive the regime. But she never thought of giving up.

Yet, despite their obvious dedication, the choristers are ordinary children. One – perhaps wanting to shock the Master of the Music – announced that her favourite records were made by a boyband called McFly. Childhood makes them friends, not competitors. Part of the secret of the choir's success is the way in which they hang together. Probationers, tots of seven, wearing the regulation scarlet cassock without a white surplice, sit with the choir throughout and join in when they recognise the music. When one probationer's attention began to wander, the senior chorister at her side administered a sharp dig in the ribs. Then, in a more benevolent mood, a guiding finger helped the novice to reclaim the lost place on the sheet of music.

What matters is the music. Sacrilegious it may be, but that is an object of veneration in itself. The result is a joy in the music which almost transcends the worship of which it is part.

At the end of Evensong, Carolyn Barrow glowed. Her son James, aged six, ran (with an admirable disregard for decorum) for the door, but she paused to speak to the choirmaster. James is joining the choir when he is seven. That was not his intention when he entered the Minster School but a teacher recognised his potential.

Ms Barrow's delight at the discovery is not just pleasure at her son's prodigious success. She knows James is about to become a part of English Church history – and English excellence.

Daily Mail 8 March 2005

Masons Giving Mother a Makeover

Canterbury Cathedral is not what it used to be. Time and weather have taken their toll. So, according to Eamonn Lee, the foreman of the masons' workshop, there is very little left of the original ancient outer wall. The process of restoration and renewal has been gradual. Only once in several lifetimes is a whole architectural feature removed and replaced.

Five years ago, the 26-foot crumbling Candle Tower – which stood above the south-west transept – was demolished and rebuilt. The job was done with such precision that not even William the Englishman (the master mason who fell to his death from scaffolding in 1178) would be able to tell the difference. But most of the masons' work ends with pieces being fitted into a limestone jigsaw.

It begins when lorries – carrying five-tonne slabs of French stone – rumble into the yard outside the Broad Oak masons' workshop. The Setting Out Mason (who keeps cricket bats beside his desk) draws a plan of the replacement for the disintegrating cornice or eroded architrave. A circular saw, which performs with the precision of a scalpel and the irresistible force of a high-velocity bullet, cuts out a block of exactly the right size. Then the laymen's idea of real masons' work begins. Men with mallets and chisels carve the stone into intricate shapes.

They are only one small part of the great enterprise to preserve 'The Mother Church of England'. Much of the conservation work is done 'on site' from scaffolding which hangs like a spider's web outside the cathedral. High on a windy platform on the wall above St Anselm's side chapel, I talked to Heather Newton – officially entitled 'stone carver conservationist' but, in fact, a mason in the great tradition of the craftsmen who built Canterbury. Women masons, said Ms Newton, rarely work at the 'hard end of the trade' – industrial building where the money is made.

Conservation, on the other hand, is 'often regarded as woman's work'. A great deal of washing is involved and 'it is more concerned with quality than speed'. In typical English style, Heather Newton 'does not want to get mealy mouthed about her job' but says that it is a 'privilege' to work on one of the great edifices of English history. Kneeling amongst the dust and debris which covered the scaffold platform, she illustrated the overriding principle of her calling – only replacing when conservation is not possible.

The delicate tracing which decorates the wall is, she announced, 'Victorian, not the original Romanesque'. The Victorians are not popular amongst the Canterbury conservationists. They recklessly cut away and replaced barely damaged stone – often in designs of their own which they thought superior to the ideas of the medieval masons. The inferior stone in which they worked quickly cracked and crumbled. Worst of all, they used cheap mortar, made of sand and cement, which rots the walls it should hold together.

Five hundred years ago, the outside of Canterbury Cathedral was painted. Whatever the aesthetic merits, and theological significance, of coloured walls, pigment protected the stone. Most of the paint was scraped away when the Reformation broke England's ties with the flamboyant Church of Rome. What remained was scrubbed off by the Victorians. Now the restored and replaced stone is covered by a protective 'limewash' in the same colour as the walls it covers. The English have no taste for painted churches.

We have, however, retained our enthusiasm for stained glass. But glass, like stone, is ravaged by time. And the great windows of our cathedrals withstood the rain as well as glorified God and honoured His saints. Old glass, like old stone, deteriorates in hard weather. Examining a soon-to-be restored window under one of the conservation workshop's microscopes, it seemed impossible that the pitted and corroded glass could ever be restored to anything like its original glory. But the conservationist dabs away with cotton wool in the certain knowledge that care and patience removes all manner of blemishes.

Dr Sebastian Strobl (head of Stained Glass Conservation and the fourth generation of glass conservationists) dismisses the myth that the vulgar colours of the 12th century can no longer be reproduced. When glass must be replaced, the problem is cost not craftsmanship. Only fragments are needed. Yet to obtain an exact match, Canterbury must buy a full square metre for £100.

Conservation costs Canterbury Cathedral

£9000 a day. And, according to Eamonn Lee, that is not enough. The cathedral is decaying faster than the damaged stone is being restored and replaced. The cathedral that marks the spot where St Augustine baptised King Ethelbert of Kent and English Christianity was born is decaying faster than the damaged stone is being restored.

All power to the new conservation appeal which is to be launched next year. Canterbury is not just a building, nor even just a cathedral. It is England in stone.

Daily Mail 19 April 2005

Ringers Seduced by Appeal of Bells

Half-past seven on a sunny Wednesday evening in Bruton, Somerset. The west tower of St Mary's Parish Church glows a soft gold against the clear blue sky. Brian Shingler, farmer and Tower Captain of St Mary's bell ringers, leads the way through the ancient oak door and up the forty-eight winding steps to the ringing chamber. The weekly practice of Grandsire Doubles, Cambridge Surprise Minors and all the other peals in the ringers' repertoire is about to begin.

Bell ringers come in all shapes and sizes. David Mills is a retired chemistry teacher. Harry, his son, is in computers. So is Christine Dunn, who describes bell ringing as a passion that she developed while helping St Mary's raise funds for rebuilding. Harry Good – the Steeple Keeper who keeps the bells and ropes in good repair – was a military policeman before he joined the civil service. The youngest bell ringer is Josh Richards, the twelve-year-old son of a stone mason. The oldest prefers to remain anonymous.

Not all the ringers are local born and bred. Ray Taylor worked in advertising and then escaped from London to the West Country. He has built his own aeroplane and is a qualified pilot. Learning to fly was, he says, far easier than mastering the art of bell ringing.

Anyone who reads the 70p booklet, which all new bell ringers buy, will have no difficulty in believing him. The little manual consists of incomprehensible instructions illustrated with unintelligible diagrams. Yet all over England men and women are working their way through its pages at the recommended speed of one every three weeks. Think of bell ringing, the book begins, as 'plaiting and weaving'. Easy. All the student ringer needs to do is remember a series of impossibly complicated patterns and the path that he or she must follow through the maze of sound – while manipulating a rope that controls a nine-hundredweight bell. That is the weight of the lightest bell at Bruton.

Yet hundreds of men and women stretch their minds and muscles with real enthusiasm. If Bruton is typical, they are not there because they feel called to ring out God's message across the countryside or summon the world to prayer. The ancient notice on the ringing chamber wall proclaims that bell ringers are expected to attend

113

at least one service every Sunday. The injunction is ignored or interpreted as the obligation to make an occasional willing appearance. The bell ringers ring bells because they like the sound they make. And they revel in the thought that they are carrying on a tradition that has been part of English life since the great parish churches were built a thousand years ago.

Juliet Bowell – a bell ringer for two-and-a-half years who still regards herself as a novice – has written an essay about her motivation. The sound, it explains, 'spreads backwards in time to all the generations of ringers who stood here before us'. Successive generations have rung the six bells of Bruton since the oldest was cast in 1528.

Bell ringing is a hugger-mugger business. The six ringers at St Mary's stand, ropes in hand, in a tight circle in the ringing chamber. Reserves and replacements – and the occasional visitor – keep well clear. Strangers who perch precariously on the bench that runs round the wall are sternly warned: 'Do not sit with your legs crossed. Or at least keep your feet on the floor.'

Ringing is a dangerous pastime. Occasionally a ringer loses control of a bell and its rope goes wild, spiralling like a ribbon on a top, up through the roof of the ringing chamber and into the bell chamber above. If it becomes entangled with legs or feet, the body to which it is attached is dragged up with it. Bell ringers have died in the line of duty.

The practice is hard work. The ringing bells do not hang and swing like decorations on a Christmas tree. They rotate through a full circle of

360 degrees. Before the ringing can begin, the bells have to be 'rung up' into their starting position, which is standing on their heads. Harry Mills, a muscular man of thirty-seven, sweats as he 'rings up' the tenor bell. It weighs twenty-six-and-three-quarter hundredweights. Bell ringing is not for the feeble.

Not surprisingly, practice usually lasts for no more than a couple of hours – measured on an ornate Victorian clock that stands on a bracket fastened to the wall of the ringing chamber. It trembles as it ticks. The clock shakes in rhythm with the whole West Tower.

When the six bells swing through their circle, the tower sways with them. Fortunately, they never all swing in the same direction at the same time, so St Mary's has survived intact for six hundred years. And for all that time its bells have rung out across Somerset.

Daily Mail 24 May 2005

Camelot Or Grail, It's Up to You...

Flaming June in Glastonbury. The pop festival is still more than a week away and most of the tourists are drifting drowsily through the hot afternoon. But on the eastern edge of the town, a handful of fit or foolhardy visitors are toiling up the steep slopes of the Tor – the 500 ft hill on which the tower of St Michael's ancient church still stands.

Those who make it to the top have no doubt that every drop of sweat was lost in a good cause. Below them, stretching out as far as the eye can see, lies what was, once upon a time, the Vale of Avalon. This is Arthur's kingdom. Camelot is only a myth away.

John Spirit – who describes himself as 'a chippy from Coventry' – looks out across the lush meadows towards Wells Cathedral, clearly visible ten miles away. He is not sure if he believes in the legend of Merlin, the Sword in the Stone and the Round Table. But the idea excites him. To him the Court of King Arthur is the beginning of England – a nation built on chivalry.

Down in the town, the legend is kept alive by a dozen shopkeepers who have incorporated the story into the names of their businesses. The brochure which describes the delights of the ruined Abbey is more circumspect. It does not even mention the claim that Arthur and Guinevere, his faithless wife, were buried side by side in front of the Lady Chapel door.

What is left of the once mighty Abbey gleams white in the sunlight of the summer afternoon. Happy families picnic between the ruins. They all have something to say about King Arthur. Admittedly one lady from Sheffield said that she had been interested in his exploits ever since she heard about him burning the cakes. But the confusion with Alfred was not typical of Glaston-bury holidaymakers. In most minds, there was a clear picture of the Once and Future King.

Julian Cooke – with an Oxford history degree –

thought that Arthur was a medieval warlord, more likely to be dressed in animal skins than shining armour. 'But the legend suggests that he was an inspired leader.' On the other hand Bar Lawson, an art teacher in the local college, held a more romantic view. Arthur and Guinevere were, she believed, 'the ultimate lovers'.

Harold Watson, a painter and decorator from Worthing, remembered that Sir Galahad was on a constant 'quest' for the Holy Grail. If Arthur's knights once rode through Glastonbury, they were looking for the sacred chalice into which Christ's blood was shed on the cross.

The old legend says it was brought to England by Joseph of Arimathea, uncle to the Virgin Mary and an early Christian who fled from Jerusalem to escape the Romans' wrath. He founded the Abbey in Glastonbury. The holy thorn – which, according to tradition, flowers at Easter and on Christmas Day – grew from the staff which had supported him during his journey from the Holy Land to the New Jerusalem.

The legend improved with the years. The journey with the Holy Grail was not, the myth-makers claim, Joseph's first visit to Glastonbury. Thirty years earlier he had made the trip in the company of the young Jesus. That story inspired William Blake to ask, 'And did those feet in ancient time walk upon England's mountains green?'

According to Susan Kastner – relying on her six years' service in the Abbey bookshop – as many visitors seek information about Joseph of Arimathea as search for facts about King Arthur. Glastonbury holds its visitors in thrall because it

117

allows them to choose which myth they prefer. Enthusiasts for the supernatural claim that the ups and downs of the surrounding countryside represent the pattern of the stars in their firmaments. The rest of us can take our pick – Joseph and religion or Arthur and romance.

Either way, the imaginary past hangs heavy in the air. That is why Bar Lawson insists, 'Nowhere else in England feels like Glastonbury. It meets a need in all of us.' John Egan – who once drove a bus in Salford, but is now the custodian on guard at the Abbey gate – is not a man to be carried away by the magic and mystery of folklore. But he speaks of the morning mist rising around the Tor and goes on to say how easy it is to imagine that the hill was once the centre of a lake. Arthur returned Excalibur into that lake as he lay dying after the Battle of Camlann.

Egan then explains the essential truth about Glastonbury and all it stands for. When asked if the tourists who buy tickets for the Abbey really believe the legends, he answers that it barely matters. 'They want them to be true.' It is their dream of England and how they want England to have begun.

Daily Mail 14 June 2005

The Great Leveller

I spent much of my early boyhood in a disused cemetery – a Gothic beginning to my adolescence which was the result of nothing more romantic than the fact that only a high wall, over which I could climb with the help of an elderberry tree, divided our back garden from the overgrown graves. From time to time, I read the inscriptions on the memorials. One tomb, which particularly impressed me, contained the mortal remains of a whole family. 'Drowned in the Great Sheffield Flood.'

The experience encouraged me to believe in 'village Hampdens ... guiltless of their country's blood' whose humble toil should not be mocked by ambition. It also permanently focused my attention on the last resting places of other 'youths to fortune and to fame unknown'. The history of England is carved on the gravestones of its country churchyards. In this village, the original burial ground is – like the cemetery of my youth – what we, in our prosaic way, called 'full'. But it is as carefully, indeed as lovingly, tended as the more recently consecrated ground on the other side of Church Lane. That tells us as much about the present village as the inscriptions on the old gravestones tell us about its past.

My favourite memorial is 'a tribute' – implying, I think wrongly, that it is merely a cenotaph and

119

the mortal remains are interred elsewhere – to Charles Morton, the founding Secretary of the Inkerman Lodge of the Grand Order of Odd-fellows. It was a duty which he performed with 'the utmost fidelity' from 1855 until his death in 1870. The forefathers of this village lived for unpredictable periods. Walter Woodroffe died in 1885 at eighty-eight. Two of his three daughters, who are buried with him – but presumably preceded him to that quiet earth – went to meet their Maker after fourteen months of life. The third lasted until she was five. Elizabeth Shinwell, who survived her husband by twenty years, was born in the reign of George IV. Then, having seen William IV, Victoria and Edward VII come and go, she died a subject of George V. Her son was less fortunate. He departed this life aged thirty-two. His sister, Elizabeth, 'died in infancy'. One hundred and fifty years ago, uncertainty must have given special force to the solemn injunction to remember that in life we are in death.

As I recall, Walter Raleigh thought of death as the great leveller which embraced the whole world in the two words 'Hic iacet'. The early nineteenth-century residents of this village did not share that view. The founding families, who have lived in these parts since the Conquest, are either buried somewhere else or have been reduced to the ranks of oblivion by the wind and rain which has obliterated so many inscriptions. But there are three tombs – gravestones would not do the massive structures justice – which seem dedicated less to the glory of God than to the glory of the Greaves and the Needhams who inhabit them. They are great oblong blocks of stone which are decorated with carving that might either be Regency teapots or Aladdin's wonderful lamp. In their time, they were protected from the passing peasantry by iron railings which have since been cut away. I like to think that they were removed during Lord Beaverbrook's drive to turn scrap into Spitfires.

There are twentieth-century lychgates at the entrance to both the old and new burial grounds – increasingly a feature of recently built country houses which have no need of a resting place for arriving coffins. In normal circumstances, I would be a critic of their modern erection even in churchyard walls. But at Saint Giles there is a justification for them. One is inscribed in letters of gold: 'Captain Hubert Bradley Dixon, 1st Battalion the Sherwood Foresters, Nuevo Chapelle, March 12 1915'. The other, in similar script, reads: 'Lieutenant William Bennet Drew, the Royal Sussex Regiment, Vimy Ridge, August 12 1917'.

There were, in the churchyard of my youth – as there are here in this village cemetery – the simple headstones, decorated with regimental badges, which marked old soldiers' graves. But, despite the exploding jam jars, my most vivid wartime memory of that old burial ground is a man, not a memorial. The verger's name was Fred Guest. He was known as Old Fred because he had a son who, everybody knew, would take over one day. And there was a third in parish line. Young Fred, his grandson, was expected to inherit the family pick and shovel. Young Fred was called up and was wounded in Normandy. While he was recovering, he sat in the cemetery watching his grandfather 'reopen' old graves so that families could be united in death. After a few weeks he was fit enough to return to his regiment. Six months later, somebody had to dig a grave for him. After I heard the news, playing at soldiers in front of his grandfather was impossible. And, almost seventy years on, when I walk through a churchyard which he never knew, I still remember his name.

Spectator 21 July 2007

Towering Beauty in a Rural Idyll

West Tanfield – on the boundary between the North and West Ridings of Yorkshire – can lay claim to being the perfect English village. It has a church of incomparable beauty, two ancient public houses, a village green once used for maypole dancing, a venerable bridge across a wide but placid river and a variety of cottages with origins and foundations which go back five hundred years. On a windy morning in April, its streets were absolutely deserted until a tourist on a bicycle arrived outside the Bull Inn. Like me, he was looking for the Marmion Tower.

Marmion is a poem by Walter Scott – and its fictitious characters, including Young Lochinvar, lived north of the border. The real Marmions were thoroughly English and appear in tales of ancient chivalry, sagas of the Crusades and accounts of land granted by various kings in gratitude for services rendered. They are everywhere. But the Marmion Tower is unique. John Leland, the librarian to Henry VIII who went in search of England at the King's behest, included it in his book of Englandes Antiqitiees after he visited West Tanfield in 1530 and found 'a fair tourid Gateway and Haute of squarid stone'. The three-storey tower is a beautiful mystery. The castle, which it once guarded, has disappeared without trace – 'lost' according to the English Heritage notice which offers free entry. And it has none of the features of a fortified gatehouse. No grooves for a portcullis to slide up and down. No cross-shaped slits in the walls through which archers could take aim. But it does have an elegant oriel window looking out to the east. Whatever glass it ever held went long ago. But most of the walls have stood the test of time. They were built during the century in which the Magna Carta was signed.

The nearby parish church of Saint Nicholas has a complicated history. Parts of it predate the Marmion Tower by a full hundred years. But aisles were added, columns decorated and windows redesigned between, more or less, the reigns of King John and Richard III. The most recent renovation was begun in 1859. The Victorians, as was their habit, decided to 'improve' what the more sensitive parishioners must have realised was too near to perfection to make improvement possible. And for once they did the work without destroying what they aimed to save. Perhaps it

123

should be called 'the miracle of West Tanfield'. The result fooled both me and another awe-struck visitor who agreed that St Nicholas's was 'untouched and unspoilt'. The Rector, the Reverend Mark Beresford Pearce, describes the atmosphere inside his church as 'combining light and peace'. He was once vicar of an inner-city parish in Leeds, but honourably refused to say which living he preferred. One of his predecessors – Thomas Sutton, who died in 1492 – is commemorated in a small brass in the chancel floor. It must have been polished ten thousand times, but the figure is still clearly engraved in the burnished metal. Another miracle.

If there was nothing else which justified a visit to West Tanfield, the alabaster tomb of the Marmions would make the journey worthwhile. Sir John lies with his head resting on his tilting helmet and his feet on a crouching lion. He wears the chain-link collar – SSSSS – which was given to him by Henry IV. Lady Margaret, his wife, rests her head on a pillow, held at a convenient angle by angels. There is a sleeping dog at her feet. And along the north wall of the church, a row of stone Marmions lie head to toe – four knights in armour with hounds at their feet and a rather battered lady in a wimple and veil. There was so much history in the air that I began to fantasise. Perhaps, when the church was closed at night, the seven Marmions talked to each other about the good old days.

The wrought-iron canopy above the alabaster tomb is said to be unique. The 'prickets' at its corners have held lighted candles on feast days for six hundred years. But I was more moved by a more recent reminder of mortality. In one corner of the church there was a Victorian bier – a cast-iron trolley on which, for a hundred years, coffins have been wheeled into the churchyard. Once upon a time priests in the Chantry – now Chantry Cottage – were paid to give the dear departed a good send-off. It seemed to me an unnecessary precaution. As Emily Brontë wrote, I wondered 'how anyone could ever imagine unquiet slumbers for the sleepers in that quiet earth'.

Daily Mail 27 May 2008

Buckfast Sunlight

As you'd expect in the grounds of a monastery, a feeling of peace and tranquillity hangs in the air over the immaculate lawns of Buckfast Abbey. Five miles away Princetown is grey and forbidding amongst the scrub and twitch-grass of Dartmoor. But, while the most famous prison in England always seems half hidden in fog, Buckfast gives the impression that it is perpetually bathed in sunlight. All things bright and beautiful might have been written with the Abbey in mind. Though one old Sunday school favourite has to be amended to suit the elegant buildings and carefully cultivated gardens. If tidiness is next to godliness, Buckfast Abbey is only a step away from heaven.

Congratulated on the immaculate condition of the Abbey Church of Saint Mary, Brother Columba pointed out a patch of crumbling stone in the ceiling of a side-chapel and says that, if the money were available, all sorts of barely noticed decay and dilapidation would be rectified. The uninformed might assume that decay was only to be expected in a thousand-year-old church. The great west door opens beneath a classic Norman arch and the tower has perfect Gothic windows which confirm that it was extended after most of the building was complete. But appearances deceive. The last stone in the building of Buckfast Abbey Church was put in place in December 1938 after fifty years of hard work by the monks of Buckfast themselves. It is a modern monastery built in the style and on the site of a medieval foundation. What Henry VIII destroyed in 1539, half a dozen Benedictine monks began to recreate in 1882.

There was no money for stonemasons and carpenters. So – out of necessity rather than choice – they did the job themselves. There were never more than six, and often only four, monks working at one time. They had no formal training in any of the building trades and very little equipment. Poles were used for scaffolding and a hand-powered winch heaved the stones up the half-erected walls. As the years passed and the church grew, other builders began to worry about health and safety. The Brothers of Buckfast did not follow suit. Yet in half a century, there were only two injuries – both of them minor fractures. There were other near-accidents. But falls were broken by fortuitously protruding masonry or ended in conveniently situated piles of sand. The monks are careful not to talk of miracles.

Buckfast is the only monastery in England that can claim to thrive in the twenty-first century in exactly the place in which its existence was recorded in the Domesday Book. But do not imagine that it still lives in the past. Buckfast is the very model of the modern monastery. It offers a 'telephone for a prayer' service – anonymity guaranteed – and, within its grounds, an ecumenical chapel offers facilities for Methodists and Anglicans in pursuit of the ultra up-to-date objective 'outreach'. The shop, in the main Abbey grounds, offers HoBo House Dolls for sale from the cocktail bar section of that collection. Charity requires us to assume that the exhibition of mild debauchery is meant as a dreadful warning. Perhaps the most dramatic symbol of the hurrying times in which we live was the monk who sprinted out of the larger of the two shops, cassock flying behind him, and – having cried, 'Sorry, Can't stop' – hurtled out of the Abbey grounds in his motor car. Not that visitors are unwelcome. Once a Guest Hall welcomed weary travellers. Now a Retreat Centre offers quiet and contemplation for pilgrims in search of spiritual peace.

There are objects of devotion on sale at the back of the main shop at Buckfast Abbey – crucifixes, rosaries and holy pictures. At the front there are shelves of produce from the monasteries of Europe – including the famous Buckfast (tonic) wine. The Abbey is, or aims at being, able to pay for its own upkeep and the wine – once thought of as a health tonic but now drunk for pure enjoyment – is only one of its products. It keeps bees and sells honey and wool from its sheep is still processed in the Lower Mill and sold to make into Axminster carpets. The Higher Mill is now the Abbey's main shop. But a giant water-wheel still turns against its wall, driven by a diverted stream which still runs through a 'leat' constructed six hundred years ago.

But the points at which Buckfast Abbey's past and present meet most eloquently are the Sensory, Lavender and Physic Gardens. They contain almost forgotten herbs and vegetables which were used in the everyday menus of the medieval monks. And they contain plants used for flavouring and plants once used for medicine – lovage and rosemary, rue and lavender. On a bright summer's morning, the blood-red roses and the golden honeysuckle gleam in the sharp sunlight. They seem like the symbols of England past and present – as indeed is the monastery itself. It stands for work as well as worship and for the indomitability which made it rise from the ruins.

Daily Mail 22 July 2008

Pits, Poetry ... and a Curious Greek Tragedy

Believe it or not, Hucknall – a pleasant and apparently prosperous town, but hardly the centre of the universe – has just achieved a special status in the constitution of Greece. The parliament in Athens has determined that, each year, the Greeks will celebrate Byron Day, in tribute to the poet who died fighting for their country's independence. And Hucknall plays an essential part in the Byron story. The inhabitants of the Nottinghamshire market town are not at all surprised by their new eminence. Bill Horton, a Saturday morning steward at the parish church of Saint Mary Magdalene, says that for years he has greeted 'visitors from all over'. Last week he welcomed parties from as far afield as Australia and Chile. As they descended from their coaches in the town square, a life-size statue of Lord Byron looked down on them from above the doorway of Kitchen Creations. Its presence is easily explained. After he died fighting the Turks at Missolonghi, Byron was refused burial in Westminster Abbey. So his body was brought home to Hucknall. It now lies in the family vault beneath the chancel steps of Saint Mary Magdalene. We know it to be there because, during the late afternoon of Wednesday, 15 June 1938, Hucknall was the scene of a macabre ritual. The Reverend Thomas Gerard Barber, rector of that parish, opened the vault to see if Byron's earthly remains lay beneath the chancel steps of his church.

When the first flagstone was levered aside, he saw three coffins – the top layer of a carefully arranged pile. One of them was covered by a faded velvet cloth. The corroded coronet, which stood on top, suggested that it contained Byron's remains. The lid was loose and the rector – fearing tomb-raiders – lifted it to look inside. All he saw was a second coffin. Undaunted, he opened that too. 'There lay the embalmed body of Byron in as perfect condition as when it was placed in the coffin... The serene almost happy expression on his face made a profound impression on me.' No one could complain that Mr Barber was not thorough. Knowing that Byron was lame, he examined the corpse's feet to discover which one was deformed and satisfied himself that it was the right. Not all of Byron was in the coffin. His heart and brains – removed during the embalming – were in an urn, kept in a casket, nearby. They still are.

The vault was re-sealed and the poet and his family were left to rest in peace, disturbed only by the tramping feet of pilgrims overhead. Now – and we may differ about its desirability – a choir stall is to be removed and the flagstone beneath it replaced by a sheet of unbreakable glass. In a year or two it will be possible to look down into the vault. For some strange reason, I think that Byron – whose poetry I much admire – would find the sight funny. Anyone who wrote 'All tragedies are finished by a death and all comedies are ended by marriage' is unlikely to regard public exhibitions of homage as anything but a joke.

But I understand why Hucknall wants to keep the memory burning bright. Five miles away is Newstead Abbey. It is the house to which he returned for rest and refuge when, for a time, he decided to 'go no more a roving'. It is in Newstead that he buried Boatswain, who (according to its memorial) 'possessed beauty without vanity, strength without insolence, courage without ferocity and all the virtue of man without his vices'. He may have been 'mad, bad and danger-ous to know' but he understood dogs. It is very doubtful if he ever visited the parish church, but Saint Mary Magdalene seems to have overlooked his impiety. He is celebrated in a manner normally reserved for saints and angels. A glass case contains the dried remains of the flowers which covered his coffin on its way from London. An embossed head, in shining gold, adorns the south wall. And the leaflet which welcomes visitors to the church proudly points out that, in the east window's stained-glass picture of breaking bread with Jesus, one of the disciples looks remarkably like the author of *Childe Harold*.

When they opened the vault, seventy years ago, the air below ground was 'tested by means of a miner's lamp'. In those days, Hucknall was coal-mining country and had another claim to fame – no doubt in some people's mind as distinguished as the Byron connection. From the top of the church tower, even on a not-so-clear day, it was possible to see five working collieries – Hucknall One and Two, Linby, Newstead and Annesley. It is twenty-two years since the last of them was closed. Colin Blackwell, shopping in the town centre, talked about his thirty years at the other Newstead – pit, not abbey Most of them were spent underground. He preferred working lying flat to standing up. The narrower the seam, the less likely it was to collapse and crush him. Hucknall's history is a combination of sweat and poetry. You cannot be more English than that.

Daily Mail 28 October 2008

Beside the Seaside

For over thirty years of my life, I spent the first few days of October by the sea. More often than not it was Blackpool one autumn and Brighton the next, but occasionally Scarborough intervened and, once, Bournemouth intruded. I never went on the beach though occasionally, at the suggestion of press photographers, I walked along the promenade so that my speech, when reported in the papers next day, could be illustrated by a picture proving that it had been made at 'the annual party conference'. Even though my visits were not in search of the 'fresh air and fun' of which Blackpool boasted, I saw enough of the real holidaymakers to realise that 'the seaside' makes a special contribution to English culture. They encourage the indomitable determination which has made England great. Holidaymakers in the coastal resorts are absolutely determined to enjoy themselves come what may.

Inland holidays encourage rest and relaxation. There may be ancient monuments to visit, tents to pitch, even mountains to climb. But none of those activities involve the hard work which is essential if you are going to enjoy yourself in Skegness or Sidmouth. Part of the problem is the weather. Seaside holidays are hypothesised on the belief that sun and sand go together. On rainy days the dreams of an all-over tan are brought to a sudden end in the gloom of slot-machine arcades and bingo halls. Yet somehow most

135

English holidaymakers manage – despite the wind and rain – to 'have a good time'. If Waterloo was won on the playing fields of Eton, Dunkirk was turned from defeat into victory on the wind-swept beaches of Morecambe and Margate.

Perhaps there is something in the sea air which makes those who breathe it unreasonably hopeful. Perhaps that was the meaning of the Delphic slogan – It's So Bracing – on the pre-war advertisement for a week in a Bridlington boarding house. Certainly the refusal to be beaten – which holidaymakers display for a few days – has sustained Liverpool and Hull through a half-century of hard times. Perhaps the wind that blows up the Mersey and the Humber contains some of the sea-born potion that makes Blackpool and Brighton full of joy in a Force 7 gale.

I know of course that there are genteel coastal towns which will resent being associated with either the ports of the north or the seaside resorts of the old working class. I have walked through Bognor Regis with George Brown before a broadcast of *Any Questions?* and I am unlikely to forget the experience. But they are not part of the 'seaside' about which I wanted to write. When the Wurlitzer organ rose from its bunker in the floor of the Blackpool Tower Ballroom and the dancers joined in the chorus of 'We Do Like to Be Beside the Seaside', they were paying homage to fish and chips and the people who eat them. I do the same.

Skegness in Winter

During March, Skegness sleeps. In part of the town the slumber is so profound that it seems impossible for the hibernation to end by Easter. Between station and sea most of the shops are more than locked and barred. Windows which, when the season starts, will plead for attention are covered with sheets of thick brown paper. They fit the panes so precisely that it is impossible to discover what dark and desperate secrets lurk within the mysterious interiors. The Beach Ball café and all the other shrouded shops and snack bars are irresistibly reminiscent of 1940 and the desperate attempts to stop blast-shattered glass decapitating grandma. They make Skegness seem desolate as well as deserted – as if an invading army had landed and marched inland to capture Grantham, leaving behind a few bedraggled sandbags and a demolished pier to remind the remaining residents of the recent occupation.

The sandbags, on closer inspection, turn out to be a protection against sand itself. The idea that they should lie across the doorways of seafront shops to insulate the summer merchandise from the almost invincible sea was treated, by normally courteous locals, with open derision. Protecting the town from the sand and the sand itself from wind are major Skegness preoccupations. Skegness is a windy town in winter. And the bracing breezes that blow in from the North Sea and swirl across the flat Lincolnshire hinterland pick up, and attempt to carry off, the tiny particles of powdered rock upon which summer livelihoods depend. So nets are strung across the beach from poles that stand in protective parallel lines – an almost invisible barrier to the sand's abduction and visible proof that the wind *can* be caught in a basket.

At any rate, most of it can. The beach is so smooth and flat and beautiful that at first it seems as if the green and orange nets have won a total victory and not a single grain or granule has been displaced since the Earl of Scarborough decided to make nineteenth-century Skegness into a holiday town. But farther inland there is ample proof of the danger of shifting sands. A khaki carpet covers the single line of the miniature railway and runs across the landing-stage of the Mini Marina. Sand has blown into little drifts against the walls of the seafront gardens and has filled the cracks and crevices in the 'shelters' which protect elderly holidaymakers, not with the usual corrugated iron and plastic sheeting but by massive stone constructions designed in imitation of either a catacomb or a wine cellar.

Pensioners, sitting under these artificially ruined arches, usually need good eyesight even to see the sea. But two years ago the waves turned savage and washed wildly up the beach and towards the town. They left the pier (which, had it remained to poke its peaceful way out into the sea, would now be preparing to celebrate its hundredth birthday) more battle-scarred than the mole at Zeebrugge.

138

Two sections were completely swept away, leaving a stump protruding fifty yards from the shore and two cast-iron islands standing on their precarious girders thirty feet above the sea.

The first is occupied by two, apparently identical, persistently white pavilions, the ideal setting for a surrealist film concerned with love and death. The second one bears on its back the splendid pleasure dome that was once the object and reward of a walk across the sea. It is dilapidated to the point of disintegration. But it has a cupola that could contain an observatory telescope and wireless masts that might send signals across the distant oceans. Seen against the background of a sharp blue morning horizon it is easy to imagine Captain Nemo surfacing between the iron legs that hold it high above the sea to revictual the *Nautilus*.

Parts of Skegness have barely changed since the pier was built. The clock tower which begins, at ground level, mock-Gothic and gradually grows into mock-Swiss is typical of the silliest sort of Victorian municipal pretension. The station buffet preserves all that was most solid and splendid in an earlier, more unashamedly prosperous, railway age. It has a marble floor and a marble top on the solid oak counter. It has long glass mirrors behind the bar and sepia ceramic tiles where inferior eating-houses have wallpaper. It sells newspapers as well as cups of tea and possesses a dartboard for the entertainment of regular customers. It is comfortable to the point of being smug – proclaiming by every detail of design that it was built to outlast a century of tourists and day-trippers.

In March, Skegness Station is like an empty cattle-shed waiting for market day and the bustle of business. In a couple of months, the visitors will be running down the long platforms and congregating under the vast wooded roofs which could protect a thousand travellers from the rain that falls too often on northern Bank Holidays. Many of them will have been attracted to Skegness by the picture that was painted by John Hassall for the Great Northern Railway Company seventy years ago. The fisherman, dancing, arms outstretched, along the beach with an agility that is improbable in so portly a white-whiskered pensioner, has remained the symbol of Skegness since before the First World War. He is an essentially Victorian figure, protected by thigh-high waders and souwester... A red muffler flutters in the slipstream behind him. The whole rig-out might have been borrowed from Mr Peggotty fifty miles down the coast in Yarmouth. As he leaps across the pure azure pool that the sea has left in the golden sands, he cries the most unlikely of advertising slogans, 'Skegness is SO bracing.'

Yet the slogan, like the dancing fisherman, endures. That they have survived into a time when the pleasures of an earlier age (Skegness Operatic Society presents *White Horse Inn* at the Arcadia Theatre) have almost been submerged by The Sands Showbar. The Beer Garden and 'Lincoln's No 1 DJ, Mr Al' is a more spectacular tribute to the designer than any award created by the Advertising Association. And the dancing fisherman looks as if he knows it. His only concession to the passage of three score years and ten is an occa-

140

sional appearance on the front wall of a pub or club with a pint pot in his hand.

It is a place for propriety as well as pleasure. The van parked in front of the kiosk that forecasts wind and weather reminds residents of social obligations that Bridlington and Blackpool have never had to accept. 'Lincolnshire Drainage Company: By Appointment to Queen Elizabeth'. Sandringham is only a 'bus-ride away'.

The coach companies which have kept going through the winter by undercutting British Rail fares to London and Lincoln will soon be plying their proper holiday trade. Soon the mechanical Bambis and Muffins and Baby Pandas that are stabled for the winter in the Golden Nugget will be shaking their infant passengers in simulated gallops for twenty pence a time. Soon the boating lake will have been drained and the bottom cleaned and then water will have been flooded back in, hiding for at least the season the old oil-drums which drainage has revealed as the pillars by which the rustic jetty is supported. By Whitsuntide the remnants of the real pier will have been reinforced and the workmen who, like shipwrecked mariners searching for warmth and comfort, on winter weekends burn piles of sea-shattered timber, will have left the beach.

In their place will sit the tourists and the trippers row on row. The now unbroken stretch of beach will have erupted into a thousand sand-castles. Mai Lee's Chinese take-away will be in hot competition with the traditional fish-and-chip shops and the National Union of Mineworkers' holiday camp will be vying for fun and frivolity

141

with its commercial counterpart. Most of the holidaymakers will be as rosy-cheeked as the dancing fisherman, flushed with pleasure and stung by the breezes that will still be blowing from the north-east. Few people will lie in the afternoon sand in sunny siesta. That would be in conflict with both the Skegness tradition and the Skegness atmosphere. It is so bracing.

Listener 6 March 1980

The End of the Line

For the last ten miles of the journey into Hull, the railway line was along the bank of the Humber. Once upon a time the trains all stopped at the little villages that guard Yorkshire's southern frontier. And as we stood in the stations at Broomfleet, Brough, Ferriby or Hessle, I always wallowed in 'the cult of the north' which George Orwell so despised. Nowhere else in the world does so mighty a river mark the boundary between civilisation and barbarism. Lord Byron could not have swum the Humber. And John Wayne, although easily able to cross the Rio Grande on the back of his horse, would never have made it from Yorkshire's sandy shore to the grey line of Lincolnshire on the far horizon.

Indeed, in the old days not even the paddle steamer that carried passengers from Hull's fish dock to New Holland was strong enough to sail in

142

a straight line across the tide. It used to struggle upstream, confident that the tide would wash it back on course towards the sea and its proper destination. I spent hours on the upper deck of the old wooden pier watching the ferry making for Yorkshire in a great arc, like a crab determined to reach the haven but desperately incapable of travelling the shortest distance between two points.

In those days, the ferry's curved course was the nearest to a straight line between Hull and the south. Further east than Goole, for there was no way to cross the Humber. Men with a taste for Jules Verne and no understanding of practicality talked of building a bridge or of digging a tunnel. But I always knew that it could never happen. Hull would remain the place at the far end of the line, the city that nobody ever passed through by mistake and few people visited on purpose.

Although an alien from South Yorkshire, I never felt a stranger in Hull. Despite its unredeemed bomb-sites, the general greyness of its skies and the forlorn foghorns that echoed over the town, it was as friendly as it was flat. And Hull is so horizontal that instead of cuttings and viaducts helping the railway across the city centre, lines cross roads in a way which proclaims the real character of the countryside – level crossings. So Hull's vast array of cyclists never experience either the exhaustion of pushing their machines uphill or the joy of free-wheeling down. Hull was neither desolate not daunting, but it was remote. Remoteness hung in the air like the smell from the fish dock.

Now Hull and the south are joined together by what locals proudly, and properly, describe as 'the world's longest single-span suspension bridge'. If you believe that fact to be one of those contrived claims which have no real statistical significance, you may be technically correct. But, thanks to the decision to cross the Humber in one great leap, what used to be Lincolnshire and the East Riding are now joined together as Humberside by an exercise in civil engineering which is more elegant than steel and concrete has any right to be.

I saw it last Monday, as once again I travelled the route that Philip Larkin took on the day that he was late leaving Hull and passed those Whitsun wedding parties on the bank holiday platforms. 'Where sky and Lincolnshire and water meet' there is now a new pattern on the clouds. From a distance, it looks like a diagram for a geometry lesson drawn on a pale grey school wall. For the cables on which the bridge is suspended hang in a perfect arc. And the road which it holds high above the water is a tangent that just touches the incalculable spot where the curve stops sloping down before it begins to slope up. Half a mile away, it looks as if a line has been drawn across the heavens with a ruler, and that earth has not anything to show more straight.

I dawdled past the place where the bridge comes down to earth in Yorkshire, on my way to a conference specially convened to remind the world that the waters which once separated Hull and Grimsby had been rolled back and industrialists with money to invest could pass over to either side. I do not know how many people we persuaded to take root and grow on the banks of the Humber. But we did show them some beautiful pictures of watery winter sunshine turning the tide from grey to silver and the rising sun itself glowing above the Lincolnshire skyline like a lightly fried egg.

Bliss must it have been, in that wide-angled dawn, to be alive. And better than bliss it will undoubtedly be if the bridge and the new roads that join Hull to the heart of England bring the long-needed jobs to the Port and City of Kingston.

In the meantime, Hull remains as I affectionately remember it, dilapidated but not derelict, sometimes a pile of rubble but never a wasteland. As we pulled slowly into Paragon Station, I noticed a half street in which the houses had been demolished but the gardens left standing. The privet still stood in line and the shaggy lilacs were ready to bloom again next year. It was like so much of Hull, a secret hidden in an unknown city. I hope that it survives the arrival of the traffic from across the bridge.

Guardian 4 December 1982

Love Letters in the Grand

At first I felt obliged to protect him from himself. So I interrupted each anecdote with the warning that everything which he said was being taken down and would be used in evidence to establish the character of the institution over which he presides. But Richard Baker, the manager of Brighton's five-star Grand Hotel, chose neither

145

to modify nor retract a single story.

'People,' he said, 'come to Brighton for romance. That is our reputation.' At the Grand, romance comes expensive. A deluxe, king-size bed and breakfast costs £170 a night. According to Mr Baker – at thirty-three still a boyish figure despite the striped trousers and tail-coat of a Mayfair undertaker – the patrons expect, and get, their money's worth.

'Most of the couples who check in at weekends are in bed within an hour of signing the register.' Some of them are married and are propelled between the sheets with 'thoughts of a second honeymoon'. Others have a less formal arrangement. The example which Mr Baker quoted to illustrate his point concerned the couple who arrived in the new Mercedes and left it for the porter to park. Unfortunately the porter drove it into the garage wall. Naturally, a responsible management sent him at once to admit his incompetence, apologise for his error and offer to sign whatever confession statement the owner's insurance required. The man came to answer the bedroom door. He was wearing a dressing-gown and was told with direct simplicity: 'I've smashed your car.' A lady's voice answered from the depth of the bedroom: 'It isn't his car, it's my husband's. Leave the keys. Go away and forget that it ever happened.'

Perhaps such incidents are commonplace in every large hotel. But, as Mr Baker points out, 'romance' – in all its various manifestations – is to Brighton what the lights are to Blackpool. It is what makes the resort famous. In both cases, Brighton and Blackpool, the reality may not be as rewarding as the reputation encourages visitors to believe. But, for almost two hundred years, Brighton has enjoyed (and profited from) the reputation of being naughty but nice, slightly rude, a little risqué and undeniably romantic.

The louche reputation is probably the responsibility of the Prince Regent. He rented 'a superior farmhouse' in the borough in order to be near to Mrs Fitzherbert, who – at the age of twenty-five – had already got through two husbands and was always described by her admirers as 'ample'. John Nash tried to transform it into a pleasure dome of the sort more commonly associated with Xanadu than Sussex-by-the-Sea. But despite its Islamic minarets and its chinoise interiors, it remained a thing of the flesh. The Reverend Sydney Smith said that it looked as if St Paul's had gone to Brighton for the day and had pups.

Charles Stewart Parnell helped to add to the dubious reputation. The leader of the Irish party spent a week there in the winter of 1890 and received John Morley, Mr Gladstone's emissary, in his suite at the Metropole Hotel. Morley (who was a journalist of the sort that the *News of the World* does not employ) raised 'one point on which I have no right to speak to you and, if you don't like it, you can say so'. The point was about one Mrs Katharine O'Shea and the divorce case being brought by her husband in consequence of her 'misconduct' with Parnell.

Morley left the interview convinced of Parnell's innocence, having accepted the assurance 'the other side don't know what a broken-kneed horse they are riding'. Two days later, Captain W. H.

O'Shea won his suit. Gladstone attributed Morley's gullibility to his 'high-souled integrity'. Morley himself said that his concentration had been disturbed by the Irish leader's disconcerting habit of straightening the prongs of the forks on the breakfast table over which they spoke. I asked a lady at the Metropole reception desk if she had ever heard of Charles Stewart Parnell. She consulted her records and told me that he had not yet checked in.

Along the road, at the Grand, they have more recent history to contend with. It is the hotel where the bomb went off, the place at which the IRA came within a whisker of murdering the whole cabinet. The picture of the devastated building – its elegant front drooping down into the road like melted candle wax – is one of the images of the Eighties, engraved on our collective consciousness. Of course, the way it is remembered differs according to character. After the hotel was rebuilt and reopened (and Mrs Thatcher had handed back the Union Jack which had flown over it on that terrible night) some guests asked to see 'the room' – the room, that is, in which the murderous bomb was planted. Richard Baker tried, politely, to persuade them that they were not really interested. He was not always successful.

And of course, at the Grand Hotel the customer is always right. Shortly after the reopening – when the massive and magnificent teak of the new bar had barely held a glass – a difficult point of etiquette arose. A gentleman wearing 'white shoes, white trousers, white shirt and dripping with gold bracelets and necklaces' booked in together with

148

two young ladies. The barman was not sure that he should be served; he wore no tie. Mr Baker was consulted and the manager responded with an enquiry about what had been ordered. When he was told two bottles of Dom Pérignon at £52 each, the rule was instantly changed. Ties are no longer *de rigueur* at the Grand.

It is thanks to such managerial flexibility that the Grand took £6 million in the first year after the reopening. In the year before the catastrophe its turnover was less than a quarter of that figure. 'Obviously,' says Mr Baker, 'the bombing gave us publicity. We were common knowledge in every house. If I ring up a newspaper they still print the story, just because we're the Grand.' But the memory of the tragedy is beginning to fade. All that the hotel can rely on now is 'romance'. That ought to keep it in business for another year or two.

Punch 26 February 1988

Walking on Water

Liverpool is different. Difference comes in a variety of shapes and sizes and, since some of the variations are not wholly attractive, it is only reasonable to describe the sort of difference that Liverpool is. I can feel it in the air when I arrive at Lime Street Station which, although rendered hideous by the dark glass and shiny plastic which now fascinates British Rail architects, is still the entrance to Aladdin's cave.

The real Liverpool pantomime is *Sinbad*. For it is sailors and the sea which make the city almost unique. But when my train slows down alongside one of Lime Street's interminable platforms, I always think of the victory over Abanazar. I expect the guard, or whatever he is called these days, to cry, 'Open Sesame.' Even his stern injunction to remember my hand luggage when I leave the train cannot quite destroy the anticipation of the magic which lies beyond the automatic doors.

Lime Street is the only station (at least in England) that leads immediately to a Greek temple: pillars perfect and crowned with Corinthian capitals, and pediment in its proper place. I like to think that the Latin motto, which has been carved into the stone, was intended to ensure that the Romans did not feel left out. Such a gesture would be wholly consistent with traditional Liverpool generosity. And that in itself is one of the attributes that make the city special. Its other peculiar attribute is the sea.

If I had been born in Southampton, bred in Plymouth, or – during my formative years in Hull – come closer to the Humber than the bar on the New Holland ferry, I might be able to accept all the signs of Liverpool's seafaring past with calm detachment. But I was brought up as far inland as inland goes. So I am entranced by the nautical cut of Liverpool's jib. Even the Atlantic Hotel is curved like the prow of a liner. Inside it is just another set of bedrooms with remote-controlled television. But it points out to sea.

On the waterfront it is dwarfed by the real

monuments to Liverpool's maritime glory: the Liver and Cunard Buildings. But I prefer the by-products of Liverpool's old prosperity: the investments which the merchants made in public esteem, national recognition and divine forgiveness. The town hall, built by Wood and restored by Wyatt, is the finest in England. It was built to combine council chamber and counting house under the same roof. The idea of two on the site of one was so attractive that St George's Hall was designed to embrace concert hall and assize courts. It became Lime Street's Parthenon.

I suspect – though I am too cowardly to be categoric – that it is ships and the sea which give Liverpudlians their special characteristic. Years ago, I was told at the Irish Centre that half the city's population is descended from men and women who paid good money for tickets which, they were told, would take them to America but in truth only entitled them to travel to the first stop on the way to Boston. Nobody, the local historian said, should be surprised that a city with such forebears was inclined to fight with its guard up.

One of the books published in praise of Liverpool provides a contemporary account of how the eighteenth century moulded the city's character. The analysis was provoked by the failure of the attempt to build an academy of art. 'What could we expect when we opened no book to the young and employed no means of imparting knowledge to the old, deriving our prosperity from two great sources, the slave trade and privateering?' James Stonehouse (himself the former master of a slave ship) went on to describe the influences upon young Scousers. 'Swarming with sailormen, flushed with prize money, was it not unlikely that the inhabitants generally would take a tone from what they beheld and quietly countenanced?'

Soon after those bad old days, a tidal wave of piety and culture raced up the Mersey, washing ashore the Botanical Gardens, the Royal Institution, the Athenaeum library, and a passion for improvement that would have satisfied even the most demanding Victorian divine. St George's Hall is probably the finest neoclassical building in Europe. The Anglican Cathedral is certainly the best medieval church to be built in the twentieth century. There are Georgian houses in Liverpool which, were they to be found in Dublin or Bath, would be photographed, printed on a poster, and sold at exorbitant prices to American tourists. But when the city comes to mind, it is not the architecture which is thought of as its principal cultural heritage. It is show business.

I blame the Beatles, aided and abetted by armies of television script writers, lead guitarists and club comics. Accessories before the fact of Liverpool's contemporary reputation were Tommy Handley and Arthur Askey. Accomplices after it are Derek Guyler, Cilla Black, Gerry Marsden, and everyone who has sung 'Ferry 'cross the Mersey' with a lump in his throat or a tear in her eye. Thanks to them, Liverpool has become engulfed in sentiment and starved of the support it needed when the tide went out.

In an essentially inconsequential column such as this, I would not even mention the continued need for houses and jobs had I not – in my most recent visit to Liverpool – fallen into a version of the romantic trap which it sets for its visitors. I drove along beside the old dock wall with its tessellated guard houses and fortified turrets. As I read the evocative names over the gates, I thought how wonderful it all must have been when Atkinson Grimshaw painted the quaysides of the great Victorian seaport. I should have thought: this city needs more jobs.

Guardian 19 May 1990

A Seaside Town from Cradle to Grave

Two weeks ago I went to Scarborough and saw the North Bay for the first time in my life. I have been a regular visitor to Yorkshire's premier holiday resort since I was in my early teens. But because of its superior status, my parents and I did no more than spend a couple of hours in the centre of the town as part of an afternoon out from Filey which is further down the coast and further down the East Riding social scale. We walked to the harbour and viewed, with conspicuous distaste, the fun fair that defiles one of its quays. But we never escaped from the hinterland above South Bay. And some of my more recent visits have been equally restricted.

I was in Scarborough on the day that Hugh Gaitskell promised to fight, fight and fight again to save the party that he loved. And I was back there

153

in the October when Harold Wilson embraced the white heat of technological revolution and welcomed Alex Douglas-Home to the Conservative Party leadership with a wonderfully bogus statement of surprise and disappointment. 'At the very time when even the MCC has abolished the distinction between amateurs and professionals, in science and industry we are content to remain a nation of Gentlemen in a world of Players.' But even at that dawn of a brave new world, I failed to get much further than the Spa and the public bars of hotels in which I could not afford to stay.

When I returned as an MP and minister, I spent my autumn days in much the same way – sitting among the delegates in the Grand Hall rather than craning my neck over the rail of the visitors' gallery and actually spending my nights in the hotels whose bars I once haunted as a hero-worshipping mendicant. The Grand was the grandest hotel in Victorian England, with central heating and a system of room-to-room communications which required guests to blow down a speaking tube like clipper captains anxious to send a message to the engine room. But I longed for the Royal.

The Royal was – and remains – more elegant. The double staircase which curves down into the foyer might have been designed as the stage set for Sheridan's *A Trip to Scarborough*. Its walls are decorated with prints of the Great Exhibition, including the immortal picture of two stands, displaying the wares of Imperial Japan and the German Zollverein, flanking the booth that advertised the products of Green Lane Stove Works, Sheffield. For years, South Bay was so full of delights that there seemed no need to venture north.

Two weeks ago, I at last saw what lies on the other side of the headland which divides the Scarborough sea in two. I climbed up towards the summit of the promontory in search of Anne Brontë's grave. I found it – neat and unspectacular – in what amounts to an annexe to the churchyard. Presumably, at some time during the nineteenth century, the cemetery achieved the status for which all Scarborough boarding houses long. It was permanently full up. No doubt the new ground was consecrated in the confident belief that when the last trump sounds, all of its residents will receive equal treatment – irrespective of the class and quality of their temporary accommodation. I like to think that Scarborough is all of a piece, a seaside town from cradle to grave.

The church from which Anne Brontë went to rest was once the headquarters of the Parliamentary army that laid siege to the Royalist castle half a mile further up the hill. Having paid my respects at the Brontë tomb, I toiled on to the ordinary ruin which began as a Roman signal station and ended its effective military life during the Civil War. Beyond its massive keep and barbican, the North Bay made almost a complete half-circle.

White-topped waves beat against the breakwaters. Sea birds wheeled in the sky and made the sort of noises which townies usually only hear at the beginning of *Desert Island Discs*. To the south, the town – Spa, harbour and hotels – looked like the model of a holiday resort. Castle Hill was magnificent and agoraphobic – so splendid in a larger-than-life sort of way that I

155

forgot that I suffered from vertigo. On the way down, I visited St Mary's once again, just to check up on the date when Anne Brontë died. My interest was historically necrophiliac. For some reason I wanted to know exactly when the main churchyard had become full to bursting.

For the first time I noticed how the holy ground had been rebuilt to help with its care and maintenance. At the far end of the cemetery, the tombstones had been carefully removed from their appointed places at the head of the graves and planted around the perimeters of the churchyard like a stone fence. Within the pale, grass had been laid and mown, if not as flat as Headingley, at least as smooth as the wickets in most municipal parks.

No doubt beneath that turf, Scarborough's rude forefathers rest in peace. Above it – at least on the day of my visit – a sort of cricket match was taking place. Five small boys were batting and bowling under the supervision of a rotund policeman, who acted as coach, wicketkeeper and umpire. The youths were not cricketers of particular merit and the bowling was so eccentric, the batting so incompetent and the wicket-keeping so obese that the ball often evaded all the participants and crashed into the gravestones which guarded the long-leg boundary I suppose that it was all the fuss about the Hardy anniversary that made me think of lines which, in content, had no connection with the contest in the churchyard. 'This will go onward the same. Though dynasties pass... War's annals will cloud into the night ere their story dies.'

Guardian 9 June 1990

The Future Hurries By

Earl St Vincent's careful prediction has passed into history as the almost perfect example of English character and courage. Confidence and gentle humour combined, but the joke was on the enemy. 'I do not say that the French cannot come. I only say that they cannot come by sea.' No doubt they laughed in Dover – and strengthened their defences just in case the admiral was wrong. The old promise is about to take on a new meaning. But the citizens of the premier Cinque Port have not changed their minds about the prospect of a French invasion. From the smart Marine Parade flats to the rundown Buckland Estate, it was impossible to find one man or woman who looks forward to the French coming not by sea but through the Channel Tunnel.

Outside the Roman Painted House – an almost perfect example of second-century domestic architecture – Lee Haines stared into his empty Stella Artois can and asked rhetorically, 'What have the French ever done for us?' The answer, whether Mr Haines likes it or not, is that Dover is a French creation. Much of the town that the Romans built as the headquarters of their fleet was destroyed by William the Conqueror – either in retribution for Harold's resistance at Hastings or in order to rebuild the town in the Norman way. The great castle which now dominates the horizon was the creation of a Frenchman, Henry Plantagenet, Count of Anjou.

In the eight hundred years since the new king laid the foundations of the keep, the city and port has concentrated most of its attention on the faint brown line which marks the skyline on the other side of the Channel. Dover existed to discourage continental invasion and encourage continental trade. But now there is a widespread fear that Europe is about to pass Dover by. The tunnel will blink into the sunlight under Shakespeare's Cliff and send its passengers hurrying north without ever giving them time to remember that Edgar once stood on the very edge of that precipice and thought 'how fearful and dizzy 'tis to cast one's eyes so far'. The Western Docks railway station is already uncomfortably close to being deserted and derelict. On what – twenty years ago – would have been a crowded Friday morning, two passengers waited for the ferry. Neither one of them was a harbinger of economic revival.

Tom Lynch, a Hampshire engineer, set out for Namur, where he was to be the judge at the Belgian Yorkshire Canary Show, a breed which, he explained, was 'bigger, better and more elegant' than other subspecies. It comes in 'all colours' and is known as 'the gentleman of the fancy'. Mr Lynch's travelling companion was an elderly German who was returning to Düsseldorf in order to have a tooth capped. Dentists in his home town charge less than he would pay in London. He was prepared to display his broken molar, but would not give his name.

Ian Williams, guard on the 11.55 to Victoria, was

less reticent. He regards the tunnel as a 'terrorist's dream' and 'the biggest white elephant going'. The Government should have built the railway line first. Indeed the whole enterprise was, 'excuse the French, arse before face'. The apology was unnecessary. France was all around us. Even the station war memorial has its honoured dead grouped around a figure who looks suspiciously like Marianne.

Tracy Nicholas, straw-hatted behind the counter of the station buffet, worried less about the French than the Irish. She is not alone in her belief that all the jobs brought to Dover by the tunnel construction companies have 'gone to Irishmen'. John Lockett, a retired caretaker who has compiled a list of all the 365 public houses which were licensed in Dover before the war, claims that 'Paddies took all the work'. His companion in the seaside shelter (a Stockport man who came home from Malta but never got past his first port of call) adds that the lodging houses are full of them.

Thomas McKeen – milk bottle and sliced loaf in hand as he contemplated the car ferry terminal at which he used to work – says that 'the locals have all been squeezed out'. Tracy Leach, feeding chips and beefburger to her little girl on the promenade, told the same story in a different way. Her husband had got a temporary job, pipe laying, because he knew the Irishman who is in charge. They both pay homage to one Larry Coleman – a Dover man born and bred – who got his name into the newspapers when he created a scene at the Job Centre after he was passed over in favour of strangers. Larry is both saint and martyr. Because of 'the row at the labour exchange' he was 'driven out' of his home town and now lives in exile in Tower Hamlets.

The camp in which the visiting workmen once lived – long dark green rows of huts surrounded by a high wire-netting fence – is now empty, and the security guard reported rumours that they were to be turned into a conference centre. A film company planning to remake *The Great Escape* ought to bid for the whole hillside whilst it is still on the market. Workers from outside the town now live in digs. What used to be called navvies are everywhere – moving earth, improving roads and travelling from job to job in hired buses or straggling columns. An assiduous afternoon's search located one Irishman pushing a battered barrow along the Military Road behind the Western Docks. He described the natives as 'very friendly'.

They are certainly indomitable. Or at least they were when indomitability was required of them. They held the castle for King John against Hubert de Burgh and, six hundred years later, used the tunnels by which the French had underpinned it as air-raid shelters. Thanks to the navy, Napoleon never came to test the garrison on the Western Heights and because of the RAF, Hitler's Operation Sea Lion did not set sail. But Dover was always in the front line. A memorial commemorates the miracle which enabled '202,306 British, British Commonwealth and Allied Troops' to be 'landed from Dunkirk between May 10 and June 1 1940'. A panel from a German gun reminds visitors that '2226 shells were fired' towards the town from Sangatte beach in Calais during the four years which followed. Joseph Pinder, a nine-year-old schoolboy, told me that the 'best memorial' was on the cliff top about St Margaret's Bay. It is a tribute to the Dover Patrol, 'fishermen who put guns in their boats to stop the invasion'.

It was from St Margaret's Bay, in times when Channel swimming was fashionable, that the grease-covered Leanders took the plunge. Captain Webb – who led the way across in 1875 – stares out to sea from the promenade, instantly recognisable to anyone who has ever bought a box of matches. Charles Rolls who, thirty-five years later, was the first man to fly to France and back, is immortalised further along the sea front. Blériot, who only made it one way, glided down to a hard landing in North Fall Meadow. Granite blocks have been sunk in the ground, at the spot where he landed, in the approximate shape of his monoplane. Another eighty yards and he would have hit the castle hill. Another eighty years and he would have crashed into trees and bushes instead of bumping along on grass.

The meadow is now a wilderness – 'perfect,' a lady with a red setter judged, 'for dogs. There's more to smell than if it was just grass.'

Which is not to say that Dover takes no pride in its past. With that grey castle and those white cliffs, it is impossible for its people to forget that it is 'the gateway to England'. It was from the battlements of that castle and from the top of those cliffs that local patriots heard Nelson 'speaking to the French' during his assault on Boulogne, and the gun platforms and earth

161

works which had been built to face the French became the southern bastion against Hitler, There is still what looks like early radar on the cliffs. It is directed towards the French coast where 'the light gleams and is gone'. Nobody in Dover could identify the hotel in which Matthew Arnold wrote 'Dover Beach'. The obvious candidate is what has become Western House. It stands, huge, square and boarded up, at the entrance to the Western Docks and bears all the marks of creeping dereliction – hotel into offices into boarded-up wreck. But Western House is at the sandy end of the foreshore. Arnold heard 'the grating roar of pebbles which the waves draw back and fling, at their return, up the high strand'. Pebbles are further east.

The problem for Dover is the prospect of a 'melancholy long withdrawing roar' as the causes and concerns which have sustained it for a thousand years are gradually overtaken by peace and new technology. The gateway to England needs no longer to be locked and barred against the envy of less happy lands and travellers to this sceptred isle are likely to burrow their way in, like Shakespeare's bold pioneer. Dover is part of the romantic past – from its Angevin battlements to its Victorian jetty. The future will hurry by to London and beyond.

Guardian 28 November 1992

A Tilt at the Don Quixotes

During the past couple of weeks, solemn environmentalists – worrying about the future of the planet – must have come to the grateful conclusion that God is green. The trivial inconvenience of panic-induced queues at the petrol pumps and the devastation that global warming has brought to America's Gulf Coast supports their arguments for developing new, and renewable, sources of energy. The case for building wind farms has become irresistible.

It always was – not as a contribution to the world's energy supply, but because they are so beautiful. It may well be that the electricity which they produce costs 5.4p per kilowatt as compared with 3p per kilowatt for electricity generated by nuclear power. I do not care. I am only interested in the aesthetics of wind power – the slim, silver masts against the skyline, reflecting the sun and emitting the gentle hum of swarming bees.

There is a wind farm in the sea off the coast at Tintagel, a sword's throw from the site of the castle in which King Arthur was conceived. When I first saw them, I thought that a dozen Ladies of the Lake were reaching out from the water to catch the discarded Excalibur. No nuclear power station has ever made me think of Camelot. Yet – to mix the chivalrous metaphors – all sorts of unlikely Don Quixotes are tilting at

163

wind farms as if they desecrate the countryside.

Their argument against is based on the belief, propagated by a Victorian missionary bishop, that in nature 'every prospect pleases and only man is vile'. Somebody should have told him that men and women are part of nature too and that they are capable of constructing artefacts of great elegance. In a thousand years' time, an inter-planetary archaeologist will discover what remains of a wind farm and put it on display as a relic of a lost civilisation.

By then, the passage of time will have destroyed the blinding prejudice that rural Britain is spoilt by anything that is new. The scars which were once quarries have become romantic with age. Ruined farmhouses which were ugly when they were complete are said to possess a Gothic charm. I want us to enjoy the sight of wind farms now. My house in Derbyshire is in the shadow of an escarpment which we call an 'edge'. A wind farm would improve the horizon. By all means build one in my back yard.

The Times 15 September 2005

Vampires, Saints and Fish 'n' Chips

Monsters, in human form, come back into our lives each Halloween and haunt us – in television series, newspaper and most recently on the London stage – until the thought of Christmas drives them from our minds. But there is one town in England where memories of the most famous monster of all time linger on. On an autumn afternoon in Whitby it is easy to understand why Bram Stoker chose the grey forbidding ruins of the abbey as Dracula's first resting place before he turned himself into a wolf and, in the best traditions of the undead, vampired his way round England.

Twelve hundred years before the Dracula story was invented, English history was changed in the Abbey – then one of the great monastic houses of England. It was the chosen meeting place of the Synod which decided that English Christianity should follow the rules laid down by Rome. Had the assembled priests chosen to go the Celtic way, we would celebrate Easter on a different date and long-forgotten saints would give their names to parish churches.

Some Saxon saints are still remembered and revered. A party from the Church of Saint Cuthbert and Saint Oswald in Winksley, near Ripon, were picnicking in the Abbey grounds. Plum cake, delicate sandwiches and buns were laid as neatly as if they had been prepared for a vicarage tea and were generously offered to passers-by. Robert Sellers, the parish priest, said his congregation 'was on a day's pilgrimage' and added that 'It was a good excuse to have a day out together.' Saint Oswald – 'Oswy' in 657 – founded the Abbey as a community of both men and women. It was not only equal opportunities which began in Whitby. During the rule of Abbess Hilda, a cowherd called Caedmon was employed as a porter. He was the first Anglo-Saxon to write verse in his native tongue and in consequence became the father of English poetry.

With so much history hanging in the air, Whitby is entitled to be the most solemn seaside town in England. Happily, it resists the temptation and attracts tourists for all sorts of reasons. On a wet and windy Saturday, the steep and winding streets of the old town were so crowded that pedestrians spilled off the pavements on to the roads. Doreen and Robert McLay, who were resting on a bench after their climb to the top of the West Cliff, had travelled the twenty miles south from Middlesbrough, because 'Whitby has the best fish and chips in the world.' John, their son – an exile from the north who was home for the weekend – happily identified the restaurant which excelled above all others. 'Look,' he said. 'It's half-past two and they are still queuing up to get in.' The McLays make the trip every time that John returns home and usually spend the early afternoon looking south from the same vantage point above the harbour.

In front of them, a statue of Whitby's most famous son stares out to sea. Captain James Cook RN, FRS, was born in a village ten miles north and apprenticed to a master mariner in Whitby's Grape Lane. He learned his seamanship by sailing coal up and down the coast and became the greatest navigator in the world – far excelling, with sextant and compass, the talents of more formally educated Royal Navy officers. The four ships – *Endeavour, Resolution, Adventure* and *Discovery* – in which he charted the oceans of half the globe and laid British claim to New Zealand and eastern Australia were built in Whitby.

The town celebrates its ancient association with the sea in dozens of different ways. On the other side of the harbour – beyond the yachts, the motor boats and a remarkably realistic replica of a Spanish galleon – a memorial to the twelve Whitby lifeboat men who died in the great storm of 1861 dominates the porch of the beautiful and clearly much-loved church of Saint Mary's. To raise restoration funds parishioners staged an 'exhibition of collections' – including examples of a 'Mrs Judy Kitchen's 2000 egg cups'. A notice read 'Admission by Donation'. Two lady helpers – Ada Roe and Christine Baker – said that white sticks should have been made available to visitors. 'Most of them must have been blind. They did not see the donation notice.'

From a distance Saint Mary's looks a perfectly normal parish church. But inside it is a riot. If the interior of an English church is ever constructed from pieces bought at a diocesan jumble sale, it will look like the nave of Saint Mary's, Whitby. Galleries were added at various levels and in different styles. Each addition to the building created pews from which it was hard to see the vicar preach his sermon. So a pulpit was extended until, today, it looks like the bridge on an ancient man-o'-war.

These days the lifeboat is employed in providing pleasure trips. Whalers sail out of the harbour no more, but there are still lobster pots on the jetties and a statue on the West Quay pays tribute to James Scoresby who invented the 'crow's nest'

167

as protection for sailors sent to the masthead to warn of approaching icebergs. Whitby is still about ships and the sea. And it is the home of the best fish and chips in England.

Daily Mail 13 November 2007

Eternal City

It is Blackpool, not Rome, that ought to be known as the Eternal City – eternally cheerful, eternally welcoming and eternally free from the pomposity and pretension that make visitors tread softly on some seaside towns. And, since it is not to be disfigured by a 'mega-casino', it will continue to be famous for the 'fresh air and fun' in which it has specialised since the railway reached the town in 1846. It was the seven miles of sandy beach – which, when the tide is out, seem to stretch all the way to Ireland – that originally attracted the holidaymakers. But a hundred years ago, the mayor and corporation decided to improve on nature by building a half-size replica of the Eiffel Tower in the middle of the town. It still dominates the landscape and is visible, against the clouds, from ten miles inland. But nothing that is an imitation can do justice to Blackpool. Blackpool is an original, one off, unique. And it is essentially English. To turn it into a second-rate Las Vegas would have been an act of high treason. It would destroy Blackpool's reputation as the 'Bank-holiday town', the favourite 'day out' in England.

Admittedly, strange foreign words, like trattoria and bistro, have begun to appear above shop fronts in the roads just behind the promenade. But they are part of suburban Blackpool – the sturdy double-fronted houses in the roads that the traffic diversions aim to keep free from the cars and coaches which are Blackpool's economic life blood. The invincibly English spirit of Blackpool was better represented by Stuart Hargreave and his partner, who, last Saturday, had come all the way from Lichfield in Staffordshire with Abbie-Leigh, their two-year-old daughter. On a cold spring morning – with a biting wind blowing in from the North Sea – they stood against the smart new wall which is being built between the South Shore promenade and the beach and counted their blessings. The forecast had warned of rain. But the day had stayed dry. And they were off to find fish and chips for lunch. 'You can't come to Blackpool without having fish and chips,' said Stuart.

Five Marshals – mum, dad and their three sons aged seven, five and two – had come to Blackpool from Carlisle for the weekend. I expect that they were staying in one of the family hotels in which the town specialises – a double bed and bunks for the boys, all in the same room. They were not so sure how much time they would spend on the big wheel, which is now dwarfed by builders' tower cranes, on the big dipper, which zig-zags across the sky-line in a crazy pattern of Z-bends and U-turns, the rest of the Pleasure Beach, which is not a beach, but the home of roller-coasters and flying machines, or the Sandcastle, which is not a sandcastle but a choice of eighteen water slides. The essentially English holiday is more than spending money. The Marshals had no doubt that they were going to enjoy themselves. When she was a girl, Colleen Marshal had visited Blackpool with her parents for their family holiday. 'Family' is one of Blackpool's most frequently used words. The biggest sign of all – in a town that seems to place no restriction on signs of any shape or size – is high on the roof of the theatre at the end of the Central Pier. It reads, FAMILY BAR. The pier's special attraction is 'family fun above the sea'.

Blackpool is clearly moving up the holiday market. The old attractions remain – Louis Tussaud's waxworks, fortune tellers, bingo and various exotic entertainments. 'Sea Life' offers the opportunity to 'come face to face with a shark'. But the kiss-me-quick, candy floss, McGill seaside postcard Blackpool is being gradually replaced by something more in keeping with twenty-first-century affluence. Visitors can judge the extent of the change from the seafront hotels – some new, some the result of the recent amalgamation of several guest houses and almost all spick and span. The names proclaim their English identity – Blenheim, Royal Windsor, Regency, Gainsborough. Forget the coffee and croissant. Order the full English breakfast.

Phyllis Hughes, who has a caravan in nearby Poulton-le-Fylde, comes into Blackpool every time she spends a weekend in Lancashire. She was walking along the South Shore promenade during a particularly gusty moment in a wind-blown Saturday morning, but it was clear that she would have been there had it been the sort of day when waves break over the tram-lines. We talked beneath one of the illuminated illustrations of the *Doctor Who* saga which decorate the North shore until the real 'Blackpool Lights' are switched on in August. With some particularly malevolent space creature looking down on us, she described the town's attraction. 'The people are so friendly,' she said. And they will prove it to the ex-servicemen when they host Veterans' Week in June – friendly and proud. Blackpool is a very English town.

Daily Mail 29 April 2008

Tired of Life

Four years ago, in a moment of pure madness, I suggested that the weekly column about England – which I was about to begin – should be called 'Tired of Life'. The title was not intended as an announcement of impending suicide. It was meant to reflect, in three short words, my low opinion of Doctor Johnson in general and my particular contempt for his silly so-called aphorism about the delights of London being inexhaustible. They are exhausted for me after forty-eight hours.

The title was abandoned for reasons which were, in part, commercial. Londoners buy newspapers too. But I was reconciled to the rejection of my idea by the realisation that to suggest that London had *nothing* to commend it would be an overstatement of my view. Admittedly I moved to the capital in 1964 because the House of Commons would not move north. But it remains a pleasant place for brief visits and the home of many events and institutions which make up England. To have put together an anthology called *In Search of England* without devoting a substantial part of it to the country's capital city would have been absurd.

Paradoxically, London's place at the heart of all things English contributed to my temporarily total antagonism to what William Cobbett – no more a favourite of mine than Doctor Johnson – called 'the great wen'. Westminster – where I live three sevenths of my life – was preparing for some ceremonial event with its usual eagerness to put pomp ahead of personal convenience. Roads were closed. Parking was prohibited. Traffic jammed the streets outside the diversions. It is the price we pay for having the Houses of Parliament, Westminster Abbey and Buckingham Palace as neighbours. In my more rational moments I realise that a constitutional monarchy and a parliamentary democracy are worth a couple of days' inconvenience – particularly since the ceremonies which are associated with them are the real thing, not the recent invention of a state impresario.

Our monarch was not imposed on us by Napoleon Bonaparte or grudgingly accepted as the quid pro quo for freedom for Austria or Imperial Russia. The sovereign – and her ancestors – have inconvenienced Westminster for a thousand years. Our soldiers, as well as closing down Whitehall while they troop (and rehearse trooping) their colours, fight in the wars which will soon be added to their ancient battle honours. Our parliamentary ceremonies were designed to safeguard free speech and an independent judiciary.

Three cheers for London. But, that being said, 'Tired of Life' is too good a title to be wasted.

Blackheath

I went back to Blackheath the other day, the first time for five years that I had visited London's loveliest suburb. Nothing had changed. The station is a full Parliament's life nearer to complete dereliction, but it still offers a glimpse of the pleasures to come, in the sunshine up above the underworld of culvert and cutting. A disused siding has become the home of more seedlings and saplings than the Forestry Commission would plant on a whole Highland hillside. A desolate, rusty wheelbarrow, half hidden among the infant elders and adolescent sycamores, adds a touch of Thomas Hardy to a place that the unfamiliar might, otherwise, mistakenly believe to be pure H.G. Wells.

Bromley – the home of Kipps and Mr Polly – is only a couple of miles away and shares with Blackheath both the confidence and the prosperity that exiles from the North once, wrongly, believed to be typical of the whole South-East. So there are bits of Blackheath – like Selwyn Court, a monument to the ugliness of inter-war architecture – that might be Bromley. And the little boys, dressed in violent green blazers and striped caps as an ostentatious proclamation of private education, would look more at home in a less fastidiously reticent part of London. But they are incongruous ripples on an otherwise calm sea. It is the serenity of Blackheath – as much as the magnificent buildings which surround it – that make it such a special place.

At least, I think that it is a special place. My judgement about the cities and suburbs that I have lived in and the villages and towns which I have visited is hopelessly confused, blatantly biased and unapologetically prejudiced. I have never been able to distinguish between intrinsic visual merit and happy memories. Thus Barnsley is beautiful; Holyhead is not. I really believe that Edinburgh is the most splendid city in Britain. But if the ravages perpetrated in Princes Street by shoe shops and teashops defiled the whole of the New Town, laid the Castle waste, invaded Holyrood and violated the granite solidarity of Morningside, I would still regard it as the Athens of the North because it is the Shangri-La of my early manhood.

So it is with Blackheath. When first I came to London, full of hope and anxiety, I lived in the next postal district with the closest friends I ever had or ever will have. We went shopping together on Saturday mornings that now all seem to have been sunny, and we rummaged around among the rubbish in junk shops that claimed they sold antiques. The houses into which I dreamed of putting the chipped Victorian china and the almost Regency fire irons (which I had enough sense not to buy) always looked out across the heath on which the Peasants' Revolt began.

Round the corner from the heath once lived the brightest and best member of my parliamentary generation – first in the sort of flat that gives Scandinavia a bad name, then in an early nineteenth-

178

century house that combined the elegance and the solid certainty of the age of progress and improvement. We often drove home together after late-night sittings, up the little hill from New Cross and over the dark brown acres of common land, bumping along on the rough country roads that criss-cross the heath like lines on an old man's hand.

In the half-light of early morning the teak and plate-glass of the Fifties and early Sixties faded into the kinder, calmer style of earlier periods. But the silhouette of the Rangers' House stood out against the trees of Greenwich Park. On the far side of the heath, beyond the ponds and the pubs, and the church which is a vertical intrusion into the horizontal world of grass and soil and sand, the Paragon was just visible – to both superior eyesight and active imagination. I longed to live in the Paragon and once actually agonised over a tiny servants' house that the Georgian architect had hidden behind one corner of its classical façade.

But perhaps the magic of those small hours was not so much what I saw as what I felt: a Member of Parliament on his way home from a late-night sitting! I expected the ghost of Anthony Trollope to pinch me awake and confirm that in a rational conscious moment I would accept that it was all too good to be true.

It took us only a couple of moments to cross the heath, for, I suppose, it covers fewer acres than the municipal parks in which I used to play. It is certainly much smaller than Wadsley Common over which I once hunted with the local

179

Wolf Cub pack. But, although these boyhood open spaces had been enlarged in my mind by the magnifying memory of childhood, Black-heath seems bigger than them all.

Perhaps it seems so large because it is so flat. Whatever the reason, the illusion is created that it is a plain. And when the explorer reaches its northern and western boundaries the illusion does not fade, it merely changes. Blackheath pretends that it is a plateau, towering over Mill-wall and Greenwich.

Classically, the view over Greenwich is the more spectacular. At the end of the tree-lined path that leads to the Observatory and the zero meridian of longitude, fastened to the ground in a metal line like a schoolboy's atlas come to life, stands a statue of General Wolfe. It looks over one of the most remarkable panoramas in London – Royal Naval College and the National Maritime Museum. Close by, the masts just poking above the trees belong to the *Cutty Sark*, a reminder to the romantic traveller that Britain's maritime history is as much about commerce as conquest.

South of the meridian the view is less heroic. Over Millwall Docks and Deptford the river is hardly recognisable as the silver causeway over which Sir Francis Drake was rowed to be knighted by Queen Elizabeth.

The view north-east is unashamedly com-mercial, unapologetically industrial, proudly urban. Its huddled houses and factories, power-stations and warehouses make up the sort of picture that a Lowry would have painted had the south been fortunate enough to produce an artist of his perception and devotion. And hanging over it all is a bronze haze made up of smoke and sun and dust – the sort of haze that has hung over London for a thousand years.

The view of London stretching out across the winding, wandering Thames confirms and emphasises that Blackheath is not really part of the mighty metropolis. The life of the capital hurries on below and is joined to Blackheath by the Southern Railway and the Old Kent Road. But once up on the heath everything changes. Cars which rattled through New Cross progress in apparent silence.

When I first wanted to live in Blackheath I thought of it as 'moving to London'. As I came to know it better I realised that, established in one of the terraces on one of the roads made intentionally bumpy to deter fast motor cars, I would have come to regard it as the place to which I could escape from Westminster, Whitehall and the West End. I would have walked each night between the kite-flyers and the amateur footballers and watched each weekend the donkeys that trot back and forward from the synthetic coffee stall.

Of course I shall never live there now. My next move will be back to the place with the happiest memories of all. When the time comes to hang up the parliamentary equivalent of my boots it will be home to Yorkshire and a grey granite house (preferably built for an assistant waterworks manager at about the time of the Great Exhibition) halfway up a Pennine foothill. I shall lie back in the recollections of my childhood and let them cover me in reassurance and comfort

181

like the water of a warm bath.

I fear that the men who were boys when I was a boy will not be there to sit and drink with me. Most of them have moved to London. It is an extraordinary thing to do out of choice. But at least a few of the luckier ones have managed to establish themselves in beautiful Blackheath.

Listener 29 November 1979

Official Rose

At two o'clock on the afternoon of the Queen's visit to the Chelsea Flower Show, only half the stands and stalls seemed remotely ready for royal scrutiny. The little alleys of prefabricated shops that cluster on the commercial boundary of the fruit and flower exhibition had turned the Royal Hospital grounds into a souk. Porters sweated. Proprietors shouted. Lorries unloading motor-mowers and water sprinklers forced pedestrians to make detours over piles of ropes and round bales of off-white canvas.

The stall that promoted garden barbecues was lining up eye-level grills and griddles that looked like intergalactic mushrooms. The company that designed and created Gothic greenhouses in the style of Joseph Paxton was putting the final panes in place. The firm that transformed tiny back yards into apparently spacious gardens ('as featured in the *Sunday Times*') was polishing the mirrors with which its illusions are achieved. A dozen decapitated concrete Aphrodites stood in a monumental mason's yard. Their heads glared up at passers-by from the polystyrene-pellet gravel.

In the suburbs of the Show only Constance Spry and Interflora were both silent and serene. Ms Spry seemed to have completed her preparations and gone for lunch – no doubt a light salad served on the chintz tablecloths of a nearby tearoom. Interflora were open for instant business, preferring to dispatch boxes of roses from the menagerie into which they had turned their shop. Each of the Interflora animals was made of flowers.

Even beneath the vaulted canvas roof of the great central marquee, only half of the little pavilions that covered the turf and tarmac of pitch and parade-ground seemed ready. The rest were being gradually assembled. Sods were being cut into strange shapes like linoleum about to be laid in an asymmetrical room. Flowers were being plucked from heaps that once must have covered whole fields, and stuck methodically into balls of bilious green plastic moss. Names that would not have been out of place on racehorses were being painted on white cards, with Latin parentheses added to prove a bit of class.

The impression of a botanical bazaar persisted; for the exhibiting nurserymen and market gardeners of Chelsea wobble uneasily between the desire to pursue floral excellence and the need to promote business. The talk is of honour. The hope is for glory. The object is gain.

Some competitors barely bother to dissemble. Fisons' garish GroBags form the foundations of a living cornucopia, plants so heavy with fruit that the aubergines, tomatoes and cucumbers had to be supported by string bags on sticks, lest the sheer opulent weight of 'Sleaford Abundance' tear it from its branch in an act of voluptuous suicide. Enough salad to feed every Chelsea Pensioner for a year had been sculpted into a nearby architectural extravaganza which climaxed in a pinnacle of spring onions. The hungriest rabbit would have been confused by the camouflage. All resemblance to nature had been successfully obliterated.

It is difficult to believe that some of the flowers had any natural origins to conceal. The intentionally surrealistic displays – wilfully stunted trees and disparate cacti grafted on top of one another – could be passed by with a shudder. The vases of blooms, unreal because they are too big, too bright and too perfect, have a magnetic fascination. Victorian ladies visiting the Zoological Gardens in Regent's Park refused to believe in the giraffes. I felt exactly the same about the begonias and the azaleas. The carnations I could understand. Like fame, they are not supposed to grow on mortal soil. They thrive in City buttonholes. In the artificial atmosphere of the Chelsea big top, they seemed absolutely at home. So, I fear, did most of the roses.

Roses dominate the Show. Some of them are so rare and exquisite that they hardly look like roses at all. White roses with each petal edged in red and red roses as flat as one of Earl Haig's fivepenny poppies stretch credulity too far. The popular patriotic concept of the rose ought not to be destroyed. A rose is round and full, or small with its bud barely open and its petals tightly compressed. It smells as sweet by any other name. But if it has been so ruthlessly inbred that it loses all its accepted characteristics, a rose is a rose no longer.

Naturally enough, the worst example on view in the entire Show was to be found at one of the rose displays. A whole BBC Television crew was crouched, intent on immortalising a single specimen. Interviewer, cameraman, sound recordist and an assortment of assistants knelt in admiration of a single blossom. The team so assiduously at work came from *Nationwide*. The specimen on which they concentrated their attention was called 'Sue Lawley'.

But it was also the roses which provided the rare touch of reality. In life, as distinct from art, roses are inclined to wither as if the worm in the bud has begun to wriggle and chew. The outside petals droop out of position and grow brown at the edges. A general air of dilapidation takes over almost before any flower is fully open. Mercifully, the same symptoms of inevitable decay were present at Chelsea. Would that the same could have been said about the delphiniums.

The delphiniums, banked at the far end of the tent, might well – like their begonia neighbours – have been brought up on steroids. That is the charitable explanation of their condition. Another possibility is that they were the ultimate product of the new technology – chemically identical to real flowers but synthesised to a perfection that would have been impossible if they had been potted by a human gardener. Or, perhaps (like the intergalactic mushrooms, disguised as bar-

185

becues), they were manufactured by an alien intelligence which knew everything about earthly horticulture but nothing about aesthetics.

The market gardeners from outer space would, no doubt, have been deeply offended by the stall set up by a nurseryman from Twyford, Berkshire. Mr Carlisle had produced a corner of the Chelsea Flower Show that was for ever England; a carefully casual garden of flowers and foliage grasses and herbs, beautiful enough to be the background to a Rural Dean's dream of paradise. A man with a trowel – for all I know, Mr Carlisle himself – modestly explained that herbaceous plants are usually indigenous and are really survivors of the glory that once grew wild.

In those days, roses blew unofficially about the hedgerows and encouraged Rupert Brooke to think of England, home and Cambridge. The wicker baskets sold at flower shows were not tin painted to look like straw, and the world was not held together by plastic-coated wire and fibreglass string.

But, apart from the roses touched by mortality, there were few signs of old England at Chelsea last week. Round, pink girls (all of whom should have been called Phoebe) pruned and planted on some of the stalls with a rural confidence that came from wearing denims long before blue bibs and braces were fashionable. There were some magnificent radishes mistakenly left unwashed, and in some of the begonias the tissue-paper illusions were remedied by their thick, furry stamens which, from a distance, looked like real bees searching for real pollen.

The rest was like the extramural department of the Ideal Home Exhibition, properly established between the King's Road and the Battersea Fun Fair. I have no doubt that by the time the Queen arrived everything was in place, that the cut flowers had been wired to stand to attention and the artificial lakes and fountains were glistening with fluoridated water. I know too that Mr Carlisle's display was in its way no more natural than the rest. But at least it made a gesture towards the Arcadian view of gardens and gardening. I hope that as the Queen passed by she was tempted to take his billhook and knight him for services to horticultural sentimentality.

Listener 29 May 1980

Talk of Alexander

One touch of cold philosophy and Trooping the Colour turns from military pageant into multiple paradox. The Queen of England, a thoroughly modern monarch, dresses in a nineteenth-century riding habit and an attenuated eighteenth-century cocked hat to attend a Birthday Parade which is not held on her birthday. Then one of the best horsewomen in the world sits side-saddle and takes the salute from soldiers of unrivalled professional proficiency. The soldiers wear the uniforms of the Napoleonic and Crimean Wars to perform a ceremony originally designed to ensure that recently recruited mercenaries knew which side they were on and around whose flag they ought to rally.

Spectators, watching the Trooping, have better ways of spending their time than considering the ceremony's intrinsic absurdity. From Downing Street or thereabouts, where the cameras are perched high above the Prime Minister's garden, the picture is almost perfect. The cleaned russet bricks and severe classical columns of the Admiralty make up half the backcloth and merge, just left of centre, with the 'Citadel' – the creeper-covered old concrete blockhouse from which the Navy fought its most recent wars. In the grey light of last Saturday's damp morning, it looked like a giant sandcastle festooned with seaweed by the retreating waves.

And in front of the sandcastle stood row on row of Guardsmen more rigidly erect, more correct in every detail, more identical in movement and demeanour than a shopful of toy soldiers cast from the same lead mould. I have seen them march on to Horseguards Parade a dozen times, watched them freeze into military immobility and gazed fascinated as they were shouted back to life. Each year as the columns wheel and apparently disintegrate it seems impossible that they will ever form an orderly line again. They always do.

In my days at the Foreign Office, when I inhabited a room designed for Secretaries of State for India, I sometimes invited comrades and friends to watch the parade from the balconies. The old India Office is oval and only one of its windows faces out from its elliptical wall directly towards Horseguards. The self-sacrificial and the cynical always volunteered for positions that afforded a view of only the rear file of the Foot-guards and the ambulance tent, imagining that they could spend a contented morning drinking to the strange enthusiasm of their fellow guests. But as soon as massed bands struck up the martial music, they invariably began to squint self-consciously around the curve of the building. By the end of the morning, they were leaning out across the guano-covered balustrades, risking the thirty-foot drop rather than let the parade pass them by. I always took the most favoured guests into the dilapidated Victorian bathroom. Crushed between wash-basin and cistern we could command almost the complete panorama.

Half the magic is, of course, the music – a boon to the general public who hear much more than they see of the Trooping. Standing in St James's Park – opposite the banks of wooden seats erected for guests of varying distinction – only a basketball player with a periscope could enjoy a good view of all that is going on. But the sound of the massed bands carries all the way down the Mall, where Her Majesty's loyal subjects stand ten deep to watch her lead the Household Cavalry home. And British military bands play a special British sort of martial music that both quickens the pulse and moistens the eye.

I suppose that sometimes they flirt with John Philip Sousa or trumpet the tune that Strauss composed in praise of the temporarily victorious Marshal Radetzky. But when I think of military music I remember the old county regiments marching to the old county songs – 'The Lincolnshire Poacher', 'Sussex by the Sea', 'To Be a Farmer's Boy' and the Durham Light Infantry dashing off to 'The Blaydon Races'. Trooping music, being picked in praise of the county from which the colour comes, always adds a touch of domesticity to the discipline. Last Saturday, because the honour went to the First Battalion of the Irish Guards, we had 'The Rose of Tralee', 'Eileen Alannah', 'Endearing Young Charms' and 'Slattery's Mounted Foot', a march which could either be a tribute to the dragoons (who were once just that) or a prejudiced joke about Irish mental confusion.

No army bandmaster anywhere in the world conducts a repertoire at once so eclectic and ecumenical as the programme played for the Guards at the Trooping. 'St Patrick's Day' is converted from march to anthem in Catholic churches each Sunday. And every year, whichever regiment's colour is carried up and down the line, there is a moment when the band seems suddenly to digress and produces a couple of unexpected lines from Martin Luther's hymn – 'A safe stronghold our God is still / A trusty shield and weapon.' While spectators are still wondering if Worms or Wittenberg appear on any of the battle honours the band is off on another apparent diversion as it beats and blows the bars of Mozart that have been captured by the Coldstream Guards.

But there is nothing theatrical about the Birthday Parade. Nobody suspects that it is under the command of a choreographer. Despite the plumed helmets of the Horseguards and the scarlet tunics of the Grenadiers nobody mistakes the Household Division for chocolate soldiers. The Army never tires of telling us that the week after the Trooping the soldiers may all be in Germany, working the computers – which seem to be the weapons of modern warfare. And the rituals they perform on the chosen Saturday in June are all very clearly a relic of what once happened in real wars. These days, the farriers' axes gleam with chromium plate, not spit and polish. But their spikes were designed to despatch wounded horses, and their blades were used to sever hallmarked hoofs, so that sceptical quartermasters could be convinced that chargers were dead, not sold.

Part of the Trooping's attraction is that, despite the jets that scream overhead, nothing much has changed on Horseguards since Queen Victoria took the salute from a landau. The Guards officers all look like the Guards officers that Alice pointed out to Christopher Robin when they went down to Buckingham Palace together. Perhaps the heavy chain chinstraps and the immense bearskins that spill down from the top like froth on an overfull glass squeeze all the faces into identical shapes and when the first Pakistani from my constituency wins a scholarship to Eton and Sandhurst he will parade on Horseguards, wearing the same expression and shouting his orders in the same Guards officer's voice.

I hope that the Household Division is preparing itself for him. But I wonder if he will fit into the spirit of the occasion with the enthusiasm that middle-aged civilians feel when the earth trembles to the tramp of boots and the air is broken by the sound of bugles. It was BBC Television, recording last Saturday both the highlights of the Trooping and the Guardsman's year, that reminded me of how carefully I had been prepared to enjoy that day.

Back in March, it was the Queen Mother's turn to present the St Patrick's Day shamrock to the Irish Guards. After the wolfhound had been displayed and the saffron-kilted pipers had blown their hearts out, the battalion gave the cheers for their distinguished visitor. On the word of command they grasped their bearskins and, literally to numbers, lifted them three inches from their heads, moved them horizontally to a point above their right shoulders and balanced them one-handed on their epaulettes. In perfect unison they gave three synchronised cheers for Her Majesty.

I had lived with an identical act of orchestrated salute for years. In one of the three volumes of a ten-volume set of encyclopedias we had bought second-hand from the Market Hall there was a full-page, full-colour picture of exactly the same scene. It was called 'Guards Cheering Victoria Before they Left for the Crimea'. It never struck me to wonder why there was no picture of how they reacted on their return.

Listener 19 June 1980

A Stroll in the Park

When, many years ago, I used to fantasise about writing fiction, the story of my dreams always began in St James's Park. I planned to produce a great political novel and I had no doubt about which sub-category of that genre my magnum opus would occupy. It would not be a novel of political ideas. Not for me allegories, parables or polemics. I wanted to write about political life. I had no wish to emulate Samuel Butler or Ignazio Silone. My ambition was to become a latter-day Anthony Trollope and the opening paragraph that buzzed around inside my head owed more to C.P. Snow than George Orwell. The square mile of lakes and lawns between the Mall and Birdcage Walk was just the right place to meet the hero of a second-rate political adventure story.

It was early autumn and the nights had already begun to draw in. The Treasury's towers, peeping over Horse Guards Gate, were only just visible in the gathering dusk. Light blazed from the long windows in the curved wall that enclosed the Foreign Secretary's great office, the chandelier above the desk seeming to burn more brightly than the other illuminations – a sure sign that the red boxes were still open and that there were state papers that had to be read before morning. The curtains were drawn on the top storey of 12 Downing Street, but a tell-tale

193

glimmer of neon that escaped the red velvet revealed that the Chief Whip was still at work. The Reform Club rumours were true. The crisis could no longer be averted. The government was about to fall.

Let me remind you – in my immediate defence – that, until now, the opening paragraph was no more than a badly written dream, one that I have only allowed to escape from my guilty sub-conscious now that the authorship of a political novel is no longer one of the achievements to which I aspire. I realise now that what I wanted to write about was not politics at all, but poli-ticians. Familiarity with that particular branch of the human race has not bred contempt but affec-tion. However, I no longer regard Members of Parliament as dashing characters, ideal to carry the plot of an adventure story. I think my judge-ment about them has improved. So has my knowledge of Whitehall geography.

It is not the Treasury but the old War Office that peers over the headquarters of London Transport into Horse Guards Parade. The top floor of 12 Downing Street has nothing to do with the Chief Whip. Some post-war Chancellor of the Exchequer spread the wing of his house over his neighbour's office. And the curved, long-windowed wall of the FO does not separate the Foreign Secretary from the real world outside. Behind it is what was once the ministerial home of the Secretary of State for India. It was designed as a Victorian tribute to the Raj in a style which is part Mogul, part Victorian and wholly elegant. Once upon a time it was my place

194

of work. I spent far too much time looking out onto St James's Park.

The touch of cold reality that came as a result of close acquaintance with politics did nothing to diminish the romantic attraction of the square mile of grass and water that runs from Storey's Gate to Buckingham Palace. Even in early autumn – when the stench from the drained ponds was almost as unbearable as the noise from the pumps that soaked up the rotting leaves and spread them into festering heaps on the downtrodden grass – the magic lingered on. Right into September I could hear the echoes of a military band that seemed always to be playing a selection from *The Arcadians*. It recreated the innocent delight of my first week's holiday in London when we went into St James's Park almost every day and sat on a carefully selected patch of hard brown earth – near enough to the bandstand to hear the music, but far enough away from the real aficionados to feel no guilt about our refusal to rent a deckchair.

In my mind St James's still retains its intangible parliamentary associations. One day, while re-reading *The Prime Minister* in an aeroplane that was making its unsteady way towards a little dot in the Indian Ocean called Gan, I reached Chapter XXII, by which time 'there was nobody in London'. So Everett Wharton and Ferdinand Lopez 'agreed to walk round the park, dark and gloomy as they knew the park would be'. The result of their recklessness was 'Wharton on the ground on his back' with 'a man kneeling on his neck and head whilst a woman rifled his pockets'. Lopez 'received at once a heavy blow on his head'. I thought of the evenings on which I had walked down the Duke of York's Steps, along the narrow gravel paths, over the little bridges and through the barrier of bushes that obscures that pathway into Queen Anne's Gate. As I sat on the coral sand waiting to be flown towards Singapore and another round in the endless battle over defence expenditure, I felt neither relief about past escapes nor fear that I might not be so lucky in future. I simply wanted to be under those damp trees on a windy day.

I have walked through St James's Park in political hope and parliamentary despair. A week after the 1979 election defeat I obstinately tramped its length on my way to 'hand in my seals of office' at the Palace. The seals themselves having preceded me by several days, I was spared the obligatory indignity of travelling in my successor's car.

A decade earlier, on the day I became Joint Parliamentary Under-Secretary at the Ministry of Labour, I crossed the park's narrowest point, hurrying in case I was late for the long-awaited rendezvous with promotion from the back-benches. My last act as Minister of Defence was to resist a determined attempt by the Army Board to pull down Wellington Barracks and replace them with a modern cubic monstrosity of the sort that now overshadows its fine, reconstructed façade. Part of the reason I determined that its classical columns would not make way for monumental concrete was the fear that the pre-stressed giant might cast its ugly shadow across St James's Park.

For all I know, it might have frightened the birds – the exotics that splash about in the fountains,

196

and the geese that swim in obsessively straight lines as if they are on the way to an important engagement, and the ducks which perform for the tourists by suddenly submerging their heads and shoulders by a rocking action that produces the exact 'up tails all' effect about which the middle classes used to learn in their nurseries. I ought to know the exact names of the geese and ganders that strut along the lakesides and the ducks and drakes that tread water at the points along the bank where seats are conveniently placed for simultaneous bird-watching and sandwich-eating. For little ornithological notices grow out of the ground on wire stalks and within their blooms there are coloured pictures of the floating and flying fauna provided to assist with their individual identification. But I just sit on the benches and take in the general impression of St James's Park, letting the spirit of it sink into me.

I was doing that last week – surrounded by couples of decorously courting clerks and shop assistants, exhausted lunchtime joggers, escapees from school outings and distressed tourists who had failed to penetrate the camouflage that protects the lavatories from public view. It was half-past twelve and the band of the Scots Guards was assembling in preparation for its lunchtime concert.

The members of the band straggled their way to the bandstand, looking comfortingly unmilitary as they struggled to fasten the last button on their tunics without dropping the instruments that they casually carried. It is impossible to carry a trombone or a tuba in a soldierly fashion and the

197

musicians did not try. Just as I thought that their approach march was over, mechanised reinforcements were brought up. A corporal appeared towing a set of tubular bells, like a scrap merchant taking an old iron bedstead to the totter's yard. A Japanese visitor, sitting next to me while he changed the film in his camera, was astonished. 'Is this not,' he asked almost rhetorically, 'extraordinary?' As always, I was thinking about the general, not the particular. 'Yes,' I said. 'It is called St James's Park.'

Listener 2 July 1981

Song of the Shirt

Just before Parliament rose for the summer recess, both Commons and Lords presented the Queen with a Loyal Address which congratulated Her Majesty in suitably archaic language on the marriage of her 'dearly beloved son, the Prince of Wales, etc., etc., etc.' – as another monarch (the King of Siam) would have said, at least according to Oscar Hammerstein II. With initial reluctance and eventual enthusiasm, I took part in the event. Anyone who has any feeling for either history or England finds it difficult to resist an antiquarian excitement at the prospect of climbing inside the time machine of royal ceremonial. The bearers of last month's formal, but affectionate, message were greeted on their arrival at Buckingham

198

Palace by a piper whose presence was clearly a relic of Queen Victoria's Highland obsession. From then on the clock moved backwards until I felt like a page out of a textbook of Tudor history – or an extra from *The Six Wives of Henry VIII*.

My Privy Counsellor's oath prevents me from describing all that took place. Indeed, it probably prohibits me from using the Privy Counsellor's oath as the reason for not describing all that took place. So abiding, as I must, by its secrecy clause (the existence of which I neither confirm nor deny), I am unable to reveal that the Lord Chancellor shamelessly hammed up his part in the proceedings. Nor can I give a full account of the way that fragments of gold embroidery fell from the Speaker's robes. Anxious, as always, to ingratiate myself with authority, I picked up the gleaming desiderata and handed them back to their temporary owner. As I did so, I felt that my role had changed. The peasant from the wild North Country who goes to court, sees the Queen and recovers the gold that has fallen from the wise man's raiment is clearly a character from Hans Christian Andersen.

If the word 'peasant' implies a life deeply rooted in the soil, it may not be the most technically precise description of my origins – although, during the war, my father did briefly rent an allotment. However, the more accurate phrase 'industrial proletariat' (which, now that I have thought of it, I propose to insinuate into *Who's Who*) does not fit into a fairytale. And in the middle of all those City of London aldermen in their red robes and bearskin caps, with the gentlemen ushers ushing away like mad, and ladies-in-waiting waiting about all over the place, a fairy story it was. And I, for reasons that my Privy Council oath in no way prevents me from explaining, had the momentary feeling of a mendicant at court. The reason concerned my shirt.

I make no proletarian claims concerning my shirts in general. Indeed, I admit extravagance in every particular – capital cost, frequency of maintenance and speed of turnover. The problem on the day of the Loyal Address was specific. It first appeared that (as a result of summer holidays at the laundry) two weeks' supply languished in some Kentish Town depot. Then hope was revived by news that a van had arrived at the Horseferry Road shop. But, instead of containing boxes of carefully ironed cotton Oxfords and Bengal stripes, complete with little cardboard bow-ties to keep the collars straight, it was filled with coat-hangers from which were suspended crumpled pieces of cloth. The presser had missed his flight back from Tahiti or some such holiday resort.

There will be those who say that I should have slipped into a heavy brown check or the little white sleeveless number with the crocodile on the breast pocket. My argument with them will have to await my years of political re-education in the jungles of Barnsley or the time when the cultural revolutionaries require me to contemplate past sins in a Lambeth cowshed.

I could have carefully pulled on a bright blue confection with dazzling white collar and cuffs. But, apart from being out of fashion, my Jermyn Street rhapsody on an original theme by Everton

Football Club had a small tear under the left arm. It was the sort of tear that would have easily survived a normal day's wear but which might well have extended itself across the front of the shirt if provoked by violent movement; like, for instance, a low bow. Since I was preparing for the only day in my life when a low bow might have been required of me, wearing a shirt which would fall apart at the moment of obeisance seemed at best perverse and at worst treasonable.

So I got the ironing-board out. I have no social or sexist objections to ironing. I send my partner (as Councillor Valerie Wise would call her) out to work as an indication of my enthusiasm for equal opportunities. And although she has not (unlike Councillor Wise herself) signed over all the property to the better half of the partnership, I try to accept some share of domestic duties. This highly moral attitude is reinforced by my actual enjoyment of ironing. Smoothing out the wrinkles and making straight what previously was crooked seems to me a rewarding way to spend a Sunday morning. With a little Rodgers and Hart on the gramophone and the smell of Sunday dinner coming round the door, it is possible to think great thoughts while flattening the final crease out of a sleeve or into a trouser leg.

Indeed, I have been accused in the past of being an ironing obsessive. I possess a travelling iron which I take wherever I go. And I pride myself on my hotel bedroom technique – folded towel on the dressing-table to provide a suitable surface, clean handkerchief soaked in water to protect the wool, knob turned round to 'v. hot' and the

Hattersley auto-valet service is in action.

I even own that special mark of ironing class, a sleeve-board. When Sarah Wilson – my agnostic equivalent of a god-daughter – was a child, she mistook it for 'an ironing thing made for little girls'. If she had asked me for the dining-room table to make into a 'Wendy house', I would have found it difficult to deny her request. But I put the sleeve-board on a high shelf, well out of her reach.

I have loyally maintained my affection for ironing through every vicissitude. Humiliating phone calls to hotel receptionists, asking for a quick check on the room to which I will soon return, 'to make sure that the iron is switched off', have done nothing to cool my ardour for applying hot pressure to bent lapels and crushed pocket flaps. The briefcase that marked my first ministerial promotion is scarred for life with a horseshoe-shaped scorch mark. But my search for suitable portable surfaces on which to make the whole world flat continues. I did not become an ironer, or have ironing thrust upon me. I was born to it. If I am not very careful, I will draw psychological conclusions about my enthusiasm. They concern the Levellers and the pursuit of equality.

Despite all that, I could not resist wondering if any of the other men at the auspicious Buckingham Palace gathering had done any ironing that day. The Speaker wore beneath his velvet suit a riot of ruffles which, if they were prepared by mortal hand, must have been the work of a team of professionals. There was no way of knowing what state shirt (or, indeed, if any shirt at all) was concealed by the Archbishop of York's stock and clerical collar. Loyalty prevented my mind dwelling on either the Duke of Edinburgh's or the Prince of Wales's laundry. But I did speculate a little about the Lord Chamberlain. As Chief Scout, he must often have started fires by rubbing two twigs together and tied securely pieces of rope of unequal thickness. But I was unable to envisage him doing his good deed for the day, stooped over some old lady's ironing-board.

I drew no conclusions from my musing, except the obvious one that ironing is, for better or worse, a wholly working-class occupation. But then, so is bricklaying, and Sir Winston Churchill boasted of that as an achievement as well as a hobby. Perhaps I should include 'ironing' in *Who's Who* when I change the entry to include a reference to my industrial proletarian origins. Of course, I could not tell the truth and put my pastime as *ironing exceedingly well*. Thinking of that in Buckingham Palace, I looked down at my shirtfront and felt with pride that, thanks to my own efforts, I was the smoothest man there.

Listener 27 August 1981

Poets' Corner

It is Saturday morning in the Peak Park and the sun is beginning to clear the mist that hangs over the Derwent Valley. Buster, tired from his early morning walk, lies across my feet under the kitchen table while I eat the muffins that I bought from the village shop on the way home. Even if it rains later in the day, the paths along the escarpments which we call 'edges' will stay hard and dry and anyone who walks up to the skyline will still be able to see half of Derbyshire's green and pleasant land stretching out towards the other clouded hills. And I, in my madness, am catching the 12.37 from Chesterfield to London.

Lunacy of so high an order demands an explanation – especially since it is a recurrent disorder that impels me south with manic regularity. The symptoms never vary. First I receive an invitation to an event or occasion which is more than a year away. Distance always lends enchantment. Ask me to speak at the Little Puddlington Labour Party next Monday and I would certainly say no. Invite me for December 1999 and I will accept at once. As the date gradually approaches, I grow more and more dissatisfied with my original decision. But, rather to my surprise, today I feel contented in my madness.

At six o'clock I am to lay a wreath on George Eliot's Memorial Stone in Westminster Abbey, and I take a strange pleasure in being associated, no matter how vicariously, with the greatest novelist in the English language. I am by no means sure that she would approve of the event. Asked about God, Immortality and Duty – strange topics of conversation to be raised during an afternoon's stroll – 'she pronounced with terrible earnestness how inconceivable was the first, how unbelievable the second and how peremptory the third'. But there she is in black polished marble on the floor of Westminster Abbey – the junkyard of the nation's vanities.

She keeps appropriate company, in a row of four disparate pagans. George Eliot would not have enjoyed a night out with her neighbour Dylan Thomas, and she had little socially in common with either Lord Byron or W.H. Auden – who occupy the flanks of the line. But, in their different times and ways, they all defied respectable convention. George Eliot, having established her personal morality, lived without the slightest deviation from its precepts. If Westminster Abbey is a temple of virtue, as distinct from established Christianity, there is no one who has a greater right to be remembered in Poets' Corner.

Over her left shoulder, there is a memorial to Henry James. Philip Guedalla said that his work could be divided into three reigns – James I, James II, and the Old Pretender. In 1878, James visited George Eliot in Surrey and, at the end of an unsatisfactory afternoon, was bidding her partner, George Henry Lewes, goodbye when he was asked a favour. Would he dispose of an unwanted book that a neighbour had brought round earlier in the week? It was *The American*, a novel from the literary reign of James I. George Eliot had not connected the author with her visitor. She simply did not like that sort of fiction and saw no reason to pretend otherwise.

I wonder what she would have thought about D.H. Lawrence, who is next but one to Henry James on her left. I was brought up to believe that Lawrence was another moralist who obeyed the call of conscience from within him rather than listened to the echoes of convention from the cruel world in which he lived. But it is hard to believe that the whining, whimpering Lawrence would have been a soulmate of the didactic and indomitable George Eliot – even though they both fell in love too easily. Gerard Manley Hopkins, immediately behind her on the Abbey floor, would have been bewildered by them both – despite approving of George Eliot spending her twenties translating a Life of Jesus from the German.

It is quite the wrong question to ask on a day when I take part in a wreath-laying ceremony, but I wonder if authors of genius should be commemorated by marble tablets laid – like Dorothy Parker's young socialites – end to end in Westminster Abbey. From time to time, there are arguments about new inclusions as if a piece of stone could enhance the glory of genius. The best way to pay proper respect to George Eliot is by reading her novels – in my case *Daniel Deronda*, at which I have taken several running jumps without ever landing on the final page.

I am in favour of the Fellowships and Societies that organise these events. They encourage reading their heroes' work and sponsor little biographical projects which, added together, produce real scholarship. But that is very different from the solemnity of a laurel wreath and an encomium. Had George Eliot died last year, I would not have even considered attending her memorial service. I loathe conspicuous grief and ostentatious mourning. Those who we love and admire should be remembered in private. But today I leave Derbyshire without a regret. I suppose that the little Abbey ceremony is as near to George Eliot as I am ever going to get. I propose to make the most of it.

Guardian 22 June 1998

Towering Triumph of the Old Soldiers

Ten o'clock in the Tower of London. The ultra-modern buildings on the far bank of the Thames are illuminated by a thousand points of light. But, within the ancient walls of the palace and fortress, a group of men, standing above the steps which lead from Traitors' Gate to the Victorian barracks, are almost invisible in the gloom. One of them carries a lantern. So it is just possible to recognise the silhouettes of guardsmen's bearskins.

The chilly silence is broken by a single voice. 'God save Queen Elizabeth.' To which the guardsmen respond in unison 'Amen'. As their prayer echoes through the night, the Tower clock chimes the hour. Once again, the Ceremony of the Keys – which has been held every night for four hundred years – has ended on time.

The Ceremony of the Keys lasted for exactly seven minutes – hence its claim to be the shortest as well as the longest-lasting of all Royal rituals. It began with a Yeoman Sergeant slamming and locking the great gates and then making his way to deliver the keys into the safe keeping of the Constable of the Tower. Halfway there, he and his escort of guardsmen are challenged by a sentry.

'Halt, who comes here?'

'The keys.'

'Whose keys?'

'Queen Elizabeth's keys.'

'Pass Queen Elizabeth's keys. All's well.'

Chief Yeoman Warder John Keohane – a lifetime of meritorious service in the Royal Corps of Signals behind him – exhibits his irrepressible pride in the corps which he leads by pointing out the correct wording of the challenge. 'Notice,' he says. 'It's who COMES here? Who GOES there? is wrong.' Keohane is a stickler for accuracy. He accepts that most people think of him and his men as 'Beefeaters' – a nickname he thinks they acquired through eating Henry VIII's leftovers. But he regrets the occasional confusion with the Yeomen of the Guard who search out the House of Commons for gunpowder before the State Opening of Parliament.

His claim to superiority is only just a joke. 'We call them the territorials. They are only part-time.' His confidence is encouraged by the uniform he wears – ceremonial red for State occasions and a more serviceable, but equally dashing, blue for performing the duties of guardian and guide. It bears the Royal Arms. Chief Warden Keohane is for Queen and country.

When I met the Chief Warder our greetings were interrupted by a tourist who told him that her daughter worked in Williamsburg – the Virginian re-creation of a town in colonial America. 'Three hundred years of history,' she said. 'How old is all this?' Without a hint of condescension, the Chief Warder replied: 'Nearly one thousand.' Boasting was unnecessary. The Tower's historical pedigree speaks for itself. On the conducted tours, the Yeomen Warders – thirty-three of them in all – fill in the details.

Each Yeoman Warder has served for at least eighteen years in the Army, Air Force or Marines and retired (usually as a warrant officer) with a good conduct and long service medal. There are no sailors in the service of the Queen and the Tower. The Navy, says John Keohane, used to rely on press gangs and expect its men to swear allegiance to the ship's captain rather than the sovereign. Yeoman Warders are free men who serve only the monarch. And they take history very seriously.

How could they do anything else? Each Yeoman Warder – married or permanently attached men preferred – lives inside the Tower. Most of their houses are built between the inner wall (constructed in 1170) and the outer wall which was erected in 1280. The back windows – all in the shape of a narrow cross – confirm their original intention. They were not designed to let in the sunlight but to provide protection for English bowmen defending the Tower against all comers. You cannot live surrounded by England's history and forget about the past.

The new recruits to the rank of Yeoman Warder have fought in modern campaigns with modern weapons. In the Warden's Hall, at the foot of the Byward Tower, Warder Terry Humphries – twenty-four years' service in the Coldstream Guards – was watching a war film as he prepared

209

for Watchman's duty through the night. He had ended his life of action and adventure with regret. But he was still in the service of the Queen. From the wall high above his head six sovereigns looked down from faded portraits. 'See that,' said the Chief Warder. 'Edward VIII signed it during the few months that he was King. Not many of those about.'

At half-past ten, Sergeant Warder Bostock – who had, that evening, carried the keys – came into the Warders' Club for a little light refreshment. Was he, I asked him, nervous when he performed the ceremony. 'Every time,' he replied. With all that history looking down, who can blame him?

Daily Mail 11 April 2005

A Hidden Beauty Going to Waste

Twenty yards inside the Albert Gate entrance to London's Hyde Park in Knightsbridge there is a manhole cover hidden in the rough grass. Below it is a shaft, eighteen iron rungs deep, which leads to the 1800 miles of London's sewers. The sewers were built – using 318 million bricks – 150 years ago. Yet they are now expected to disperse the effluent of a city which is ten times greater than when they were designed, after 'The Great Stink' of 1858 closed the House of Commons.

Their success in keeping the sewage flowing is

a tribute to Joseph Bazalgette who designed them and the Victorian workmen who dug the tunnels and lined the walls. If you want to see the best brickwork in British history, go down into London's sewers.

You will not find the descent easy. The regulation thigh boots, with tungsten-studded soles to prevent slipping without causing sparks, are hot and heavy. The harness – strapped on above the compulsory white shell-suit in case injury or illness requires a quick evacuation to the surface – is tight. And the emergency breathing apparatus which is hung from the belt feels as if it weighs a ton.

Although the necessary precautions create more anxiety than reassurance, once underground the spirits rise. Much of London's sewers are more than six feet in height – although there are places at which the roof is so low that the workmen, appropriately known as 'flushers', can carry out their duties only on hands and knees. And the effluent – which flows along the sewers' floor – often looks like water clean enough to drink. Appearances deceive.

But there are good days and bad days. Sometimes – since much of the effluent is water from land drainage systems – the 'flow' is several feet high. And there are parts of the system where blockages are common. The Piccadilly branch, below Leicester Square, has a particular problem – hundreds of tons of fat washed down, warm and liquid, from London's fast–food restaurants. It sets solid once it reaches the low temperatures underground. Thames Water offers statistics to illustrate the cost of clearing it away – sometimes with picks and shovels. Of the hundred thousand blockages each year, half are caused by all the fat that is flushed into the system. The annual cost of clearance – distributed among everyone who pays water rates – is £300 million.

Without the expert knowledge of the men who maintain them – only thirty-nine these days compared with the four hundred when the system was built – the sewers would have failed London years ago. Rob Smith, a 'catchment engineer' with fifteen years' experience, says that it is important to 'know the flow'. The flushers who work with him have memorised the pattern of the sewers in the way that men who work on the roads have learned the street map. They point out 'landmarks' as they make their way under Hyde Park. One stretch is actually labelled 'Knightsbridge' with what looks like a road sign. But most of the features have to be identified from memory.

'That,' says Mike McLaughlin, the team leader, pointing to the end of a pipe, 'is the sewer that comes straight from the French Embassy.' We all make the obvious jokes before we squeeze through a narrow gap, ducking under a low roof, and suddenly are able to see daylight. Ken Young, a supervisor, identified it as the Serpentine Overflow. In places, the sewer system is barely a couple of yards below the ground.

Like all men in hazardous occupations, the flushers minimise the risks of their job. At the front and rear of every working party a man carries a gas detector. Both methane (smelling like rotting vegetables) and hydrogen sulphide (smelling like rotten eggs) pollute the air from time to time. During my time down below, I smelt not a whiff of either – nor of anything else. Nor did I, as expected, wade through a river of what looked like untreated sewage. The effluent is normally 95 per cent liquid and 5 per cent solid – largely because rainwater has entered the system though the drains. There are remnants of toilet paper hanging from the iron stanchions which protrude from some of the walls. But it does not look very different from the garbage which clings to the banks of many country rivers.

And I saw only one rat. It was briefly caught in the beam of the light which shone from the front of my miner's helmet and scurried away into the darkness of an overflow drain. Rats are part of the myth of London's sewerage system – as is the invention that flushers spend hours under Hatton Garden looking for diamonds that jewellers have dropped down the lavatory. However, one fact is beyond dispute. When Parliament decided to build the best sewerage system in the world, their objective was magnificently achieved. Underneath London lies one of the engineering marvels of Victorian England.

Daily Mail 12 July 2005

Arms against Oblivion

The College of Arms in Victoria Street, just inside the boundary of the City of London, is an imposing Restoration building which shelters behind magnificent, gilded, wrought-iron gates. Everyone assumes they were specially designed to add to the College's splendour. In fact, they were erected after the war as a replacement for the originals which had been commandeered in 1940 and melted down to make tanks and Spitfires. The gates used to stand outside Goodrich Court in Herefordshire and they look at home outside the College of Arms because it is not the sort of establishment which could possibly conduct its business behind a wooden fence or brick wall.

Richard III granted the College of Arms its Charter in 1484, shortly after (according to William Shakespeare) murdering the two young Princes in the Tower just down the road. It remains under the supervision of the Duke of Norfolk, the hereditary Earl Marshal of England, and the Heralds who run it are appointed by the Queen. Yet in the foyer of their historic building, books on heraldry and history are on sale – each one carefully labelled with its price. That is not at all the sort of thing you expect to find in an extension of the Court of Saint James. But the College of Arms is a strange English combination

214

of pomp and practicality. It has to pay its way in the world by selling its wares.

The head of the College is Peter Gwynn-Jones, official title Garter King of Arms. You can see him in action on television next Wednesday morning as he performs his ceremonial duties – in scarlet tunic and gold tabards with the Coat of Arms of England front and back – when the Queen attends the State Opening of Parliament. He takes part in all the great ceremonies from the Garter Service in St George's Chapel, Windsor, to the Coronation. Yet, when he interviews new Peers – discussing their titles and arrangements for their inauguration – he always suggests that they buy a Coat of Arms to add to their distinction. That is how the College of Arms pays its bills.

Coats of Arms are not just for peers. They are available to anyone of standing. In his office – a portrait of his grandfather, a general, on the wall above a framed collection of the distinguished soldier's medals – Gwynn-Jones describes who qualifies. Could this week's lottery winner obtain an heraldic device to celebrate his good fortune? 'Not just for having won the lottery,' Garter King of Arms replies. But what if he or she was also head of a successful secondary school? 'Certainly.' Gwynn-Jones could quote a price.

Indeed he has a printed price list. The standard price for a peer who wants the full works is about £5000 – with an extra £1000 if the parchment on which it is painted is decorated with a border of chivalric symbols. A Coat of Arms without supporters – the allegorical figures who hold each side of the shield – comes a little cheaper at

£4500. Buy one and it is yours in perpetuity to pass on from generation to generation. 'Garter' as he is known certainly regards that as a bargain.

High in a room in one of the College building wings, two artists were hard at work designing and painting Coats of Arms for recently en-nobled peers. Gillian Barlow – who also paints exquisite and botanically precise pictures for Kew Gardens – was working on a shield sup-ported by two scarlet greyhounds. Her colleague, ex-guardsman Christopher Collins, was clearly meeting the specifications for a lord who was musical as well as a noble. Symbolic trumpets were spread across it and it was surmounted by a representation of a violin bridge.

Peter Gwynn-Jones keeps a copy of every Coat of Arms which the College has granted in his time. One, which he displays with particular pride, was designed for a judge who often presided over the prosecution of what Garter calls 'dubious ladies'. The main motif was a dozen legs in fishnet stock-ings, copied, according to Gwynn-Jones, from a picture of Barbra Streisand. The background was white (for good) and black (for evil).

They are not the only trophies of Gwynn-Jones's long years at the College. He is also, as his name suggests, an Officer of the Order of the Garter and grants its Knights crests as well as Coats of Arms. When KGs die their banners go to their families but their crests remain in the College. They stand on the top of cupboards and in half-empty book cases – a red dragon for Jim Callaghan, a green knotted snake (the traditional symbol of the Cavendish family) for the Duke of

Devonshire and an elephant holding a sword in its trunk for General Kitchener.

A visit to the College of Arms is like an afternoon in Camelot. But David White, hurrying to his office in shirt sleeves, was just as typical of the work it does. Although his official title is Somerset Herald, he – like his colleagues – spends much of his time answering the questions from the general public. Some of them go on to ask for what the College has on offer. In England a Coat of Arms is available to every person of distinction.

Daily Mail 14 November 2006

Sweet Serenity of Parliament's Secret Society

The Houses of Parliament or the Palace of Westminster – as some people still prefer to call that Victorian Gothic masterpiece – really was the property of the Queen not long ago. Her Majesty is landlord no longer, but there are still parts of the building which television cannot see, tourists cannot visit and remain in her possession. The most beautiful is St Mary's Undercroft, known as 'the crypt'. It is hidden away down a staircase which begins in the Elizabethan Westminster Hall. Officially, St Mary's is neither a church nor a chapel. It is a Royal Peculiar – a status which it shares with Westminster Abbey across the road.

On a wet Thursday afternoon, two young

couples stood self-consciously by the crypt's double doors. They were waiting for wedding rehearsals. Direct descendants of peers and Members of Parliament can be married there and have their children christened at the ornate font. The rehearsal was to be conducted by Terry Eiss, the Verger of St Mary's Undercroft, an employee (via Black Rod and the Lord Great Chamberlain) of Queen Elizabeth II. He is a former church warden from Northampton who – after a spell in marketing which included 'being captain of a Russian submarine which tourists visited on the Thames' – answered the advertisement for what amounts to manager of the crypt. As well as organising weddings and baptisms he makes sure that everything is in order for the Parliament's communion which is celebrated every Wednesday at 12.45. The services are conducted by the Reverend Robert Wright, Rector of St Margaret's Westminster, the parish church of Parliament which nestles in the grounds of the Abbey. Worship at Westminster is organised by a procedure as complicated as the Rules of Order which its inhabitants observe when they debate the future of the nation.

The doors, by which the anxious brides and grooms were waiting, are one of the quaintest features of a building on which work began in 1292. A lion's head is carved above each lintel arch. One lion pokes its tongue at the world. The other has its mouth firmly closed. Exit and entrance are thus clearly marked by signs which separate the ways in and out. According to Terry Eiss they were meant to guide generations of worshippers who could not read a written notice. He confirms that the guiding animals are lions but adds that the 'bosses' (complicated carvings on the ceiling) are not as leonine as they look. 'They are' he says 'green men' – the mythical spirits of the forest who evolved into Robin Hood and the protectors of the English countryside.

The bosses – carved to celebrate the martyrdom of Saints Lawrence, Margaret, Catherine and John – have a practical purpose. They are the joints and junctions of the unique double arches which first curve upwards and then turn down before they come together, high in the roof. The elaborate vaulting lifts the visitor's eyes to heaven. Looking eastward from the door, everything – gilded wood and golden stone – seems to glow like a burnished sovereign. The chapel looks like a home for angels. Three of them balance on the pinnacles of the mighty organ. Four more decorate the elaborate organ case. Each one is appropriately winged and playing the instruments of paradise.

In 1834, most of the Palace of Westminster was destroyed by fire. But the Undercroft – much changed during the five hundred years since it was completed – survived, though badly damaged. And the Victorians restored it to more than its former glory. The gilding was made more golden than in the glory days and the painted figures more vivid than they had ever been in medieval England. The elaborate carving of St Lawrence – being martyred on a gridiron – shows the burning coal beneath him glowing red. One tormenter, with bellows, keeps the fire burning bright. Another, with a shovel, feeds the flame. The saint himself observes the proper rules of Victorian respectability. He dies in agony, wearing long spotted underpants.

After the wedding rehearsals were over, the silent chapel seemed far removed from the hustle and bustle above – the armed police on duty at the public entrance to the House of Commons, the visitors queuing for a seat in the gallery and the parliamentary staff hurrying towards the canteen at the far end of Westminster Hall. The crypt was serene in its secrecy. Cynics will say that it could not be less like the House of Commons which it serves.

Yet there have been moments when the two worlds met. On 1 January 1911, the night of the national census, Emily Wilding Davison – a militant suffragette – hid in a St Mary's Undercroft cupboard. As a result, her entry in the census recorded her address as 'the House of Commons' – a declaration that she had a right to sit, as well as sleep, in Parliament. She died when, as a more dramatic protest, she ran in front of King Edward's racehorse on Derby day. The memorial plaque, inside the cupboard, is a tribute and an apology from the MPs whose predecessors denied her access for so long. It adds to the tranquillity of the most peaceful place in the whole Houses of Parliament.

Daily Mail 24 July 2007

Perfect for Trafalgar's Sweet Plinth

London ought to be ashamed of its statues. I make no complaint about their quality – even though President de Gaulle seems to be wearing Eric Morecambe's comedy riding-breeches and Nelson Mandela appears to be illustrating the size of a recently caught fish. Nor do I object to the number of politicians and generals who stare down upon us. The fault is the failure, on the part of whichever body of worthy citizens decides these things, to pay proper homage to England's writers and composers. There is, in particular, a deplorable absence of William Shakespeares – the man whose work defines our country and enables us to feel that, whatever else may go wrong, we are a special people because he was born among us. The best memorial on offer in London – the capital of the nation which he personifies and the city in which he wrote and acted – is a crude likeness in Leicester Square. It is currently surrounded by the whirligigs of a travelling fair. There ought to be a proper statue on what estate agents call a prime site. Fortunately one is available. It is known as the 'empty plinth' in Trafalgar Square.

I confess, at once, that I would rather keep the plinth empty than have it occupied by some of the entries for the competition which will decide what adorns it for the next twelve months. Their fatuity was admirably illustrated by Jeremy Deller, whose submission – a burned-out motor car – is called *The Spoils of War* and is subtitled *Memorial to the Unknown Civilian*. A sculpture that needs a subtitle – not to mention its creator explaining on television what message he means to convey – might be said to lack visual impact. At least Tracey Emin's *Something for the Future* is instantly recognisable as four bronze meerkats – and as preposterously inappropriate for anywhere except the entrance to a safari park. But the real scandal is the sheer stupidity of having an empty plinth and even considering filling it with anything except the man who was not of an age but for all time.

Letters keep appearing in newspapers demanding that we reaffirm our national identity, take pride in our history and promote what is best about us to a sceptical world. Generals Napier and Havelock, on two of the Trafalgar Square plinths, recall our colonisation of India. George IV, on a third, reminds us that the monarchy can survive even the most deplorable of monarchs. Does anyone doubt that William Shakespeare has at least as great a claim to represent our national heritage as those three gentlemen? He is, to put his greatness in more prosaic language, our highest-quality product and most spectacular export success. Nothing would do more to improve our prestige in the world than a statue which reminded tourists, as they wander across Trafalgar Square, that he was 'Made in England'.

The Times 10 January 2008

High Hopes

I was sixteen before I noticed that there were parts of England in which the land stretched out, low and flat, as far as the eye could see. We had spent two family holidays in London but, as the train raced through the market towns en route, there was no reason for me to suspect that this land to the west of Newark and Grantham was barren of hills. All I knew was the Peak District and the Pennine foothills. So I took gradients for granted. When I learned that there were tribes of Native Americans (I called them Red Indians in those days) who worshipped mountains, I was first surprised that anything so commonplace would attract veneration. Then I wished that I had thought of the idea first.

In my School Certificate year we spent a summer fortnight in a tin hut on the Lincolnshire coast. We travelled to our 'holiday bungalow' by hired car and the full horror of Lincolnshire was revealed to me. The thought that Norfolk was even worse never entered my innocent adolescent head. But I did begin to believe that hill country was special. The ancients thought that people who lived in high places were close to God. I cannot bring myself to share that view, but I have no doubt that we inhabit an earthly paradise.

Hills are heroic. Moses would not have made much of a stir if he had brought back the Ten Commandments from an alluvial plain. And when Governor Winthrop – founding father of the

Commonwealth of Massachusetts – wanted to impress the importance of integrity on his fellow colonists, he told them to behave like a house on a hill, not a homestead in the valley. Hills are a synonym for power and nobility. We speak of the commanding heights of the economy and urge our disputing politicians to occupy the high ground. They are also, in the proper sense of a much misused word, awesome. Looking down from the top or up from the bottom, man puts his tiny existence into proper perspective.

Where I come from, and where I now live, we are inclined to call hills mountains – in the belief that everything is biggest as well as best up here. But it is hills – accessible to anyone with a stout pair of boots and moderately healthy heart and lungs – that provide a panorama of England. From Ingleborough in North Yorkshire I have looked west and seen the Blackpool Tower. From the 'edges' of the Peak District, Chatsworth House is clearly visible. Skiddaw provides an unrivalled view of the northern lakes. It is Moses again. From the hills he looked down into the Promised Land. I have the good fortune to inhabit it.

Riding the Rails in the Peak Park

As far as I recall, it was ghostly heartbeats and the rustling of phantom skirts that convinced Rudyard Kipling that there was once a way through the woods. The Monsal Trail – although trees meet in archways overhead – provides more tangible evidence of what used to be. For the way was once permanent and there are still sturdy stone bridges and remnants of country platforms to prove that, years ago, steam trains raced that way along the Midland Railways line from Manchester to London. Now it is a gentle stroll which begins south of Bakewell and ends in the Peak Park, somewhere north-west of Miller's Dale.

I will not pretend that it is my favourite morning walk. It is too man-made. And, because of the steam locomotives' reluctance to climb hills, all the ups and downs were smoothed out more than a hundred years ago when the track was laid. It is the ups and downs which give limestone country its special charm. So the less cultivated footpaths, which cut across the contours, offer better views and more exercise. But I used to tell myself that the attractions of the horizontal would grow with the years.

Now there seems a real possibility that the delights of the Monsal Trail will be denied to me just as I begin to need them. There is serious talk of bringing the railway back to Derbyshire and running it along the ancient route – not a theme-park steam train but the real, 100 mph express. The proponents of the scheme are not directors of the existing railway companies – who have difficulty enough in maintaining a decent service on the lines which they already mismanage. The enthusiasts are the conservationists of the Peak Park Planning Board and the environmentalists of the Derbyshire County Council. You may find it difficult to believe, but tracks and trains will actually preserve the countryside.

I certainly found the idea hard to swallow, though I now realise that my intellectual digestion was disturbed by prejudice. I wanted the Monsal Trail to be there for me to walk. And, although the railway line will be almost a mile from my backyard, I was offended by the thought that the far end of the village would be disturbed by the rush of locomotives. Ironically, the houses which will be mostly affected are the children of the railway. Manchester merchants wanted to enjoy the beauties of the Peak and then dash down to London after stopping a train (by request) at the local halt. But history, I thought, be damned. A modern railway would, I feared, spoil the Peak.

The suspicion still occasionally sneaks its way into my mind. But in my more rational moments, I realise that the Peak is more likely to be spoilt without it. Our limestone escarpments are being cut away to provide hard-core for motorway maintenance. And, although we are resisting the more destructive quarrying, thousands of tonnes will be shipped south and west over the next ten years. Most of it is taken away in eight-axle lorries. It would be better transported by rail. We welcome visitors to the Peak Park but regret that so many of them crowd the roads with their motor cars. They ought to be encouraged to travel by train.

I know all these things yet I remain ambivalent about the railway – a perfect example of personal prejudice colliding with considered judgement. I am told that the historian George Kitson Clark faced a similar dilemma when it was suggested that women be admitted to Trinity College,

228

Cambridge. Knowing the proposal to be right he decided to vote in its favour. But finding the idea uncongenial he determined to speak against it at the Fellows' meeting in the hope that his colleagues would be persuaded by what he knew to be an irrational argument. I have searched for a similar compromise, but I have not found one.

So, if the railway enthusiasts organise a poll I shall vote in favour, And I shall not take part in the form of protest suggested by the late Duke of Rutland, for the leader of the council tells me that if I threaten to lie down in the path of the first train, he will look forward to travelling on the inaugural footplate.

Instead, I will campaign for the railway's development and luxuriate in the self-righteous feeling that I am doing what is right in defiance of all my atavistic instincts.

Guardian 23 August 1999

On the Edge of a Barren Landscape

The Peak District village in which I spend half my life has chosen to celebrate the Queen's Jubilee sotto voce. There is bunting on the post office and the village hall, and a couple of union flags hang from bedroom windows like sheets put out to air. But Main Street – every shade of green, dappled with red hawthorn and white horse chestnut – encourages, as always, the patriotism which simply comes from living in England in June. I have never understood why Robert Browning's home thoughts from abroad were confined to April and May. There is not one month of the year in which I would choose to live anywhere else in the world.

English topography is as varied as the weather which creates this green and pleasant land. My home and hearth – including a village green on which I ate my sandwiches during a youth club hike half a century ago – is at the heart of the best walking country in Britain. The White Peak is rough enough to require some physical effort, but not so rugged that only athletes can manage more than a couple of miles.

However the Peak came about – earthquake or erosion – its special quality is the relationship between earth and sky. There are always hills to look up to and the horizon is usually an almost perfectly horizontal escarpment that we, with the familiarity of affection, call an edge.

Edges are the defining characteristic of our part of the Peak. This weekend they will attract to Derbyshire men and women from all over the north of England. The real enthusiasts – dressed in knickerbockers and woolly socks to look like Victorian alpine mountaineers – follow their plastic-covered maps for mile after adventurous mile. The weekend ramblers – most of whom seem to change their driving shoes for walking boots while sitting on my garden wall – follow the recommended routes. It is the right reasonably to roam that they celebrate this weekend.

It was not won without a fight. The Dark Peak to the north is the land of the Kinder Scout trespass

230

by which, between the wars, protesters asserted the English ramblers' rights to walk on English moorland. The fracas with gamekeepers which followed ended with some of the trespassers being sent to prison for offences which today would not even attract a caution. Now, with varying degrees of reluctance, the right to roam the Peak has been generally accepted. Unfortunately, part of the land is being literally removed from beneath the walkers' feet. The edge is being quarried away.

The hillside up which it is approached already bears the marks of quarrying. I do not call them scars because, after a hundred years or so, a quarry becomes romantic. I spent part of my boyhood playing King Solomon's Mines in excavations which, a century before I was born, had sent dozens of quarrymen to their deaths, coughing sandstone particles. But the great gash had grown to look benign. It is new workings which desecrate the landscape. And that is what is happening to our edge.

Fortunately for our village the damage is being done on the other side of the hill. For the moment we are spared everything except piles of debris breaking the clean line of the horizon. But somebody somewhere looks out each morning at what should be a miracle of nature and sees only the brutality of commerce. The Peak Park Planning Board had no choice but to acknowledge the ancient mining rights of the quarry company. An old lease entitles the company to mine fluorspar. So, happily for its balance sheet, it can remove and sell millions of tons of limestone, in which run veins of that mineral. Promises have been made about eventually restoring the land. But every time I see a heavy lorry racing towards the motorway with a load of aggregate, I know our inheritance is in jeopardy.

A community which carefully closes gates and rarely strays from footpaths deserves better. Yet the only way of preserving the edge intact is to buy out the quarrying company's mineral rights. That would cost more than the Peak Park Planning Board can afford. Tomorrow, as I walk up toward the site of desecration, I shall consider who – in the judgement of the gods – are the true patriots, the people who endorse whatever it costs to finance the four-day jubilee celebrations or the men and women who would rather spend the money on preserving the splendours of the English countryside. God save the edge.

Guardian 3 June 2002

Arcadia – a Nice Place to Call Home

It is my good fortune to spend half my life in one of the Peak District's pedestrian villages. We boast neither a car park nor a historic church. So we are spared both bikers whiling away their afternoons by revving up their engines and motorists who think that they have done their duty to culture and the countryside by driving slowly past something that was built five hundred years ago. People come to our village to walk.

They come all year round – teenagers with huge backpacks and bedrolls, bare-kneed geriatrics supported by exotic walking sticks, and earnest students of limestone landscape with plastic-covered maps hanging upside down from lanyards round their necks. Today, spring bank holiday Monday, the hardy annuals will be joined by seasonal reinforcements: the casual walkers for whom our village has a special significance. They stop here to change their shoes.

Middle-aged ladies in twinsets and pearls who travel together in sensible family saloons behave in exactly the same way as the courting couples in wire-wheeled sports cars who kiss before they disembark. They remove whatever is on their feet with the conscientious solemnity of a pious Muslim at the door of a mosque. There the comparison ends. For, rain or shine, they pull on expensive hiking boots in preparation for an afternoon or pre-prandial stroll in the best walking country in the world.

W.H. Auden wrote that what made limestone country special was its inclination to dissolve in water. That is only part of the story. Great faults run through the substrata of rock and, during the years before we began to calculate time, the earth split open. The result was towering escarpments which we call 'edges' and horizons that are always sharp and clear against the sky. When I walk my modest four miles in the early evening, I can see halfway to eternity.

The ruined barns and byres are relics of a dead civilisation as well as a more simple sort of farming. But farmers are rebuilding the dry-stone walls that have separated the fields since the enclosures. They are being recreated along exactly the lines that the rude forefathers of our hamlet accepted when their grazing rights were stolen, and they will be remade with the stones that built the original boundaries. Today's visitors will walk across living country built out of old England.

We take pride in the Peaks' unyielding landscape. But the visitors who change their shoes outside my house today will walk over hills and fields that have been made to look gentle by the colours of May. In the meadows that are already mowed, pale earth shines through the paler green of the stubble. The fields where the grass still grows are speckled with buttercups and behind them, at the foot of the hills, Queen Anne's lace and May blossom dapple the slopes with patches of dazzling white. Even the gorse at the crest of the escarpments has changed from violent yellow to modest amber. Rabbits in the hillsides sit in the entrances to their burrows like extras from *Watership Down*, and hares tiptoe to reconnoitre the land before racing away with the skip and jump that made our ancestors believe that they were mad.

The farmer who writes agricultural notes for our parish magazine caused some surprise by asking his neighbours to accept that the foot-and-mouth epidemic – which passed us by but forced us into quarantine – was not without its blessings. Wildlife that he had not seen since he was a boy returned to his land. His reaction was unusual. But what else would you expect from a citizen of Arcadia?

Let me not give the impression that there is no grief and sorrow here. Each spring morning, we

234

have a daily sadness. Frogs, which have swum happily in one of the underground streams beneath my garden, squeeze their way through cracks in the wall above the lawn and luxuriate in the dew on the grass until the sun comes out. Then they dehydrate. Those which I cannot revive with a watering can wither into desiccated corpses that remind me of the dead in Pompeii. But next spring there will be frog spawn in the old horse-trough by my garden gate.

And next spring bank holiday, the walkers will be back to change their shoes. They will park in front of my house, sit on my wall and occupy the undivided attention of my dog as he lies on his window seat. As I try to work nearby, he will draw my attention to each arrival. The years of our companionship have taught me to distinguish between his various messages – welcoming, warning or suggesting (in the politest possible way) that the visitors should move on. I tell him just to rejoice. They are there because we live in the best walking country in the world.

Guardian 31 May 2004

Stones That Will Never Roll...

A windswept country road five miles from Buxton on the A515. The sky is an unclouded blue and, even at noon, the ground is still hard with overnight frost. On Brundcliffe Farm, sheep

235

graze alongside cattle, black plastic bags of winter food are piled high outside the cow sheds and a ginger feral cat hunts among the rusting agricultural machinery. It looks like all the other farms along the road which stretches back to Ashbourne. Even the signpost, announcing that it is the home of a pedigree Ayrshire herd, is not exceptional. They take cattle seriously in north Derbyshire – cattle and stone walls.

It is the stone walls which make Brundcliffe Farm special. In its fields, Trevor Wragg – in his time the National Stone Wall Champion of England – teaches the trade in which he is a certified Master Craftsman. Wragg is, in appearance, the typical ruddy-faced northern farmer. But he has made an art out of the craft by which, for more than a thousand years, Derbyshire has divided its fields. His walls rely on neither mortar nor cement. Building them has become a local growth industry – and therapy for men who work in factories and offices but long to create something that will last.

The old walls on Brundcliffe are as straight as the Roman road which runs alongside the A515 – a sure sign that they were built during the 'enclosures' which divided up the common land among the local gentry. Some sections are as solid and safe as they were in 1780. But other parts have collapsed into heaps of rubble. Each summer weekend it is possible – on payment of a modest £50 – to learn 'stonewalling' by rebuilding them. The traditional technique will guarantee that the new walls last for another two hundred years.

Master stonewallers are scarce in Derbyshire.

Their order books are full for a year or more. So Mr Wragg loses money by teaching rather than building. He makes the sacrifice because of his enthusiasm for walls in general and limestone walls in particular. Limestone is the rock that gave the White Peak its name. North of Buxton walls are made of millstone grit and south of Matlock wallers use sandstone. Both are easier to work. But real craftsmen prefer limestone – because it is too brittle to be 'dressed' into shape.

'The sound is important' says Mr Wragg. 'A good piece has a ring to it.' To illustrate his point he prepares to tap a stone which, because it is split from end to end, will not ring true. But he is distracted by a fossil. 'Coral. Three million years old.'

Time has turned the once white walls dark grey. But they are blotched with particles of fawn and green. 'Living lichens,' says Mr Wragg, 'each with its own environment. Move them and they die.' There are, he adds, twenty thousand species. Everything about walls fascinates him. 'Walling' is a hard way to earn a living, especially in the driving rain of north Derbyshire. But he would have no other trade.

Building a dry-stone wall is an art. The secret is the cross section – four feet high, two feet across the bottom but tapering towards the top like a capital A. The right shape can be ensured with the aid of a wooden template – though Mr Wragg scorns to use anything except a piece of string stretched between two sticks. But, even with a template, the waller needs the talent to pick up the right stones from the heap at his feet. There is no time for trial and error. Each must fit in first time.

Dry-stone walls are a sandwich. 'Facing stones' look out from front and back. But the 'middle fill' – with the romantic name of 'hearting' – makes the wall one piece. Hearting is no more than rubble. But, without the rough interior, the handsome face stones could not withstand the wind and weather. There are all sorts of morals to be learned from dry-stone walling.

One is that sometimes what seems hard and unyielding can provide a home. 'There is,' says Trevor Wragg, 'more wild life in dry-stone walls than in hedges. It is safer and warmer. At the bottom there are toads, newts, snails and snakes. Birds nest higher up. Fifty different species of spider live in the spaces. Butterflies, bees and wasps hibernate in them.' He draws a line with the toe of his boot in the grass. 'There'll be a mole run, just there. It's sheltered by the wall.'

The dry-stone wall ought to be the economists' delight. It is built out of local material with no other investment except talent. These days the process is complicated by health and safety legislation. Trainees are required to guard against everything from back strain to bee stings. School walls must be secured by mortared coping stones to guard against broken toes.

The men who built Derbyshire's old stone walls – the walls that Mr Wragg is rebuilding with the original stone – could remember Bonnie Prince Charlie's clansmen streaming across the Peak in their triumphant march from Manchester to Derby. Wragg – a purist – will work in exactly the same way. The result will, in the long run, be far cheaper to the farmer than barbed wire or wicker fences. Dry-stone walls are part of England's heritage. And they are built to last.

Daily Mail 15 March 2005

Ah, What It Is to Be Well Dressed!

Over Haddon is a village which justifies its high-sounding name. Even by the standards of Derbyshire, a county which boasts some of the best views in England, the prospect looking south is extraordinary. Over Haddon stands halfway up a hill that is the northern slope of Lathkill Dale. Below, the river runs through a deep wooded valley and beyond it, green fields roll on to the skyline. The people who live at Over Haddon must feel on top of the world.

Yet high though the village is, there are springs in Over Haddon. For years cattle drank at two troughs where the water has no obvious origins. Most of the cattle have gone. But according to Pat Thirlbey, who has lived in Over Haddon all his life, 'The troughs never dry up.' Nearby, an ancient cast-iron pump still works. Not surprisingly, in common with other northern limestone villages, Over Haddon holds an annual thanksgiving for its constant supply of mysterious water.

In some parts of limestone country, water comes and goes with an unpredictability which primitive people could not understand. In the villages where streams suddenly disappeared, they held rituals to propitiate the gods of drought. At some date in the Middle Ages, the Christian Church took over and 'blessed the wells' which never failed and prayed for the inconsistent springs to flow all the year round.

Canon Edmund Urquhart, vicar of Bakewell with Over Haddon, gave the blessing. He wore a leaf-patterned stole, which he rightly thought appropriate to the occasion, and spoke of man's obligations to the animal kingdom. Asked about the pagan origins of the ceremony which he performed, he replied: 'A lot of what we do began that way. The Christmas tree, for instance.'

His blessing is only the formal beginning of what has evolved from a primitive rite into an annual celebration. The wells are decorated each summer with pictures that, true to the primitive origins of the festival, are made from 'natural' materials – petals and leaves at the beginning of the season, nuts and leaves at its end.

Well dressing, as it is called, has been going on in most Staffordshire and Derbyshire limestone villages since long before the Romans built their crude, but straight, roads across the countryside. But not in Over Haddon. For some reason, at a date no one can remember, well dressing was abandoned. But in 2004 Over Haddon decided to reconnect itself with history and keep faith with the past. Now, to make up for lost time, it produces a pair of flower pictures. One – created by the whole village – is close by the water troughs. The other – made by local children – is outside the village hall. Both are genuine works of art.

By the water troughs, the picture of a packed Noah's Ark seems – at first glance – too good to have been made from what the villagers have picked from their gardens and plucked from the hedgerows. But it has. Two anxious giraffes tower above the rest of the animals. A pair of monkeys peer out of a porthole. Ducks swim on and fish swim in the surrounding waves. The whole seascape is bordered by a pattern of leaves – olive green, carefully cultivated cotoneaster on a lime-green background of the wild silverleaf.

Over Haddon has been lucky. Tricia Gillies, a professional designer, lives there. She supervised the creation of both flower pictures in a disused barn which was put at her disposal by a local retired farmer. But she had a terrible confession to make. Desperate for a bright blue to give a startling colour to the sea on which the ark set sail, the village agreed to buy a hydrangea. 'At least,' she added by way of mitigation, 'it was natural.'

The children's picture in front of the village hall was of the same superb quality. It paid proper respect to the pagan origins of the event by putting a vivid golden sunrise above the representations of individual animals. Like its parent picture, it received a blessing from Canon Urquhart before he announced that light refreshments were available in the village hall. Asked if he had performed an act of worship or taken part in a village fête, he said that the two things could not be easily separated. That was one of the joys of living in the country.

Before the prayers at the well dressing that all the village had created, we sang two verses of 'All

Things Bright and Beautiful', a children's hymn which might seem more appropriate to the children's well dressing. But looking out over Lathkill Dale, it was absolutely right for that place at that time. We were celebrating more than water and the view Over Haddon had re-established its connection with the folklore of limestone country. We were reaching back into England's history and drinking deep.

Daily Mail 5 July 2005

Stop This Peak Practice

No other country in the world would allow its national parks to be vandalised by casual commercial development. But in Britain areas of 'outstanding natural beauty' – created as safe havens from industrial expansion and urban sprawl – face an increasing threat of quarries cutting open wounds into the land. And, because of the law's ambiguities, the planning authorities – created to protect them – cannot, or will not, come to their rescue.

Dartmoor, the Yorkshire Dales, the Lake District and the Peak are most at risk. But there are, in all the national parks, 'permissions' to quarry which were granted when men with picks (and the occasional stick of dynamite) provided stone for local builders. Now giant 'earth movers' rip away whole hillsides and lorries thunder

242

through country villages with loads of 'aggregate' for motorway maintenance.

'Active' sites – quarried continuously since 'permissions' were granted – are virtually unregulated. When a 'dormant' site comes out of hibernation, the operating company must observe minimal rules about depth of digging and land restoration. Inevitably the law is stretched as far as it will go. 'Dormant' sites are said to be 'active' and 'active' sites quarry more than their original permissions allowed.

According to the Peak Park planning authority, only fluorspar should be extracted from the Backdale site in north Derbyshire. Last year, Merriman of Leicester mined 400 tonnes. None of it was processed. At the same time, it quarried 175,000 tonnes of limestone. All of it was sold. After what local residents regard as a lifetime of wrangling, the authority issued an 'enforcement notice', requiring the company to limit its work. The inquiry which followed was adjourned for seven months. Meanwhile the quarrying continues.

The 'enforcement notice' is the national parks' weakest weapon. A 'stop order', as its name implies, has automatic and immediate effect. But the more robust the defence of a park's integrity, the greater the penalty of losing the lawsuit which inevitably follows. When a 'stop order' is overturned, the planning authority pays compensation for the loss of earnings.

Planning authorities do not have that sort of money. They cannot even afford the legal costs which are tax-deductible for the quarry companies. So the blasting goes on. The dust rises.

Great gashes are cut into the land. The government has a choice to make. It can either legislate or watch while giant holes are dug in all our national parks.

The Times 29 September 2005

One Step from Paradise

I was brought up in a vanishing village. It did not disappear overnight under the waters of a reservoir. Nor was it suddenly deserted on the orders of the Ministry of Defence. Wadsley was slowly submerged under owner-occupation. Our house – bow windows, drive with space for garage and garden front and back – was one of the culprits. But when we moved in, just before the war, the village still had a limestone-and-millstone-grit individuality. From my bedroom window I could see – over the churchyard, beyond the almshouses and past the cottages in which the knife-handle makers used to live – moorland hills that stretched on, only interrupted by farms and quarries, until they reached the Peak District and what was to become Britain's first national park.

We thought of ourselves as entirely distinct from the borough within whose municipal boundaries we lived. A trip 'to Sheffield' was an adventure which we faced with great equanimity when, in the course of two tram rides and a bus journey, we passed through the city centre and emerged into

Derbyshire on the other side. There, the villages were still unspoilt and intact. For the next half-century it seemed to me that living where the horizon is the top of a hill not the roof of a house was only one step away from paradise. It still does.

For more than thirty years – living and working in London SW1 and visiting the decaying central area of Birmingham – I knew that, one day, I would go back to the Peak District and to a stone village which has remained, more or less, the same since long before Wadsley was swallowed up by suburbia. It took eight years to find the right house. But I never doubted that I would settle in before long and before legs made it impossible for me to climb the hills that end a thousand feet nearer to heaven than the city lights in the distance. I just about made it.

No doubt my village (the possessive pronoun denotes affiliation not ownership) is like hundreds of others. We have a village green with a war memorial and a market cross. The Post Office closed a couple of years ago, but there is a general store which sells almost everything, a butcher and a garage that does not sell petrol but gladly mends our cars. There are two public houses, about which many of us became unnecessarily alarmed when the licensing laws changed. Every application for planning permission is fiercely resisted. We like things to remain as they are.

There is a farm just across the road from the church. One of the farmer's sons breeds prize-winning Charolais and accustoms them to the hurly-burly they will face in the show ring by walking them through the village. The primary school has such a record of success it is always mentioned in the estate agents' advertisements. In the late spring, hawthorn and horse chestnuts glow with pink and white blossoms which, after a week or two of glory, cover the pavements like confetti. We hide away our wheelie-bins as soon as they have been emptied.

All villages have vices. Ancient animosities live on in a genteel sort of way. Matters of little consequence – most recently the relocation of the post-box – are treated as matters of great concern. But, with one or two exceptions, we get on well together. We knock on each other's doors uninvited, warn of windows left open, organise posses to search for missing cats. We close gates after we walk through fields and keep dogs more or less under control. In our way, we are a 'community' – though most of us would be embarrassed to use such a word.

If we are in any way special, it is because we live in limestone country. But most English villages have defining characteristics. The feature which they have in common is the power to convince the people who live within them that – four-by-fours and television aerials notwithstanding – they live in an idyll of England. That is why, as I report each fortnight on how we spend our days, I shall call my despatches 'Letter from Arcadia'.

Spectator 3 June 2006

We Lift Up Our Eyes to the Hills

According to family folklore, my parents took me to Castleton on the day that war broke out. I was five at the time. So I remember very little about my father's attempt to distract our attention from the dark days that lay ahead. But I have been told a hundred times how we climbed the steep slope to the Norman keep of Peveril Castle, marvelled at the stalactites that hung from the roof of Speedwell cavern (explored by boat on the sub-terranean lake) and – with the extravagance of desperation – paid two shillings and sixpence for scones and jam in one of the tearooms which still abound in Derbyshire's Peak District.

At about the same time W.H. Auden was setting sail for America, later writing a poem of self-reproach which had been inspired by his boyhood visit to Castleton. It speaks for those who have never left, as well as those who have abandoned, limestone country: 'If it form the one landscape that we, the inconstant ones, / Are constantly homesick for, this is chiefly / Because it dissolves in water.'

To be exact, most of it does. Some of the Peak District is millstone grit which, for something like 300 million years, has stubbornly refused to be washed away The millstones which gave the rock its name have become the symbol of the Peak national park and the great hills, made of the stone itself, stand out from the limestone plateaux to provide some of the Peak's most memorable scenery. Monsal Dale, a couple of miles from where I live, owes its spectacular beauty to the hard rock which made the River Wye – cutting its way south – turn through ninety degrees. Looking down the valley from Cressbrook, the rushing water seems suddenly to disappear into the sheer cliff face. The view north from Monsal Head – the bluff below which the river bends – combines all the best features of the Derbyshire Peak: limestone farmhouses with fields separated by limestone walls, steep slopes which race up to a skyline and the mottled green of grass, gorse, heather and trees. In this part of the world, we lift up our eyes to the hills.

The Monsal viaduct – which once carried the railway line between Manchester and London – is now accepted as a thing of beauty which adds to the valley's wonder. Plans to demolish it would be resisted by an army of conservationists. But 120 years ago, John Ruskin – who thought Monsal Dale 'divine as the Vale of Tempe' – denounced the viaduct as the vandalism of fools who wanted to travel between Bakewell and Buxton in half an hour.

Despite being generally complimentary about the Peaks, Ruskin must take his share of blame for following in the footsteps of J.M.W. Turner and William Wordsworth by overselling the Lake District. We have no way of knowing if Turner would have wanted to paint the traffic jams at Windermere or if Wordsworth would have composed a sonnet in praise of Beatrix Potter – posthumously one of Cumbria's greatest attractions and likely to become more so now the film of her life and work has hit the cinemas. But we do know that the Peak District, well under two hundred miles from London, remains generally unspoilt by commercialism and that its clouded hills have a rugged beauty which often amazes but never intimidates.

Thank heavens the Peak District has never been 'fashionable' in the way that the Cotswolds are. But it meets the needs of our time. Walking in the Peak leaves no carbon footprint. Cars touring the 'beauty spots' are not welcome. A holiday, hiking across the hills, is good for the hiker and good for the environment.

It is not the landscape alone, but the ease with which the landscape can be seen, which makes the Peak District special. Climb its hills or walk up its escarpments, and you can see halfway into infinity. Hills follow hills – first green, then brown, then grey And the air – even on cold winter days – is clear and bright. It was because of the air that the Peak became Britain's first national park, created to provide breathing space for the industrial towns and cities of the north Midlands.

The park's 555 square miles cover country that constantly changes. The millstone and shale 'Dark Peak' stretches north past the Pennine Way which begins at Edale. The predominantly limestone 'White Peak' runs from the borders of Sheffield in the east to the outskirts of Manchester in the west. The boundary between the two is roughly marked by Mam Tor and Kinder Scout – two hills (which we are inclined to call mountains) that are just about the right size and shape for the Peak's purposes.

The national park is walking country. The tracks are long enough and the gradients just about steep enough to require some effort but still be within the capabilities of reasonably healthy adults and, if they have any sense, their dogs. The athletic and the energetic walk further and faster than the rest of us, climb precariously up the faces of crags and descend deep into potholes in pursuit of a hobby they call caving. There is even a gliding club at Great Hucklow. It catapults enthusiasts into the air from the edge of a ridge and provides them with a panoramic, if slightly bilious, vision of the hills and dales below. Hills make all things possible and walking irresistible.

It will be wrong to claim that walking, or hiking as it used to be called, was invented in the Peak District. The 'right to roam' was certainly tested here long before the government enshrined it in law. In 1932, the Kinder Scout mass trespass asserted the people's rights to walk across open land that belonged to the Duke of Devonshire. After scuffles with gamekeepers, the trespass leaders were arrested, prosecuted and imprisoned. After the war, and the creation of the national park, attitudes changed. And the story has a happy postscript. Three years before he died, the 11th Duke arrived in his Bentley at the annual trespass celebration. He had come to apologise 'for the great wrong which had been done' by his grandfather. He added that visitors to Chatsworth – house, garden, estate – were invariably impeccably behaved.

Chatsworth – the stateliest of stately homes – is

the greatest of the Peak District houses. Its size and splendour (together with an extraordinary collection of paintings, ornamental gardens and an enthusiasm to welcome visitors) have made it synonymous with the Peak Park. Haddon Hall, as near to being its next-door neighbour as it is possible for two stately homes to be, is almost as grand. On the way to the park, there are two other great houses: Kedleston Hall to the south, and Hardwick Hall – 'more glass than wall' – add elegance and distinction to junction 29 on the M1. And there are many more smaller houses that are well worth a visit.

One of them is Eyam Hall in the 'Plague Village' where in 1665 the villagers decided to stay and die, one by one, rather than spread the pestilence throughout the county. The 'Plague Cottages' still stand as a monument to their extraordinary sacrifice in one of Derbyshire's many unspoilt limestone villages.

There is a lot of history about in the Peak District. There were Iron Age forts on Mam Tor and Fin Cop which overlooks Monsal Dale. The Romans mined lead in the Castleton caverns and the straight lines of dry-stone walls mark the fields that were common land before the 'enclosures' drove the peasants to the towns in the eighteenth century. And, for visitors who like more recent history, there is the Lady Bower reservoir at the foot of Snake Pass where Guy Gibson and his 'dam-busters' practised dropping their 'bouncing bomb'.

Those of us who live in the Peak Park think of it as a peaceful place – as witness Dovedale, which is tranquil even when, in the summer, a regular procession of tourists walk the river bank or make the perilous crossing on the stepping stones. Again, the river has cut deep into the rock and once more it bends when it meets hard stone. But the Dove has a special claim to fame. It was in its waters that Isaak Walton, author of *The Compleat Angler,* learned to fish. Now Dovedale is a national nature reserve, its plants, no less than its animals, protected and preserved for ever.

Because the Peak District is walking country and because the Peak Park was created to meet the needs of industrial England, it is often regarded (especially in the south) as a bed-and-breakfast sort of place. Certainly the Peak boasts some of the best B&Bs in the land, but there are also good hotels with excellent restaurants such as the Cavendish at Baslow and the George at Hathersage. Hassop Hall Hotel has a special neoclassical elegance, and at the entrance to its long (and often torch-lit) drive there is the sort of public house that tourists dream about. The Eyre Arms has open fires, home-made food and half a dozen 'guest beers'. Half of the public houses in the Peak Park welcome walkers in their often muddy boots. Quite right, too. For this is walking country. If you want to see a mountain hare (turned white in winter), a spangled golden plover or a peregrine falcon, pull on a pair of boots and come to the Peak. Remember that it is made glorious by its geology.

Dear, I know nothing of
Either, but when I try to imagine a faultless love
Or the life to come, what I hear is the murmur

Of underground streams, what I see is a
limestone landscape.

Guardian 20 January 2007

It's Top of the World – and Sheer Poetry

At the foot of Skiddaw, the mountain which overlooks Keswick in Cumberland. Two grey stone
paths lead over the startling bright green grass to
the summit. One is the dead straight route to the
top. The other zigzags to make the ascent easier
for the less than fully fit. The walk to the top of
Skiddaw is not a suitable afternoon's excursion
for the feeble or faint-hearted.

Kevin Roycroft from Stafford is preparing for a
hard seven-and-a-half-mile trek over Skiddaw
and beyond. He spends much of his retirement
walking and he had made a longer and tougher
walk a couple of days before. He looks fit enough
to romp to the top without breaking sweat. Long
canvas gaiters, protecting his legs from knee to
ankle, complement his purpose-made royal blue
jacket and trousers. His appearance confirms
that, while there may be novices on the mountain, one walker knows exactly what he is doing.

Another couple, preparing themselves for the
climb, lean against the dry-stone wall which borders the field from which Skiddaw rises towards
the skyline. He is wearing the regulation anorak
and woolly bobble hat. She is similarly attired.

Their devotion is made obvious by the way she adjusts the straps on his rucksack and he carefully helps her through the first gated stile. They prefer to remain anonymous, but he admits to being an environmental health inspector from Liverpool.

Asked if they will make the summit, he says they will not even try and goes on to explain their reticence. He booked the holiday months ago with the firm intention of completing the climb. But then his wife discovered she was pregnant. 'Please don't mention our names. We're telling our families when we get back.' They walk off, clearly feeling that – although they may not make much progress up the hill – they have wings on their heels.

It is not necessary to walk all the way up Skiddaw to enjoy the wonders of the Northern Lakes. In the valleys, the cliffs and crags of Cumbria intimidate. From the hills, the rugged landscape inspires. Where they touch the sky the mountains are dark grey. Their lower slopes are mottled brown and black with heather and bracken which, in March, has not yet come to life. And the lakes themselves, Bassenthwaite in the north, Derwent in the south and Buttermere to the west, sparkle in the sharp sunlight of an afternoon in which winter is just turning into spring. And the little town of Keswick nestles peacefully in the valley.

Keswick is clearly a tourist town. Even the new buildings have been constructed in the picturesque slate which makes the shops and the bed and breakfast boarding houses look as if they would be perfectly at home in the Swiss alps. Its pavements are crowded with men and women who carry the adaptations of spiked ski-sticks which are the sign of serious walkers. Shops specialise in waterproof clothing, hiking boots and all the other paraphernalia of walking and climbing. If there is an amusement arcade or any of the other detritus of the modern holiday resort, it is well hidden.

The Northern Lakes became famous because the area attracted poets and painters. J.M.W. Turner included Adam and Eve in his picture of the fells to emphasise that he had found a new Garden of Eden. Thomas Gray – having completed his *Elegy Written in a Country Church-Yard* – announced, as he approached Keswick, that he was entering 'a second Elysium'. In April 1815 Robert Southey, a Keswick resident, organised a bonfire and roasted an ox on the Skiddaw summit to celebrate Wellington's victory at Waterloo. Samuel Coleridge wrote from his house in the town that there was nowhere in England that 'commanded a better view of Mountains and Lakes, Woods and Vales'.

Visitors are still attracted by the landscape which, even in the fabled Lake District rain, still has a breathtaking grandeur which wind and weather cannot spoil. But Keswick also bustles with the young – and not so young – who are there to enjoy more robust pleasures. Some of them are as breathtaking as the scenery.

Jason Chambers arrived at the foot of Skiddaw on his mountain bike ready to ride off down the road to Keswick. He was almost apologetic that, on that morning, he had not been all the way to the top. But, in the past, he had often pushed his cycle to the summit for the joy of riding it down again. There was, he conceded, some difficulty –

perhaps even danger – in riding over the loose cobbles which geologists call 'scree'. But the feeling of elation, as he raced down the mountainside, made the risk well worthwhile.

Elation and Skiddaw go hand in hand. Carl Hathaway, a laboratory technician from Norfolk, and his wife, Lyndsay, are typical of the men and women who are drawn to its magic. Veterans of Snowdonia, they had climbed Skiddaw four or five times before but that day expected a harder ascent than usual. After months of inactivity they were stiff following a walk a couple of days before. As they disappeared up the steep gradient, the sun came from behind the clouds and the sheep on the rough grazing came out of the shadows into the new warmth. However far up the mountain the Hathaways climbed, they must have felt that it was good to be alive and in England and on their way to what seemed like the top of the world.

Daily Mail 13 March 2007

Hidden Wonder Whose Beauty Lies in the Scars

Malham at the head of the River Aire – one of the carefully kept market towns of north-west Yorkshire. The fields around are mottled with limestone 'paving', great slabs of white rock which push through the grass in a strangely symmetrical pattern. The gradient on uneven ground makes it hard walking country. Yet Malham High Street is packed with men in hiking boots and women with Ordnance Survey maps in plastic covers to protect them from the rain. They are serious ramblers and they have come for serious rambling. But they expect Malham to provide more than mere exercise. Peter Nugent, an engineer from Stoke, pointed north: 'We're going up there.' Then he added an invitation. 'Come with us and see what heaven will be like.'

Up there is Malham Tarn – a lake in the sky. One hundred and fifty acres of shining steel-grey water which is trapped 1200 ft above sea level by rock and stone that was left behind by a retreating glacier. If it does resemble heaven, then behind the pearly gates the air is cold and clear, bird's-eye primroses speckle the rough pasture, curlews, mallards and crested grebes nestle in the woodland and, from time to time, peregrine falcons hatch their eggs in the undergrowth. On 7 May, two peregrine chicks were found close to Malham Tarn. They had made their home in a disused rabbit burrow.

Once upon a time Malham Tarn spilled over the ice-age rubble which blocked the neck of the valley. Then the water cascaded over what is now called Malham Cove – a curved crag which towers over the landscape and can be seen from twenty miles away. Its white surface is smudged with dark mosses and lichens which Charles Kingsley – whose Water Babies would have been at home in Malham Tarn – suggested were the result of a chimney sweep falling over the cliff edge and sliding down its previously spotless surface.

Wordsworth wrote a sonnet about Malham Cove – 'No mightier work has gained the plausive smile / Of all beholding Phoebus!' But it was not the sight which most impressed him when he visited Malham in 1819. Another sonnet left the reader in no doubt about his preference. 'Let thy feet repair / To Gordale-chasm.' Last Thursday afternoon half of the visitors to Malham were taking his advice. They approached the object of his veneration through a campsite largely composed of teenagers whose spirit seemed undimmed by both the wind and weather. In front of them was what looked like an impenetrable mountain. But, had they followed the curving road alongside Malham Beck, they would have entered into the hidden heart of the Pennines.

Around the rocky corners and past the protruding rocks was one of the wonders of the English countryside. It is called Gordale Scar – a limestone gorge 150 ft deep and a mile long. It was a tunnel cut through the living rock by water from the melting glacier. At some time, millions of years ago, the roof collapsed. The gorge which the upheaval caused still has the curved walls of the old cavern. They overhang the footpath on the floor of Gordale Scar and convince nervous hikers that the rock is about to close in on them. When Thomas Gray, author of *Elegy Written in a Country Church-Yard,* visited Malham he said that he could survive in the gorge for only fifteen minutes and even then he trembled from start to finish.

Artists have always been fascinated by its rugged majesty. Turner completed a massive canvas almost two hundred years ago and since then thousands of painters have followed him north. Last week (one of the few bright days in all the summer) half a dozen easels were perched in front of the waterfall which is the southern entrance to the gorge. Janet Wilmott from Manchester described the attraction. 'The challenge is to catch the strength that comes from so much solid stone.'

Jack and Harry Harris – seventeen-year-old twins from Leeds – did not view the waterfall with such solemnity. In normal weather there is a steep but manageable descent by the side of the tumbling water. At the end of a wet July, the rocky path had turned into a second cascade. Nearing the end of their long walk south along the cavern, the Harris brothers had decided to make the wet descent back to the campsite. Both agreed that the experience had been 'Great', and Harry – like his brother, dripping water – added, with the reckless confidence of youth, that 'Damp feet never did anybody any harm.'

North-west Yorkshire around Malham is hard, unyielding country. Its spectacular beauty offers none of the cosy warmth which visitors feel in the Cotswolds or the Suffolk Downs. It is more likely to take a traveller's breath away than to bring a sentimental tear to his eye. But in Malham Beck, the stream which bubbles through Gordale Scar, there are 'cave pearls', tiny pebbles that have been polished so bright by the running water that they glow like precious stones. There are no brighter jewels in all of England than Malham Tarn and Gordale Scar.

Daily Mail 31 July 2007

View from the High Ground

It was, I think, Governor Winthrop, one of the founders of the Commonwealth of Massachusetts, who said that politicians must think of themselves as a house on a hill. I have never been sure if he meant that they had the advantage of being 'looked up to' or the problem of being constantly visible to voters on the plains below. The last couple of weeks have, however, left me in no doubt about the benefits of literally occupying the high ground. The rain, which has swamped the road to junction 29 of the motorway, has passed us by. It has fallen in great quantities. That was only to be expected, since it rains on the just and unjust alike. But that which has not been absorbed into our porous limestone landscape has rushed away to the valleys. Sometimes it has flowed down the road outside my house like a living stream. When I saw the pictures of the Sheffield Wednesday football ground under four feet of water, fifteen miles away, I realised – with a very bad conscience – that some of the damage had been done by rain which had initially fallen on my garden.

The miracle is that it did so little damage as it fell. The peaches – which have no right to survive outdoors in even the best of rugged Peak District climates – still cling tenaciously to their espalier branches against the wall. The quinces seem indestructible. So do the damsons – a mixed blessing, since we are still trying to give away the jam from two years ago. It has been such a record year for raspberries that I am thinking of preparing a paper for the Royal Horticultural Society to reveal my discovery that soft fruit does best in hard weather. The young apple trees are bowed down with heavy Granny Smiths and Cox's Orange Pippins, and a solitary pear has appeared on a tree which we only planted last year. Neither mulberry bush has given birth. But then they never do – even though we bought the second one to keep the first one company and to perform whatever intimate act was necessary to bring about the miracle of creation.

Admittedly, the roses along the front of the house have taken a beating. But I have always regarded them as more 'quaint' than is acceptable in this essentially un-chocolate-boxy part of the world. The hardy perennials in the borders have lived up to their name and the camellias have survived. I have every expectation that next year, as in every other, they will come into bud in late October and excite the hope that they will keep their promise to blossom on Christmas Day. Then, as always, the rotting but unopened bud will fall off in March. Most important of all, the grass prospers. Indeed, in the absence of cutting weather, the grass in the orchard has grown to the length which I prefer but which is never acceptable to the man behind the mowing machine. Adjacent long grass is very important in wet weather. Despite, or perhaps because of, his first year living rough in King's Cross, Buster does not like to go out in the rain. So, when he is feeling sick, eatable grass within vomit distance is a boon both to him and to me.

There was only one regular cause for concern. When the rain was at its worst, there was always the fear – irrational but unavoidable – that the water, having seeped into the limestone, would first settle on a layer of slate or millstone grit and then bubble up in some inconvenient place. The inconvenient place I had in mind was my kitchen, in which there once was a well. The underground stream, which surfaces below the churchyard and runs through three horse troughs, was in spate last Wednesday. I tried to follow the example of my neighbours and prepare for the flood with typically English stoicism.

We enjoy the inestimable boon of a cheerful farming family, all of whom are more inclined to sympathise with the suffering in the flooded valleys than to complain about the problems that a wet summer creates in the hills. So they talk about their good fortune in grazing on high ground and managing to reap the early silage rather than the costs that they will have to bear because of damage done to the main crop by the summer rain. They still hope to mow the fields of now-bedraggled grass. But its nutritional value will be low. So winter feed will have to be augmented with extra 'concentrates', and concentrates are expensive. This week the weather has improved and the grass begun to dry out, so it should be all hands to the mowing machine. But the Bakewell Show is only two days away and the son and heir has two Charolais to scrub and primp in preparation for their appearance in the show ring. An indulgent father will not stand in the way of a winner's rosette.

So, by and large, we have withstood the weather well. I am not quite ready to regard myself as half of a double act called 'Darby and Joan who used to be Jack and Jill'. But what a blessing it is to number among the folks who live on the hill.

Spectator 4 August 2007

Also England

I am not sure when I first realised that there was an England of the very poor, but I can remember the exact moment when I discovered that the whole nation did not possess skin of the faded pink colour that we call white. At the performance of a Christmas pantomime, in about my fifth year to heaven, I turned round in my seat and saw a black – Afro-Caribbean we would now call him – Boy Scout. I was amazed and profoundly impressed. Oh brave new world that has such people in it. I doubt if I even thought again of England's ethnic diversity until, sixteen years later, a retired naval officer – who was the warden of a Leeds University hall of residence – reassured me that, if I achieved a place in his establishment, I would not be asked to share a room with a 'Blackman'. The selection as parliamentary candidate for the Sparkbrook Division of Birmingham in 1962 was the equivalent of enrolment in a crash course in race relations.

By then, I knew about the poor. One lesson had been learned during a summer 'vac-job' on a Co-operative Society milk round. Looking back I realise that I was no more suited to the study of poverty than to the understanding of economics. I dimly remember one Christmas Eve when my mother – who liked to drive home a moral message – told me that we had agreed that Santa Claus should divert one of my presents to a little boy whom my father – then an official of the

267

National Assistance Board – had identified as, otherwise, unlikely to find anything in his stocking. I hope that I did not complain. But I cannot be certain.

Sparkbrook completed my education. Indeed, it is not too dramatic to say that it changed my life. It was my introduction to the other half of the two nations of which Disraeli said England was composed. My constituents were, in the sociological phrase, the victims of 'double deprivation' – poor and what was colloquially called black – although most of them were light brown and, rightly and reasonably, deeply resented everyone who was not 'white' being classified by one inaccurate adjective. It was, as somebody bitterly said, 'enough to make you a socialist'. And it did.

Politics had only a subliminal influence on much of what I wrote during the years which followed my election to parliament. But from time to time it burst into what I was, intended to be a diversion into nostalgia, literary criticism and uninformed polemics on architecture, drama and poetry. But, thanks to my 'advice bureaux' every other Saturday morning and the Friday evenings in between, I was never allowed to forget my submerged fellow citizens who, for one reason or another, were denied the delights which I described in my spare-time occupation. And, despite all I wrote about Shakespeare and Elgar, Constable and Turner, I felt entirely at home amongst Sikhs, Pakistanis and Kashmiris who admired other heroes and worshipped other gods.

Whenever I went to Pakistan – which I loved and love still – I worried that I had inherited the

Englishman's imperial attachment to the mysteries and magic of the subcontinent which had inspired the Raj. But when I got home I was always reassured by my adjustment to reality. Like the ignored and discounted poor of every race, the descendants of the immigrants who came to this country fifty or more years ago are an integral part of England. Most of them now are legally so because this is their place of birth. Unless we understand them, we do not understand England.

Carnival in Sparkbrook

Summer really ends when the party conferences begin and the silly season tales of teeth lost on the Blackpool sands give way to stories of reputations won in the Winter Gardens. The party leaders may be photographed smiling their way around the big dipper. But they – and their supporters – have only been allowed in the hotels and boarding-houses because the genuinely joyous holidaymakers have gone home to save for next year.

From the moment the first delegate arrives we can only count the days until the signs of spring inevitably appear again. A trumpet of a prophecy, oh wind! If winter comes, can the Sparkbrook Carnival be far behind?

The Sparkbrook Carnival takes place each spring. It is certainly not the biggest and probably, by objective standards, not the best of the summer celebrations in my constituency. At Acocks Green the crowd is twice as large and is offered delights as diverse and diverting as a caged-bird show in the billiard-room of the 'Sons of Rest' pavilion and a tug-of-war competition in which local public houses heave away for the coveted 'Hattersley Shield'. There, real ale is on sale for all the afternoon and most of the evening, the streets are closed to traffic, and children ride on donkeys so recently brought from the seaside that they still have sand between their toes. But, for me, the only sure sign that another summer is really on its way is the Sparkbrook Carnival, for in Sparkbrook they have a contest for the best decorated lorry and usually I am the judge.

The lorries – or 'floats', as we experts call them – draw up in line alongside the iron railings which once enabled Farm Road Park to be emptied and locked as soon as dusk, and its attendant moral dangers, descended. Most are decorated by (and with) the youth clubs, play-groups, Wolf Cub packs and infant schools of the area. Some are the permanent coach-built advertisements of the armed forces and national-ised industries. A few are so crude and casual that they are not really part of the competition, just the teeming, huddled masses of black and white Sparkbrook youth out for a joyride.

The professional displays sent, for example, by the Midlands Electricity Board in a heroic bid to improve its sponsor's popularity, I mentally dis-qualify at once. In my mind, if not in the published rules, the real contest is between the groups of local children – nursery classes turned

270

by their teachers into hosts of cardboard daffodils and fields of paper poppies; self-conscious 'Schools of Dance' pirouetting uncertainly on the back of coal lorries as they attempt to keep their tutus clean; whole crews of primary school pirates, every man blind in one eye and forced to wear a black patch; West Indian girls' football teams, augmented by guest appearances of men with balloons inside their shirts and bright red patches painted on their cheeks.

There is always a comic policeman who helps the real policeman to marshal the crowd for the presentation of the huge tissue-paper rosettes that the organisers have made in caricature of what they have seen at the *Horse of the Year Show* on television. Occasionally the Air Training Corps band, the drums and fifes of the Boys' Brigade and the bugles of the Scouts all parade together, raising delicate issues of precedence that are always settled with honour and amity.

St Trinian's is regularly represented – a commentary upon the ease with which their uniforms can be obtained or the psychology of forty-year-old ladies. The elderly pupils always offer improper inducements to the judge and shake their hockey sticks in mock rage when they are rejected.

But the hazards of choosing the winner do not compare with the dangers of deciding who shall take part. The basic rule is simple enough. The competition is open to any decorated vehicle. No problem ever occurs about whether a vehicle is, or is not, decorated. For the organisers, quite rightly, regard twenty or thirty singing children as a decoration in itself. The real difficulty arises when decorators arrive without a lorry to carry them.

It is almost impossible to believe how improvident daleks, knights in armour and leprechauns can be. They will spend weeks building turreted castles and crocks of gold (complete with rainbow ends), only to discover on the morning of public manifestation that their creations are too big to fit the Co-op milk-float or that the promised lorry on which they were to be assembled is, after all, needed at the abattoir. Improvidence turns to anger and despair, then to the demand that, lorry or not, they take part anyway.

Of course we always capitulate – or at least allow them to take part in the competition. Parading along the busy main road that joins Birmingham to Warwick and Stratford is difficult. Thirty teenage crusaders carrying a plywood portcullis are inclined to overlook the sudden arrival of a double-decker bus. The risk of Humpty-Dumpty falling off the back of his bread-van is bad enough. No sensible organiser will risk the paper centipede (with thirty-four legs but only one pair of eyes) being trapped between the brewery dray that carries the evangelical message of local Nonconformity and the steam engine that advertises the arrival of Leyland's latest model in the neighbourhood showrooms.

The same rule applies to bands. The purveyors of martial music, who can be relied upon to move forward at a regular and steady pace, are encouraged to march. Other musical ensembles – Hard Rock, All Steel, Irish Accordion, and, for all I know, Senior Citizens' Gipsy Violin – can only participate if mechanised, for it is assumed that they will make irregular progress, varying in both speed and direction and simultaneously holding up the procession and risking death from traffic moving in the other direction.

Imagine, therefore, my surprise when in 1977 I was told that nothing could begin before the arrival of a 'walking float' – an idea that seemed either to possess biblical connotations or be a contradiction in terms. It was a unique, if not a special, year for the Carnival. Much to the organisers' surprise the cameras of *Panorama* were present. They had come to Birmingham to film an interview about immigration. Without much difficulty their attention had been turned to a small example of the multi-racial society in triumphant action – the Sparkbrook Carnival. The BBC, of course, believe that God made the world in six days simply so that it could be televised on the seventh. They were impatient. As the man responsible for their presence their impatience infected me.

It was then that I saw the 'walking float' appear over the stony, grassless mound of earth that is Farm Road Park. First came a line of children, sixty or eighty abreast. Behind, there was a second line, and behind the second line a third and fourth. Three hundred children, of many races, most creeds and every colour, marching in something approaching unison is, in itself, a formidable sight. But these children bore a banner with a wonderful device and were dressed in celebration of their message.

There were little Frenchmen wearing their mothers' berets and carrying strings of Spanish

273

and Israeli onions; Indians disguised as Red Indians; Jamaicans in their national costume of white flannels and cricket caps; Trinidadians in grass skirts with assegai and oval Zulu shields; Pathans dressed in the sort of clothes their grandfathers wore when they fought the British Army on the North-West Frontier; a disproportionately large contingent of cowboys representing North America; young Sikhs resolutely dressed as adult Sikhs; and two or three incipient Englishmen in paper bowler hats. Above, the banner proclaimed 'Children of the World Unite'.

It did not seem a moment for a rigid adherence to the rules. We pinned the paper rosette on an infant Chinese from the nearby takeaway and formed the children up into a column of four at the head of the procession. Most of the other competitors applauded. The ladies of St Trinian's wept a little. We marched off to the massed bands of the Scouts and Boys' Brigade. I think that the tune was called 'Imperial Glory'.

Listener 11 October 1979

Make Cowards of Us All

Most mornings I walk past little groups of London's homeless poor. A few of them have just come from the front steps of the nearby Catholic convent where soup and sandwiches are handed out at breakfast-time. The rest are huddled hopelessly around the Salvation Army hostel, doing nothing very much except wait for the moment when the drab, grey building has been swept and aired and its inhabitants allowed back into their home. They loiter in twos and threes under the protection of shop doorways or sit on low window-sills in unspeaking and unsociable couples.

Sometimes there is among them a close-cropped, clean-shaven young man from Ireland or the North who has come to the capital looking for hard but well-paid work and is bedding down at the Sally Ann until he gets a shovel in his hand and a room of his own in Kilburn or Wands-worth. But pink faces shining with health and hope are the exception. Most of these men are not wanderers and wayfarers by choice. There is not a W.H. Davies or Jack London in sight. They are the dispossessed who no longer bother to despair, but sink down through society without struggling to swim or even wanting to float.

From a respectful distance down the road, two ladies with walnut complexions, wellington boots and carrier bags stuffed with their worldly posses-sions, watch the men from the mysterious depths of tattered top-coat worn over tattered top-coat. The men ignore these strange, brown, round bundles and appear not even to notice the brisk and well-dressed commuters who hurry on their way towards shops and offices. The regular pas-sers-by have progressed through all the appro-priate emotions from impotent compassion ('Surely there is *something* we can do') to irrelevant callousness ('Things are much worse behind Charing Cross Station'). Although they look they

275

do not notice, but simply pick their careful way through the litter.

Strangers passing that way for the first time feel an immediate impulse to press small coins into the men's hands. Normally they resist it. The honourable urge is suppressed for fear of rebuff or assault. There is also the terrible possibility that other passers-by will notice the act of wanton charity and mentally condemn such flamboyant philanthropy as emotional exhibitionism. Anyway, ten-pence pieces have to be hoarded for parking meters, one-man-operated buses and the ticket machine at St James's tube station.

Nowadays nobody – whatever his political persuasion – needs to be ashamed of stifling the generous impulse. Philosophy, psychology and sociology have provided a wide selection of compelling arguments against alms. They range from the Victorian absurdities about encouraging indolence and alcoholism to modern sophistries no less nonsensical but much more subtly seductive. Dole degrades both the donor and the recipient. It merely confirms the difference in rank and status between the giver and the given. It blunts the edge of the poor's indignation and is really no more than hush-money paid to quieten the conscience of the rich.

Observers of a radical disposition are inclined to speculate about fundamental solutions to the problems of these men – often confusing the practical difficulties which they face with the moral dilemma they create for others. In my time I have favoured invasion of the area by armies of determined social workers in white coats who would shave, scrub, dress the men in carpet slippers and V-neck pullovers and sit them down with mugs of tea in front of television sets – preferably to watch racing from Kempton like proper old age pensioners.

I am constantly assured that the independent spirits from General Booth's citadel would not succumb to such tyranny. That is not my experience. The octogenarian ship's carpenter with bandaged feet who used to steal my milk and tell ingratiating lies about his boyhood in Sheffield would gladly have become a slave to the small screen. Once established in an easy chair he had to be prised away from golf at Sunningdale, *Juke Box Jury,* or the Open University Foundation Course on industrial archaeology. He exhibited all the signs of a man willing and anxious for the welfare state to make unreasonable intrusions into his private life.

But in the real world – as opposed to the realms of Fabian fantasy – there is really very little that the welfare state can do to help. The welfare state is geared to the needs of people who live in houses, hospitals and local authority homes – well-ordered people, disciplined enough to sign on at the job centre or sufficiently domesticated to be visited in their own living rooms by officials of the DHSS. Men who do not bother to claim benefit, who are never absolved from prescription charges because they never visit a doctor to get a prescription, who have no idea about discretionary payments for much-needed clothes, cannot be fitted into Lord Beveridge's scheme of things.

Even the Community of Corpus Christi has to

impose strict rules on the distribution of bacon sandwiches. Man does not live by fried bread alone, and if the nuns cut into another loaf every time their doorbell rang, there would be no time for *panis angelicus*. The stern note pinned on their front door – 'No more breakfasts today' – indicated neither a shortage of food nor feeling: just an inclination to teach and pray a little as the obligation of the Order requires.

But the nuns and the Salvation Army are doing something. The rest of us really just wish these men would climb out of our consciences, sweep themselves under some sort of social carpet, and enable us to enjoy rainy evenings at home without wondering if they are getting wet. Because of their nature, these mendicant men will not go away. They will remain a permanent reproach.

They are a reproach not only because they suffer in public, but because they demonstrate that our conventional cures for suffering do not always work. Neither does our conventional defence against the charge that many of us have too much while others have too little. John Kenneth Galbraith says that a rich man, committed to the creation of a more equal society, has a single moral obligation – 'never press for a wage increase, never argue for a tax cut'. Quite right. But such high principles do not make old boots waterproof or old bones lie more easily on hard beds.

Sometimes the old bones and the leaky boots venture some distance from the purple door of the Salvation Army Social Centre. One Christmas morning, some of them got as far as Parliament Gardens and sat on the wooden benches looking out across the Thames at St Thomas's Hospital and space. In anticipation of eating too much I was out for my daily run. At the other end of the park the Cardinal Archbishop of Westminster walked in solitary contemplation.

The men from the Salvation Army did not share our problems. They had no need to worry about either the sin or the penalties of gluttony. They got all the fresh air and solitude that they wanted. At that moment, the argument for taking all that you have and giving it to the poor seemed irresistible. Back home, I decided not to do it. But I still cannot think of one decent reason for my decision.

Listener 18 October 1979

Turbans, Bangles and Beards

If you ever come to visit me in Birmingham, be sure to arrive without holes in your socks, for you will not escape from a day in my part of the Second City without taking off your shoes at least once. And, to my certain knowledge, few experiences are quite so embarrassing as sitting cross-legged on the floor, surrounded by polite Sikhs or courteous Muslims, all of whom are carefully *not* looking at the big toe which is protruding from their guest's frayed extremity.

I represent that part of Birmingham where temples stand side by side with tenements, and mosques are just across the road from maisonettes. They look like old, dilapidated suburban houses. Often even the faithful can only recognise them by the small green flag that flutters over the front door, or because of the little holy picture that hangs in the bay window. Without me to act as native guide, a stranger might not notice them at all. But they are there, little pockets of piety, worshipping their way through the West Midlands day.

Occasionally, there are accusations about sacrificed lambs seen peeping out of attic windows and allegations of garlanded bulls led through the front gardens and tethered in the kitchens to await ritual slaughter. Such stories are about as theologically credible as the notion that vestal virgins are essential to the rites of the Anglican Church. But they get reported in the evening paper. When they are disproved, corrections never appear because the stories were provided by 'usually reliable sources'.

In only two parts of Birmingham has the influence of the East been visibly reflected in brick and stone. In a more prosperous area than mine a purpose-built mosque boasts a minaret, and windows suitable in shape to be scenery from *The Desert Song*. And in the centre of the glass and concrete confusion that is known as Birmingham University there is a red sandstone fortress which would not look out of place in Lucknow. The prophet in whose honour it was built is called Joe Chamberlain.

His other shrine is the Birmingham Council House. In an ordinary city it would be called the Town Hall. But Birmingham gives that name to an early nineteenth-century Parthenon built for symphony concerts and public meetings. So the place where the council meets and the Lord Mayor entertains his civic guests has to share its name with ten thousand non-parlour-type dwellings built under the Housing Act of 1923. But it has everything for which any town hall could wish. It has a clock tower and a dome.

It has a marble staircase leading up to a statue of Queen Victoria. It has a pillared portico to protect carriage-driven visitors from the rain and a vast fresco stretched out across its front. The fresco figures wear neither togas nor crowns of laurels, but frock-coats and top hats. They represent the Victorian virtues – thrift, industry and ingenuity – on which the city prospered.

For me, the Council House is a place of occasional terror. It is where they count the votes on general election night – where I pace, paranoid, between the piles of ballot papers, trying to calculate the size of my always anticipated defeat. But last week I turned up in committee room four to see imperial justice done.

It was a public inquiry into the refusal of planning permission – the prosaic end of Portia's profession, the dull and dusty side of the law. But this was no ordinary Appeal. Seventy Sikhs were demanding the right to worship as free men. For almost twenty years they had used a Baptist church hall as a temporary temple – moving the furniture early each Sunday morning and setting in position their holy book. But by the summer of 1978 they had decided to buy a place of their own, a couple of semi-detached houses twenty yards along the road from the borrowed hall which they had used in peace for almost two decades. The council refused planning permission. They were worried about traffic congestion.

So the Sikhs appealed and filled Committee Room Four with turbaned, bangled and bearded men. To support their cause they brought with them a brace of Nonconformist ministers, a matching pair of Labour MPs and an assorted bag of city councillors. Two ladies – potential neighbours – came to argue the other way. They handed out chewing-gum to the adversaries with whom they proposed to battle later in the day.

The presiding inspector wrote everything down and quoted sections from Acts of Parliament about which only the lawyers had heard. One MP questioned the council's motives. The treasurer of the Sikh temple explained, with infinite courtesy, why a permanent building was necessary. The local ladies were too friendly to be anything but half-hearted in their objections. We were told that a report would go to the minister and that we must await his decision with patience.

That is exactly what the Sikhs will do. Next Sunday the chairs in the church hall will be pulled back and piled up once more. The sweets – like concentrated Turkish delight – and the Cornish pasties filled with gunpowder will be passed round as usual. Occasionally a visitor (perhaps with a hole in his socks) will be given a ceremonial sword. It will all be certain and serene.

For the Sikhs are in Birmingham to stay, and they know it. They are now as much a part of the city as the patron saints of truth and honesty that decorate the Council House fresco. They came possessed of some of the Birmingham virtues, for no one in the city works harder or takes material advancement more seriously. They have acquired Birmingham habits and some wear Aston Villa Supporters' Club badges to prove it. Joe Chamberlain ought to smile on them from his grave. The old empire *is* closer to the mother country than ever before. It *will* prove to be a blessing for all the members of what was once the imperial family.

Listener 8 November 1979

Afternoon at Home

My Christmas festivities always begin at Clifton Infants' School with a Friday afternoon party at which little Muslims and young Hindus join together with more conventional celebrators called O'Connell, McManus and Kelly to sing the songs of the Nativity. Father Christmas, his ascetic Indian features hidden beneath a conventional cotton wool beard, wears a scarlet coat that can compete in neither splendour nor brilliance with the saris worn by visiting mothers. Thanks to Clifton School, when I think of Advent I always remember the coming of strangers into Sparkbrook and how, in the end, they found room in our inns, our schools and – for the most part – our affections.

Christmas memories are, I admit, a strange beginning to a high summer essay. But I have an excuse. Last week I 'opened' the new Clifton

School – a supernatural building in which architectural legerdemain has scaled everything down to the needs of four-foot/six-stone pupils without causing six-foot/fourteen-stone visitors to bang their heads on ceilings or become wedged in the apparently narrow doors. But the Clifton 'opening' defied laws of time as well as space. Children and teachers had been in happy occupation for nine months.

Although we did not know it at the time, our little ceremony took place on the day that Mr Enoch Powell spoke of the 'active volcano' of racial violence that he proclaimed was about to erupt in Britain. In the Clifton School playground, a hundred little lumps of Mr Powell's potential lava glowed in anticipation of the afternoon ahead – the food and festivities that were to be enjoyed after the red ribbon that fastened the handles of the new front door had been untied.

The food disappeared almost before the last echoes of the opening speeches died away. Sponge cake, on which cream had been spread like mortar, fastening a top layer of strawberries to the three-storey structure, was the first to go. Dhokla, a Gujarati sweetmeat made of semolina, flour and ground rice, was the second-fastest down. Of course, we all drank tea. The cup that not only cheers but binds together the two continents and is, I believe, particularly enjoyed by Englishmen who resent alien intrusions and revere our traditional customs – among which they number the enjoyment of an Indian drink. Refreshed, we took our places in the school yard and looked apprehensively at a sky that was

284

greyer than the tarmacadam.

We need not have worried. It rained, and it would be sentimental nonsense to pretend that we did not notice or that we did not mind. But although the tiny drops of moisture glistened in my neighbour's hair, I knew that nothing could dampen either Mrs Bi's spirits or mine. We had seen the children in their classrooms, possessed of a passion to perform that was far too strong for the elements to exorcise. Mrs Bi is a parent governor of Clifton School. Ten years ago I helped to get her husband into Britain. In rather different ways we both felt responsible for one of the performers whose enthusiasm defeated, if it did not deflect, the rain.

The performance began with the arrival of a clump of walking trees; not so well disguised as Birnam Wood on its way to Dunsinane, but an obvious clump of trees nevertheless. Each sapling wore a pair of paper leaves sewn together to make a forage cap of which Robin Hood would have been proud. Each seedling carried a stick festooned with green paper streamers. When the action demanded it, the sticks became branches that shook in the wind and the streamers turned into foliage that fluttered in the breeze. The trees were, in fact, the wood into which it is unwise to go on the day the teddy bears have their picnic.

The teddy bears – Pakistani teddy bears, Brummie teddy bears and Jamaican teddy bears, indistinguishable under their ochre cardboard masks – danced and pranced in orderly, though unregimented, delight around the wicker hampers. The school gramophone played a jazz version

285

of the song my own teddy bear was always brought downstairs to hear whenever it was broadcast, at a slower tempo, by Henry Hall on the old Marconi radio. Neither their energy nor their exuberance was exhausted by the time the lyrics required 'tired little teddy bears' to be taken off to bed. They were still pawing the air – and obscuring the view of seated parents – when the next act began. 'Teddy bears, sit down at once!' cried the headmistress with an authority and success that Mrs Barbara Woodhouse would have envied.

Following the teddy bears was not an easy task, but it was carried out with dignity – a comparatively rare quality in seven-year-olds – by half a dozen Asian girls dressed, I suspect, in their first adult saris. They swayed rhythmically and clapped in perfect unison to the slow music of the subcontinent, mimed the winnowing and grinding of corn, and then made way for folklore and fantasy of a more European sort. Even the severest critics of modern education could not complain that the curriculum at Clifton lacks breadth. There was a traditional fairy story in which Aniel, Smya and Hazifa played Hansel and Gretel and the witch. The human forest came back into verdant action. A classic prince rescued a classic princess. There was a dragon dance. A chorus of imitation tulip pickers wearing pointed paper Dutch hats sang about a mouse ('with clogs on') from old Amsterdam.

Of course, things went wrong, as things always will go wrong in infant schools. A huge eight-year-old called Mahmood, dressed in a pink leotard, looked so much like an Indian wrestler that from

286

time to time the desire to act like one overcame him. A claret-coloured turban began to slip over one of its wearer's eyes, and a proud parent darted forward to set it straight. The mulberry bush around which the reception class danced had some trouble climbing into his bark-covered trunk. But the overall success was obvious, overwhelming and both audible and visible.

There was one moment – shortly after 'the dingle-dangle scarecrow in the flippy-floppy hat' – when one class struck up a tune that I have heard plagiarised at a hundred football matches: 'If you're happy and you know it, nod your head.' There was so much assent and affirmation on every side of the playground that I feared that a few small heads would be shaken off. Nothing was damaged. When the Hansel and Gretel song reached the moment for the wicked witch's laugh, the whole school joined in with a noise that broken necks would have made impossible.

By five o'clock it was all over and we were back inside the school, cleaning and clearing up. The sweet blue and pink popadoms had been taken for safe keeping into the staff room. Little girls collected, to carry home, the dolls which had been on display. The school pictures and paintings, hung from classroom walls, had become bedraggled from the brushing past of anxious parents and confident performers. A thin film of greasy city rain covered the golden circle and the wriggling yellow snake that had been painted into the playground. Walking down Ladypool Road, I bought a copy of the *Birmingham Mail* and read Mr Powell's volcanic metaphor.

287

The first thought of any decent reader at the end of such an afternoon could only be of the children – those of them who were old enough and wise enough to discover that the world is not always as welcoming as Clifton's friendly classrooms. But losing the optimism of innocence is the fate which we are heir to, and the urban poor have always suffered it earlier and more brutally than other people in other places. The second thought concerned the possibility that the eruption could happen.

I suppose it is possible that one day the children with whom I spent last Friday will burn down Clifton School. The rule that governs the writing of this column prevents much speculation about why that might happen or how it could be prevented. But were it to happen, through fear or failure, malice or mistake, one thing is certain. They would be burning down their own houses, their own schools, their own country. There is no question of their going home. They are home already.

Listener 24 July 1980

Hull and High Water

North of the Arctic Circle – where Sweden reaches out towards the Pole – an eighteenth-century adventurer carved a record of his visit on the door of a Lutheran missionary church. 'I have looked upon Montezuma's temples and I have drawn water from the Indus. Now, soldier of

France, I stand at the edge of the world.' Although I had not enjoyed Raynard's heroic preparation for his terrifying experience, when I first arrived in Hull I knew exactly how he felt as he looked down into the abyss. Paragon Station is the end of the line. Beyond it, there is only shore and sea. And back in the 1950s it seemed that, for Hull, the tide had gone out for ever.

Whilst the rest of Britain rejoiced at never having had it so good, Hull remained stubbornly and visibly poor. In the twenty years that followed Macmillan's conspicuous consumption, deep sea fishing – a source of boundless pride but decreasing income – became the casualty of the Cod Wars which successive governments fought with Iceland and always lost. Fred Gray – fifty-two years at sea and thirty of them as a trawler skipper – can remember when 'more than 170' ships regularly landed their catches on the north bank of the Humber. Now it is 'nearer ten. Three of them, big freezers'. Captain Gray, now eighty, is master of the *Catherine-M*, a little motor boat named after his granddaughter and the first craft to be moored in the Marina which was built in the old Humber Dock ten years ago.

Graham Barnes, a lock-keeper on the Marina, says that it is possible to 'buy a good boat for the price of a decent motor car'. A year's berth costs 'about as much as an old van'. That is at the bottom end of the market. In the boatyard, *Magic Moon, Amaryllis, Kalamandas* and *Fancy That* are tall, sleek and self-consciously expensive. Fred Gray, who once ferried motor yachts between port and port, says that some of them 'must be

289

owned by millionaires. It costs £1180 in fuel to get from here to Ocean Village in Southampton.' Yet when he went to Puerto Buenos in Spain, the pride of Hull's Marina 'looked like rowing boats'.

Gray would like to live aboard his little boat. For he feels safer with water under his feet. But the council now forbids boat-owners to sleep aboard for more than twenty-one nights out of twenty-eight. So for one week each month he lodges with his daughter. To him, the corporation's ruling 'makes no sense'. But he is an admirer of the council. It has 'done well with the heritage'. From the fishing museum in what once were the offices of the Hull Dock Company to the Prince's Quay Shopping Centre, apparently afloat on the old Prince's Dock, Hull now proclaims its confidence that the sea can become an asset again. On the footpath in between, one paving stone in six is decorated with an embossed fish.

Sometime during the 1980s the tide turned. Nobody is sure why it happened or when the improvement in spirits and prospects began. But everybody agrees that the smell of success has replaced the tang of fish in the cold winter air. Some commentators attribute the upturn to the prospect offered by closer ties with Europe. Others give credit to a Labour city council that is anxious to forge a partnership with private business. The stimulus may have come from the Humber Bridge and the M69. Romantics proclaim a victory for the indomitable human spirit which suddenly enthuses men and women at the moment of greatest adversity. But no one doubts that Hull is fighting back against history.

The old fish dock, St Andrews, has been filled in and become the site of a Leisure and Retail Park – Furniture World, Eyre's Carpets, 34-Alley Bowling, a casino, cafés and coffee bars. On the edge where the trawlers dock today, a man from the Hessle Road – who preferred not to be identified – stood and explained that the change for the better came about when the old Dock Labour Board was done away with and the dockers 'stopped being so bloody greedy'. He once was a docker himself but had, in his youth, 'made a fortune in the salvage business'. His wealth had not changed him. He stood, dirty and dishevelled, by the derelict remains of a warehouse and stared wistfully at the *Novina of Fleetwood*. It was, he said, the only ship sailing that night.

The dredger which was making its ponderous way towards the sea had just pulled a G-registration Polo and a Toyota van from out of the silt below the steel-grey water. 'Joyriders,' said the man from Hessle Road. 'About two a week. Most of them brand-new.' That is more than can be said for the ship over his shoulder. It seemed barely possible that the *Lord Shackleton* (registered in Port Stanley, F.I.) once crossed the Atlantic. The man from Hessle Road will not comment on the state of the survey ship. 'What this country needs,' he says, 'is a bit of discipline and a bit of pride.' He would undoubtedly be happy in the lavatory in Nelson Street.

Nelson Street is really not a street at all. It is a promenade, a jetty, a landing stage, an esplanade, a waiting berth and a lesson in social history. The New Holland Ferry once sailed from the Victoria

291

Pier which stood at its eastern corner. The ship crossed the river in a great arc half-steaming and half-drifting with the tide. Now – with Barbara Castle's toll bridge hung across the heavens from Yorkshire to 'where sky and Lincolnshire and water meet' – the ferry is forgotten. But the lavatory, in which its passengers once prepared for their journey, retains its old magnificence.

The attendant, Douglas Glasby, was a sailor for twenty-two years. Now he polishes the brass rings around washbasin plugholes as if they were the handrails on the admirals' flagships and a chief petty officer was looking over his shoulder. The lavatory itself he has turned into a conservatory. Baskets of flowers hang from the roof – 'These are the winter plants, I change them in the spring' – and above the stalls and contraceptive machines, exotic ferns and homely sweet williams thrive in boxes which have been lovingly fastened to the wall. Nelson Street was Loo of the Year in 1990 and, much to Glasby's annoyance, was not allowed to take part in the 1991 competition. He is anxiously awaiting the announcement of the winner for 1992. 'Whatever job you do,' the old sailor said, 'you ought to want to do it well. You ought to want to be the best.' Hull, he added, was getting better. The 'old double deckers' had gone from the ferry, but new container berths were 'being dug at the North Sea depot'. The city and port were looking up.

On the corner of Nelson Street, the Minerva Hotel is prospering because of the landlord's decision to stick to the principle that he learned as a Rugby League professional. He is moving forward

292

whilst looking back. The Minerva is a traditional public house – not part of a synthetic past with designer wallpaper and reproduction antiques, but as down-to-earth and as wholesome as it was a hundred years ago when bed and breakfast was five shillings a night and the nearby rivals (Pepi's Marine Palace and the Smuggler's Bar) were no more than the shape of happy hours to come.

John McCue is more than a publican. He is also a brewer who, in a summer's fortnight, can sell a thousand litres of his own beer. Ask him what makes it special and he looks at you as if you had asked a silly question. Better and stronger, as well as real. He invents exotic names for each brew – Angel Tipple and Riverside Pride – and sells it, as an alternative to Tetley's, with the meat and potato pie, the sausage and tomato casserole, and the special hot chilli which are cooked (with three choices of potatoes) by his two chefs for lunch. McCue neither eats nor drinks in the middle of the day. For he is still in training.

The top storey of the Minerva – where merchants and ancient mariners once passed the night – is empty. McCue has plans to buy his lease from the old Dock Company and rebuild seven bedrooms. All of them looking out across the Humber and therefore enjoying one of the best maritime views in England. Julie, his wife, hopes that the council will demolish the dilapidated Pier Café which is only open in summer but an eyesore all the year round. Then only the new-laid cobbles of traffic-free Nelson Street will separate the long bar of the Minerva from the sea and McCue's special brew will be drunk on the waterfront ('only plastic glasses outside please') in even greater quantities. The Minerva and its landlord are typical of the best of new Hull. The past has become the engine of progress into a successful future.

Guardian 30 January 1993

On the Milk

During my last summer at Hull, I delivered milk – naturally enough for the Brightside and Carbrook Co-operative Dairy. It was my second choice of vacation jobs, for I had hoped to dig holes in the Hull roads. But rather a milk round than nothing. My experiences gave me enough confidence to deal with a left-wing trade union leader who, when I became deputy leader of the Labour party, objected to my parliamentary candidature being sponsored by the Shop, Distributive and Allied Workers. Anyone who has never tried to get a handful of coppers out of a dirty milk bottle on a cold morning is in no position to talk about the class struggle.

My days on the back of the Co-op milk float also provided an example of why, in Matthew Arnold's words, we should 'choose equality and flee greed'. My milk round was in Shalesmoor, the scene of my political baptism, and there were, amongst our regular customers, a number of women who, by the end of the week, could not afford the price of a pint. The regular milkman

294

believed that he could distinguish between the deserving and undeserving poor and he had invented a way of helping what he described as 'genuine cases'. He would carefully remove the tinfoil top from a full bottle and pour the milk, free of charge, into the virtuous pauper's jug. Then, the top being replaced with equal delicacy, he would smash the bottle and enter it in his records as 'a broke'. I was full of admiration for both his compassion and his ingenuity. But I believed it to be far too selective. Much as I detested smoking, it seemed wrong that anyone with a packet of Woodbines on the sideboard was disqualified from help. At the other, more salubrious, end of the city nobody was expected to choose between milk and smoked salmon, milk and their golf club subscriptions or milk and dinner in one of Derbyshire's country hotels. I had become a class warrior. I also became – more or less absent-mindedly – a graduate.

Who Goes Home? 1995

A Guided Tour of the Gutter

The Salvation Army played a regular part in the ritual of my boyhood Christmas Days. Between the ceremonial present-opening and the unusually formal family breakfast, the band appeared at the end of our street. More adventurous families stood in a little huddle on the pavement and joined in the better-known carols. We watched from the window as the Salvation Army did what it does best – prove that joy and religion can go hand in hand.

Anyone who grew up in a city during the Forties and Fifties learnt two things about the Salvation Army. Its officers braved the saloon bars of public houses, selling the *War Cry* and demonstrating that not all total abstainers were po-faced bores. And it helped the very poor by distributing tea and sandwiches. I knew very little more about the 'Sally Ann' when I began to write a biography of its founder, William Booth.

Booth had all the strengths, and many of the weaknesses, necessary in a man who founds a religious movement which, in his own lifetime, acquired a worldwide membership. One of the weaknesses was the habit of claiming credit that others deserved. His 'cab horse principle' was plagiarised from Thomas Carlyle. When a London cab horse fell, passers-by helped it up and sent it on its way without first demanding to know if the animal's stumble had been its own responsibility. Surely, Booth argues, we should behave towards men with the same compassion we showed to horses. That principle – help where help is needed without blame or recrimination – is the basis of the Salvation Army's social work.

Halfway through writing the biography, I felt compelled to see how the modern Salvation Army helps the 'men living under bridges' whose belated discovery had so distressed Booth before he published *In Darkest England*. So, one Saturday night, I joined the patrol covering the Strand and the Embankment, downstream from Parliament Square.

The battered minibus in which we travelled was driven by an out-of-uniform officer. But his platoon of helpers was, to my surprise, made up of ladies who would not have looked at their best wearing sweaters emblazoned with the motto 'Blood and Fire'. They were women who wanted to do good. But they were not 'do gooders'. I have never met less self-righteous people – or a group that was more devoted to the task of providing succour and comfort.

Having represented an inner-city constituency for more than thirty years, I imagined that there were few sorts of human degradation which I had not witnessed. I was wrong. The men and women huddled under dirty blankets in the archways behind Embankment Gardens were more wretched than anything I had ever seen. Most of them were either mentally or physically ill. There was little evidence of drink (the curse of Booth's day) but much of drugs. I assumed – perhaps because it was what I wanted – that we would pass out tea and sandwiches and swiftly move on. Instead the ladies started conversations.

At first, they talked about everything and any-thing – the weather, the traffic, the stars. Then, gradually, they got round to the subjects that were the real objects of the conversation. 'Wouldn't it be sensible to see a doctor? It could be done without any embarrassing questions being asked... What about a clean shirt or warm jumper?' No one was asked to pray or give thanks to the Lord. In the small hours of the morning, after the last call had been made and the night's work was done, we drove to a cul-de-sac near Gray's Inn and, after eating what was left of the sandwiches, said a prayer of thanks for being allowed to be of service. Although they made clear that atheists were not expected to feign religion, I joined in.

About a year ago, I made my second sortie with the Salvation Army's care and comfort battalion. In Leicester a young man in the doorway of the ironically derelict Citizens' Advice Bureau had to be roused from a deep sleep. Would he not, on such a cold night, prefer a place in a hostel?

The minibus was available to take him there at once. The offer was declined for the not altogether rational reason that the hostel was 'no more than bed and breakfast'. Then there was a moment of anxiety. 'You will be round in the morning, won't you?' He was assured that breakfast would, as always, be served in the shop doorway. Would he like a new sleeping bag then? The young man took offence at the suggestion. For he retained a perverse pride in the few worldly goods he still possessed. 'I have,' he said, 'one which is state of the art. It was given me by the Salvation Army.'

Anyone who thinks that such young men are treated with too much indulgence ought to pause and consider the conversation in the minibus as we moved away. 'I'll get him off drugs if it's the last thing I do.'

The next stop was a municipal park notorious for muggings and rape. The baseball cap and sweater that bore the insignia of the Salvation

298

Army were, I was assured, a guarantee of safety. Everyone knew that the Salvation Army existed to help, not to pass judgement. So it does. But it also works to rehabilitate. Its strength is the way it encourages a return to the paths of righteousness without seeming righteous itself. Officers of the Army regard exhibitions of moral superiority as a sin. They believe in a strict, indeed a rigid, code of personal discipline and religious belief. But they do not impose their beliefs on those they aim to help. They share Booth's conviction that deprivation is the Devil's ally and that a man or woman, raised from the gutter, is more likely to find God than one who is left to rot in squalor.

It is not necessary to share the Salvation Army's theology in order to admire its work. I list the volunteers who work the streets at night among the best people I have ever met. I wish that I had the courage and grace regularly to join them. In my inadequate way I do no more than assert that they are worthy of your support.

The Times 15 December 2005

Support You Evermore

Although he was not a man to make his feelings public, my father was so romantically inclined towards my mother that he had little romance to squander on other objects of his affection. Towards me he displayed – if that is the right word – an austere and slightly detached affection. But, when we went together to football matches – almost every Saturday in the season for more than a decade – he demonstrated an anxious attachment to me and an unusually overt enthusiasm for the aspects of the game which make little boys dream of scoring Cup Final goals. And he was positively sentimental about the past glories of the game – or, at least, the limited number of great moments which had been enjoyed by Nottingham Forest and Notts County.

I was told about the great players of the city's footballing past (a forward called Sam Wellar Woodison invented the goal net as a way of checking whether or not the ball had crossed the line between the posts). And I was given recitals – from my father's memory – of the Nottingham papers' reports of great, and not such great, games. One match, in which the ball was kicked from end to end with more height than accuracy, was dismissed with a phrase which my father found particularly memorable. 'Only angels play up there.' For over ten years – as I stood, for safety's sake, *in front* of a crush barrier on Sheffield Wednesday's Spion Kop – my father repeated the criticism every time the ball rose more than ten feet above the ground. It was not his only joke. On the way to the ground he always bought two quarters of Mintoes – one for him and one for me. We ate them all before the final whistle. At suitable intervals, he would point at the growing pile of sweet papers between our feet and ask, 'Who dropped these?'

It was my father's reminiscences – as much as Wednesday's distant victories in Championship and Cup – which encouraged the feeling that football was part of the fabric of society. Reading J.B. Priestley's essays – part of my fourth-form syllabus – I shared the view that football was 'conflict and art' and that to describe it as 'twenty-two hirelings' chasing a ball was like calling a Stradivarius 'so much wood and catgut'. Though I was not quite sure what a Stradivarius was.

The feeling that football – playing in the morning and watching in the afternoon – was part of my national heritage was my winter emotion. In the summer I felt exactly the same – though more intensely – about cricket. Once again the past was Nottingham. My father devoutly believed that Harold Larwood was the best fast bowler in history. The present was Yorkshire – particularly Len Hutton. I talked without doubt or inhibition about 'our national games' and took it for granted that, since we invented them both, we knew how they should be played. We did not always win but – I fondly imagined – we played like English gentlemen.

In fact, football and cricket were the two parts of my life about which I was an unapologetic chauvinist. England – not Britain, which in terms of both the games did not exist – always deserved my unequivocal support. Sixty years on – when I still miss the complaint about only angels playing up there – I feel the same.

Never Walk Alone

The season is over. I suppose that a handful of fans maintain a sort of interest in the FA Cup and will make a short journey across London to watch, at Wembley Stadium, a contest which is now of purely local interest. (That year, the Cup Final was played between Arsenal and West Ham United.) But for most of the country the passion is spent, the hopes are fulfilled or frustrated, the fears are confirmed or confounded.

Watching football is a pastime for partisans. And an all-London Cup Final denies most of us the opportunity to offer even vicarious support. Next Saturday I shall sit in front of my television set committed to neither red and white nor claret and blue. As it has turned out, my three usual tests of which commands my allegiance cannot be applied.

First, I want all teams playing against Sheffield Wednesday to lose. Secondly, I hope that all clubs managed by Malcolm Allison and Tommy Docherty will encounter the same fate. Thirdly, since these prejudices cover only three teams in the whole Football League, I have constructed a criterion that determines where my loyalty lies in most other matters – I am on the side of the team that hails from the farthest north. Since I have no idea how the lines of latitude divide Highbury and Upton Park, I have nobody to shout for and therefore no real interest in the game.

There well may be, scattered somewhere between Newcastle United and Exeter City, a few thousand purists who see the game as an art and watch it to enjoy the objective beauty of rhythm and form. The rest of us want to see *our* team win. We will follow it right on to the end of the road. We are the tribe and the team are our warriors. They will never walk alone.

Of course, the songs of love and loyalty ring out with especial fervour on days of victory. On the day that Nottingham Forest won the Football League, their highly disciplined red and white regiments stood in well-ordered rows on the terraces and gesticulated with ferocious composure in the direction of the vanquished Coventry counterparts. This year, at Liverpool, the fourth championship in five years was greeted with songs of praise sung with a practised precision of which the Huddersfield Choral Society would have been proud. Last Saturday at Hillsborough, where Sheffield Wednesday are less accustomed to triumph, escape from the Third Division was simply celebrated by a good-natured riot. Long before the final whistle blew, the spectators began to come over the fence that divides pitch from people, like a mass escape from Colditz. Using the wire mesh as ladders, they rolled across the top and down the other side as if commando training were an entrance requirement for the Owls Supporters' Club. For a while, the police stemmed the tide, waiting until they were poised for the descent and pushing at their exposed point of balance. The first few toppled over backwards like Aunt Sallies at Wadsley Fair. But when the referee signalled quietus by spreading his arms like a man embracing martyrdom the frenzy really began. Suddenly the police at the palisades were outnumbered by a hundred to one. It was Rorke's Drift without the Zulus showing mercy. The thin blue line was overrun and the pitch occupied. A constable's helmet curved through the air, following a route taken a few moments earlier by a long, low goal kick.

The team vanished, totally submerged in their ardent admirers. In the apparent safety of their box the Directors sweated at the sight of life being squeezed out of their investments. From time to time a shirtless player reappeared, bobbing uncertainly on the shoulders of jubilant fans whose determination to pay their respects transcended all concern about whether or not their idols would survive the idolatry. Gradually, the strikers, the midfield men and the back four struggled and squeezed their way into the dressing-room, rashly to reappear in the front row of the reserved seats.

It was then that the fans invaded the Directors' box, mountaineering up the north face of the stand, roped together with blue and white scarves. Long after the evacuation and occupation, when the hands had been shaken and the champagne opened downstairs, I climbed back to the scene of Sheffield Wednesday's triumph and their Directors' rout. A giant snake of teenage celebrators was zigzagging across the pitch in an endless conga. What grass remained had been trampled a damp brown. The low spring sun cast fluttering shadows across half of the pitch, images of the flags that have fluttered over the grounds since the glory days of the World Cup.

The fans had been waiting for fourteen years for something to celebrate. Some of them had barely been alive that long, but the folk memory stretched back to Wembley in 1966 and they had inherited their fathers' frustration with the failures that followed. Last week's match itself was wholly uneventful, a goalless draw with few shots, no spectacular saves, and most of the players huddled together in the centre circle for the largest part of the proceedings. But the single point had confirmed Sheffield Wednesday's position – third in the Third Division table. We were promoted. We were up. We had overcome.

It had been a long campaign since relegation from the First Division in 1970. For me the high point had come in Oxford in March. We won 2-0, and I stood with the real fans behind the home team goal. I admit at once that my original intention had been to sit in the luxurious ease of the stand. But all seats being sold, I queued for standing room on the bank of Bunker's Hill, or whatever Spion Kop is called at Oxford. The terrace of my initial choice turned out to be enemy territory so I set out, complete with kid gloves and blue Burberry, to find the homeland of rosettes and rattles at the other end of the ground.

The last obstacle on my escape-route was an iron gate manned by a commissionaire with three rows of medal ribbons and no respect for travelling Northern fans. The contempt in his voice was more for me than for the band of dancing dervishes who were intoning a ritual imprecation within their cage. The imprecation concerned the victims of 'the Boxing Day massacre' (Sheffield Wednesday 4: Sheffield United 0). The commissionaire's contempt concerned my ignorance of the fate that would befall me inside. 'You can't go in there,' he said, 'that's for them.' In a South Yorkshire accent, thickened by emotion, I told him: 'I *am* one of them.' The gate clanked shut behind me.

I spent most of the afternoon next to a young man in a sleeveless cricket sweater, which, at first sight, proclaimed membership of either the Free Foresters or I Zingari. The impression of gentleman cricketer was, however, undermined by the absence of a shirt. But the pink exposed arms and the parts of the neck and chest visible beneath the long, lank hair proclaimed an enthusiasm for games that Raffles himself would have admired. There were owls tattooed on both biceps and the message – 'We are Jack Charlton's army' – running from wrist to elbow.

At the end of the long embrace with which we celebrated Wednesday's second goal, he asked me with deep suspicion whether or not I was Roy Hattersley. I admitted it. Had I, as he believed, appeared in 1977 on a local radio programme and proclaimed my undying affection for 'the Wednesday'? I pleaded guilty again. Without an iota of irony he held out his huge right hand, displaying the word 'hate' etched on the knuckles. 'Shake it,' he said. 'In those days it took a real man to say he followed Wednesday.'

Last Saturday it was easy, for success was there to be shared by anyone who wore the blue and white. So we waved our banners and threw our caps in the air with an enthusiasm that almost excelled the joy in victory over Germany in 1966. Third in the Third Division is not one of football's great achievements. But it provided a taste of supremacy for thirty thousand fans to whom life had provided few opportunities for exultation. For most supporters, football offers them the one chance to become acquainted with glory. As long as they are there cheering on the terraces, they never walk alone.

Listener 14 August 1979

Family Failings

I was brought up within the sound of the Sheffield Wednesday football ground. In Wadsley Lane, the noise of every near miss had reverberated through the house. But at Airedale Road, only the exultation of actual goals ricocheted through the walls. By 1947, I was at the ground in person to witness the triumphs and tragedies. Judged big enough to stand on Spion Kop, I took my place with Uncle Syd and my father on the shale terraces at about two o'clock on alternate winter Saturday afternoons. When Wednesday played away from home we agonised about whether to watch the reserve team or make the journey to Bramall Lane and Sheffield United. Uncle George – my father used to tell me in order to keep the memory green – was a Unitedite. And much as I disapproved of that affiliation, I used to scan the terraces in the hope of sighting the long-lost uncle. I suspect that Syd had secret meetings with his brother – secret even from my father. For my father's anxious loyalty would not allow him to parley with anyone who was in dispute with my mother. I have no doubt that he longed to see George. But he disapproved of – and suppressed – the longing, because he felt it was disloyal to his wife.

So the three of us stood on the Spion Kop together. At Bramall Lane we were protected from the rain by a corrugated iron roof, but for me at least there was not the warmth and shelter of being at home on the exposed slope of Sheffield Wednesday's uncovered terraces. I spent most of the afternoon staring anxiously at the 'results board' that had been erected in front of the pavilion. The half-time scores of all the major matches were hung from its iron frame, and the latest score in the game that Sheffield Wednesday was playing away to some far-flung and exotic opponent like Luton Town or Cardiff City was exhibited at fifteen-minute intervals. I was really at Sheffield United's ground to chart the quarter-hourly progress of Sheffield Wednesday, to cheer in company with other Wednesdayites

311

when we were ahead, to groan in unison with my desolate co-religionists when we were behind, and to live in agonised anticipation of the revised score when a draw was displayed.

At Bramall Lane we existed vicariously. But at the Wednesday ground we lived life to the full, experiencing every emotion known to man, boy or beast. For me it was fantasy time. I really did expect the crackling tannoy system to splutter into life with an announcement that Goodfellow, Morton or Mackintosh (the delusion survived several generations of goalkeepers) were injured and a request for Roy Hattersley to make his way to the players' entrance complete with football boots and jersey. Even when the game started without me, I felt that I was down there on the pitch tackling the opposing forwards with Swift and Westlake, nodding crosses clear with Packard and Turton, and creating all manner of opening and opportunities with the hero of those early adolescent writers, Jackie Robinson. When Robinson swung at the ball the man in front of me felt the kick on the back of his legs.

Jackie Robinson was the last relic of Sheffield Wednesday's pre-war Cup-winning team. In fact, he had not played at Wembley. But Wednesday fans claimed for him the esoteric record of being 'the youngest man ever to play in a semi-final'. And starting from such juvenile distinction he had gone from personal strength to strength as the team he served declined into the second division. He played a couple of times for England and in the mid-Forties was north Sheffield's answer to Jimmy Hagan, the city's other international inside-forward who played in the south for United. Robinson was my winter hero. Even after he left Wednesday for Sunderland I looked anxiously at the Green 'Un each Saturday night in the hope that he had scored. But if Sunderland had ever played Wednesday there would have been no problem of divided allegiance. I always wanted Wednesday to win. Unfortunately, during the early years of my fervent enthusiasm, they rarely played such elevated opposition.

When Wednesday were in the second division the great clubs only came to Hillsborough for Cup ties. And then only for what, in those ancient days, was called the 'third round proper'. For that was the round when Wednesday entered the competition, and the round when they left it. But on the first Saturday after Christmas we were sometimes given a tantalising glimpse of greatness. In 1947 we were drawn against Arsenal – the team of the Comptons, Joe Mercer, Logie and Lishman – who had beaten Grimsby ten-nil at the end of the previous season. My father and I looked forward to the game for weeks.

In those pre-floodlight days, winter football matches began at two o'clock to make sure that they ended before the wintry sunlight faded into early evening darkness. If a fixture was postponed because of snow or ice, the game was played on some subsequent weekday working afternoon. The long-awaited Arsenal match – planned for the third Saturday in January 1947 – had been scheduled for the beginning of the worst winter of the century. At the time of the intended kick-off, the pitch was a foot deep in snow. Volunteers had dug away at the edges of the avalanche, but the following week rumour insisted that the amateur groundsmen had merely pressed the soft flakes into hard pack ice and prejudiced the real reclamation work that the groundsman began when the blizzard ended on Sunday morning. By mid-week, assiduous sweeping and shovelling had made the field fit for play, but the ground was still covered by a thin layer of compact snow and the pitch was marked on it with blue paint. There were great mounds of snow piled along the touchlines, and the steps of uncleared terraces were obliterated under a sheet of ice which made the fans feel as secure in their foothold as if they were attempting to balance on a steeply sloping glacier. I can describe every detail because, despite the problems involved in a Wednesday afternoon game, I was there.

I cannot remember if I left for school that morning with the calculated intention of playing truant, or if I had a sudden fit of madness during the morning. But the evidence suggests premeditated irresponsibility for I took with me, when I left home in the morning, the hand-made rosette which I had secretly constructed from two lengths of blue and white plastic ribbon which I had bought from a Hillsborough haberdasher. I pinned it on my blazer as soon as I was out of sight of City Grammar and travelled by bus to Wisewood with an acquaintance whose mother was out at work and whose house was therefore available for a surreptitious sandwich and an undercover cup of tea. Wisewood is at the summit of a higher hill than Wadsley. But both villages are the source of roads that run down into the Don Valley like tributary streams. On match days the Wednesdayites flowed down those roads towards Hillsborough. On the day of the rearranged Arsenal match my father and I met at the confluence of Fair Lane and Mardcliffe Road. I think that his embarrassment was far greater than mine.

To this day I cannot be absolutely certain that my father was also a truant. It seemed inconceivable then, and it seems inconceivable still, that he had filled in an official leave form and agreed to an official half-day's holiday being recorded against his name. But since he was proceeding to the match from the direction of Airedale Road it seemed as if my mother knew of his afternoon's intention. Indeed, I could not have imagined him taking time off work without using some of it to bask in the pleasure of her company. It was clearly my mother's tacit approval of his brief and unusual irresponsibility that confused my father about our relative culpability. Neither of us should have been at the match. But I had committed the added sin of being absent from school without my mother's knowledge. We walked together to the ground in mutual guilt and common confusion. 'You must,' he said, 'tell your mother'; desperate lest it become his duty to turn Enid's evidence. After Arsenal had won their anticipated victory and I had walked back up the hill to home, I made my confession. The recriminations were as predictable as Wednesday's defeat. At school the next day, the Headmaster spoke to me for the first time. It was obvious, he said, that I had been to the football match. Did my parents know that I had

315

taken the afternoon off school? With absolute conviction I answered 'Yes'. For the next three years I was branded a bad lot, with character deficiencies compounded by uncaring parents.

A Yorkshire Boyhood 1983

The Free Seats at Lords

At half-past two on a summer's afternoon I can become a vagabond who need not return to middle-class respectability until stumps are drawn at close of play. I rest my caravan in the Free Seats at Lord's. (*Now replaced by the 'press facility'.*)

They are only free inasmuch as spectators who have already paid entrance money are allowed to park their posteriors upon them without extra charge. But the view which they afford the enthusiast is beyond price. For high above the boundary at the Nursery End the bowler's line and length and the batsman's ability to get his foot to the pitch of the ball can be judged without interference from either umpire or wicketkeeper. Certainly balding fielders have the signs of age more cruelly exposed to the occupants of the Free Stand than to the MCC members in the pavilion or the weather-conscious troglodytes who huddle in the subterranean depths of the barrack block called the Lord's Grandstand. But the Free Stand is the perfect vantage point both for the expert witness and for the casual caller who means to

316

pass the afternoon with only one eye on the ball.

For it is flanked by horse-chestnut trees which, though still to blossom at the start of the season, are in full conker before the championship is decided. And the native fauna are just as interesting as the indigenous flora.

Ancient workmen set up benches on the tarmacadam paths around the ground and plane pieces of wood which become the bevelled backs of Long Room chairs and rasp away at steel rods that are destined to reinforce the railings which keep Middlesex members quarantined in the Q stand. And all these sights and sounds of Old England are accompanied by the cries of MCC young professionals practising in the nets and a soft drone which is not the sound of a bumblebee, but a mysterious noise that drifts out of the Ladbroke betting tent.

The Free Seats are also the proper place for the aficionados who want no diversion from rigorous concentration on the game, the absolute antithesis of the private box hired by the limited liability company or public corporation. Official hospitality is an organised conspiracy to prevent the uninterrupted watching of cricket, based on a constant invitation to 'have a drink' or 'meet our sales manager from Slough'. Just as the true devotee turns his back on the pitch to have his glass replenished or to shake hands, a wicket always falls.

In front of what used to be a real Tavern at Lord's, the distractions are different but barely less disconcerting. It has become the home of hard drinkers, and the haunt of Australians with hairy chests and huge stomachs. These days my ambition, once I am established in the Free Seats with cushion and scorecard, is not to leave my seat at all.

During my impatient boyhood, I used to hate the tea interval. It was simply twenty minutes with nothing to do except count the seconds to the pavilion bell and the reappearance of the umpires. Now I think of it as an essential opportunity for meditation. For cricket is a contemplative game and these days, unless there is a pause during which I can take stock, I miss part of the pleasure. Cricket's true beauty lies in the way it interleaves a moment's frenzied action with a minute for reflection. Now, after 30 years of concentrated watching, I need time to pull my memories together.

The Free Seats at Lord's are the perfect place for controlled nostalgia, with Father Time pointing in whichever way the wind blows. On a clear day Don Wilson – once Yorkshire's left-handed pride and now the senior MCC coach – can be seen in the nets. And other spectators are always willing to jog the forgetful memory about how many runs Denis Compton scored in 1947. Indeed the regulars in the Free Seats are the ideal cricket companions.

Ask one of them if a catch carried or if byes were signalled and the reply will be brief and courteous. There is neither rambling about weather or traffic nor the beginning of a fleeting conversational friendship. The true cricket enthusiast needs to pass freely in and out of solitude with concentration only occasionally broken by comment and reverie, rarely disturbed by raconteur. That bliss is allowed in the Free Stand. And sometimes there is quite a good cricket match going on down at ground level.

Guardian 7 May 1983

To Be Disliked Again: Reflections on Yorkshire Cricket

On a warm afternoon in the late summer of 1946, my father – normally the most reticent of men – danced a jig on the promenade in Morecambe. He had, as was his invariable summer habit, bought an evening paper to find out the cricket scores. To his delight he discovered that Yorkshire, already the county champions, had lost to Hampshire. He addressed my mother and me in a voice of triumph. 'At least they haven't gone all season without being beaten.' It was then I realised that the Yorkshire County Cricket Club attracted the animosity that goes with near-invincibility. With any luck, we will soon begin to attract it again. (*Yorkshire had just won the County Championship.*)

The complaint, in those days of constant Championships, was that the three Ridings were so big that the county club had a bottomless pool of talent from which to choose. Now, the contract system, which regrettably grows ever more like the football transfer racket, has ended all that. But when I first watched Yorkshire, there was an abundance, in a way an excess, of potential first-

319

class players within the Broad Acres. In 1946, a 43-year-old spin bowler called Arthur Booth took a hundred wickets and topped the national averages. Before the war he had played only the occasional game when Hedley Verity was on Test match duty. But he had soldiered on in the Yorkshire Colts without a thought of playing for another county.

For years, Yorkshire ignored cricketers of the highest quality. Bob Appleyard took two hundred wickets in his first full season with the county, 1951, and, as he was a 'mature' man at the time, John Arlott (commentating later on a Test in which Appleyard was playing) wondered aloud how he'd spent his summers during his early twenties. Long after his retirement, I met the overnight sensation and asked him the same question. 'Bowling myself silly in the Bradford League,' he told me. Nobody has been able to explain why it took the Yorkshire committee so long to discover him.

League cricket – particularly the Bradford League – was half the secret of Yorkshire's success. Hundreds of tributaries flowed from the club grounds towards Headingley. The two Pudseys – one produced Sir Leonard Hutton, the other Raymond Illingworth – are the most famous examples of that secret strength. But there were dozens of other clubs that thought it their duty to prepare players for the county. In Sheffield, border country in the far south, we always suspected the northern leagues were as far as the county committee ever looked. The prejudice, if it ever existed, has clearly passed – though the young Darren Gough and Michael Vaughan were far too good to be ignored whatever part of the county they came from. What a pity that, now there are South Yorkshire players in the county team, the county team never plays in South Yorkshire.

Perhaps the idea that South Yorkshire got a raw deal was always a myth. But we certainly believed it. In the week that I was born, my father, a temporary Labour Exchange clerk after years of unemployment, was sent to work in Wath upon Dearne. Eating his midday sandwiches in the deserted cricket ground, he fell into conversation with the groundsman and naturally told him about the baby boy at home. 'He'll never play for Yorkshire,' the groundsman said. Thinking the dismissal of my cricket ability a little premature, my father asked why he was so certain. The reply allowed no contradiction. 'Comes from South Yorkshire.' The pessimist's name was Turner, and his boy, Cyril, was finding it hard to break into the team. He became a regular member of the side that won the Championship four times before the war and once immediately afterwards.

Sixteen years on, when I was batting in the nets behind Spion Kop at Bramall Lane, the anti-Leeds feeling still persisted. There were rumours that a great fast bowler, a colliery craftsman by profession, was about to emerge from Maltby and there were dark suspicions that 'the committee' would not do him justice. But nothing could hold Fred Trueman back. To the day of his death, my father (a Nottinghamshire man) argued that Harold Larwood was both more accurate and more aggressive. Filial piety requires me to conclude that Larwood and Trueman were the two greatest

321

English fast bowlers of all time. Neither of them should be anything other than flattered by the comparison.

In the years that followed the war, we Yorkshire members grew used to success. Indeed, in the 1950s, when the team began to fail, we felt that the natural order of things had been disrupted. In 1958, when we came eleventh in the Championship, Johnnie Wardle, an ingenious spin bowler, prehensile close fielder and irresponsibly entertaining batsman, was sacked for defending himself from committee criticism in a newspaper. I attended the county club's annual meeting with the intention of causing trouble about his treatment. The chairman welcomed members to the 'AGM of the champion county' and added, 'We know which the champion county is, whichever team happens to be at the top of the table at the end of any one year.' After that, no criticism was possible.

After the 1950s the county recovered but continued in its profligate ways. Ray Illingworth left for Leicestershire – and became a highly successful England captain – following an argument about his contract. The accusation was that he was disloyal because he did not regard a year with Yorkshire as better than three with any other county. Brian Close, who led the last Championship-winning team, moved on to Somerset. Bill Athey went to Gloucestershire, and dozens of other players, less talented but highly able, drifted away. For a time, it seemed that nothing could go right for Yorkshire. After the pride of a century was forgotten and an overseas player recruited, two of the world's greatest batsmen wore the white rose for a single season. Neither Sachin Tendulkar nor Richie Richardson was a success. Yorkshire remained in the wilderness.

Perhaps, even in the early 1990s, Yorkshire was still suffering from the repercussions of 'the Boycott affair'. Whatever the merits of the argument – Boycott versus the committee – the damage that the conflict did to the county was immense. In 1978, members were asked to vote on what some thought were rival propositions: endorse sacking Boycott as captain or ask the committee to resign. I voted 'yes' to both, hoping that a clearout would put the damaging disputes behind us. It dragged on for year after year, making life impossible for some of the best Yorkshire cricketers of the age, John Hampshire, captain in impossible circumstances, amongst them.

It was all desperately different from 1938 when, as well as winning the Championship, Yorkshire provided five players for the final Test at the Oval. More than half of England's highest-ever total of 903 for seven was made by Len Hutton, with his record-beating 364, and Maurice Leyland, whose century he overshadowed. Hutton, the greatest English batsman of his time, remains the example of what Yorkshire cricketers should be. Genius is not enough. Determination and dedication are equally essential. When I read of Yorkshire fast bowlers who worry about the strains of playing two Championship matches in a week, I wonder if they recall that Hutton lost two inches of bone from his arm in a wartime accident, came back to first-class cricket and almost immediately faced Ray Lindwall and Keith Miller.

Not all the Yorkshire fast bowlers whine about being overworked. Much to his credit, Matthew Hoggard, asked if he had fears about touring India, replied that he wanted to play for England and therefore had never considered refusing to go. Suddenly – partly owing to their academy and the new coaching regime – Yorkshire have a surfeit of fast bowlers and enough batting strength to make a second successive Championship a strong prospect. I still regret that Darren Lehmann, the star batsman of 2001's success, is Australian, and I wish that Michael Vaughan had been born in Yorkshire as well as being a clear candidate to succeed Nasser Hussain as England's captain. But the clock cannot be turned back – except in one particular. There is real hope that Yorkshire will become so successful that we are really disliked again.

Wisden 2002

Freddie Trueman, the Perfect Bowler

Fred Trueman was the greatest fast bowler of his generation and, arguably, with only Harold Larwood as a competitor for the title, the greatest English fast bowler of all time. Richie Benaud put Trueman in his team of all-time international greats. The fabled West Indians – Holding, Hall, Griffiths and Marshall – were not included in his list of immortals. But the rough diamond from

Maltby in South Yorkshire who, on his test debut, took three wickets in eight balls was there.

The statistics are only a small part of the story. But they are, in themselves, extraordinary. He was the first bowler in history to take three hundred test wickets – a record broken only by cricketers who played far more tests than Trueman. And in twelve consecutive seasons, he took more than a hundred wickets for Yorkshire. When he chose he could also bat. Some commentators said that, if he put his mind to it, he could become a great all-rounder. They were wrong. He was, by temperament, a fast bowler. If concern about batting had distracted him from his destiny, the essential Trueman would have been lost.

The essential Trueman was more self-opinion-ated than any man I ever knew. We never met without him reminding me that he was on the other side of politics – and that I was in the wrong team. Ten years ago, during the summer, I chaired a radio discussion programme from Manchester about class distinction and Fred Trueman – always at odds with authority – was invited to discuss the difference between gentlemen and players. He accepted. So did the Duchess of Devonshire. After the broadcast was over I heard Fred say, 'If you ask me, Duchess, only you and me had the faintest idea of what we were talking about.' Perhaps he was right.

Under that aggressive exterior there was a man of charity and grace. During a Test Match lunch at Headingley, someone – probably me – was insensitive enough to raise the subject of his exclusion from the 1954–5 tour of Australia. According to legend, his omission was the result of his conduct in the West Indies during the previous winter. The whisper was that he had insulted local politicians.

Asked if the story was true, he replied, 'It was Sir Leonard who kept me out' but went on to say that Leonard Hutton 'was the greatest batsman I ever played with or against. And a real gentleman.' That generosity of spirit was rarely revealed in his fast bowling.

Fred Trueman was a proud man. That characteristic was often revealed, to my irritation, by insistence that he had been a 'colliery bricklayer' rather than a simple miner. His greatest pride was not in playing for England but in playing for Yorkshire. When the county fell on hard times, his anguish was genuine. His remedy was a return to the old virtues – players born in the county, hard work, self-sacrifice and batsmen and bowlers who were more interested in contributing to victory than attracting commercial sponsorships. Fred Trueman was the quintessential professional from a more innocent age.

Neville Cardus, the greatest of all cricket writers, believed that the game gave 'aesthetic pleasure to men who had never heard of such a thing and would be terrified of it if they had'. Fred Trueman personified that process. His bowling action was near perfect – high right arm at the point of delivery, elongated last stride, left foot hard down on the pitch and the entire movement performed 'side on'. One of his aphorisms was 'Cricket is a sideways game.'

When, during his days on *Test Match Special*, a listener telephoned to ask if the rule applied to wicketkeepers, he said that he had no time to bother with 'that sort of clever, clever talk'. His broadcasts, as a regular cricket commentator, were so didactic – and so unstintingly critical of the players whose performance he evaluated – that listeners wondered if, in his playing days, he had ever bowled a full toss, dropped a catch or given his wicket away. The question showed profound ignorance of the real Fred Trueman. He never hesitated to admit that he had made mistakes. But he had worked hard to correct them. And that, to him, justified the identification of mistakes in cricketers who were not so committed to self-improvement. His commentaries were always made up of the simplicities in which he believed. Fred Truman could not dissimulate.

Great sportsmen are not always accommodating companions. I remember one day being on the fringes of a conversation about the hook shot – a stroke which Fred, in accordance with the classical coaching manuals, believed that right-hand batsmen should play over their left shoulders. 'You have,' he said, 'got to get inside the ball.' Then he added: 'Even Roy knows that and he was a nothing cricketer.' I did and I was. But I was also an unambiguous admirer of Fred Trueman. I recall seeing him on television at a Conservative rally during the 1983 general election and thinking, unusually for me, that it did not matter that he worshipped Margaret Thatcher.

He was the greatest fast bowler of his age – perhaps of all time. And he was also an honest cricketer. Even now, he will be pacing out his run in heaven, sure that he is going to take a wicket with every ball and prepared to argue with the great umpire if the decision goes against him.

Observer 2 July 2006

A Hero and Hero Worship

The old Oval changeth, yielding place to new. But the new cantilevered 'stadium' will never have the charm of the dilapidated cricket ground in which, long ago, I sat on the grass outside the boundary rope and watched Len Hutton make 200 against the West Indian spin of Ramadhin and Valentine. Len Hutton was my boyhood hero and the Oval was the pitch on which he made the highest score in Test Match history – almost exactly seventy years before England's One Day victory over South Africa. During the war, while I was waiting impatiently for the return of county cricket, I chanted the magic spell which I hoped would turn me into a great batsman. 'Caught Hassett, bowled O'Reilly, 364 : 13 hours, 20 minutes.'

For summer after summer, I pursued Len Hutton with pleas for his autograph. They were always rejected. Then, in the early Eighties – when he was the knighted ex-England captain who had won back the Ashes and I was the relic of a recently defeated government – we met. On a Test Match Saturday, as I waited to pay my bill at the Queen's Hotel in Leeds, I saw him in the queue immediately in front of me. I was nerving myself to speak when he turned round and said, 'It's wonderful to see you.' My elation lasted for about ten seconds. Then he added, 'Are you back home now or still coaching in Tasmania?'

During the hasty explanations which followed, only I was embarrassed. Nobody who had scored runs off the fastest bowlers in the world was likely to be disconcerted by a confusion over names and identities. And, joy of joys, he offered me a lift to Headingley. On the way he talked in a stream of consciousness about cricket and cricketers. Victor Trumper's life had been ruined by superstition, George Hirst never carried his own cricket bag to the tram stop. Hedley Verity had 'looked after' him during the Sunday break in that record innings. He did not mention the interruption in his career and the two years of anguish which followed – the time in his life when he exhibited the courage and character which made him a genuine hero.

When war broke out, Len Hutton – still only twenty-four – joined the army and became a physical training instructor. A fracture of his left forearm – following an accident in the gym – would not heal. After months of surgery, the break mended. But the arm – with which classically correct batsmen 'lead' – had lost two inches in length. It was generally assumed that he would never bat for Yorkshire and England again. Len Hutton thought differently. Instead of cursing fate and wallowing in self-pity, he bought himself a 'Harrow' (youth size) bat and started to learn the game all over again.

The eye, the footwork and the power of concentration were still there. By any reasonable definition, he was physically handicapped. Yet, thanks to his indomitable will, by 1945 he was back in the England team for the Test series against All India. For the next ten years he was the regular opening batsman – with the exception of one solitary match for which he was controversially dropped in favour of a Gloucestershire batsman whose name I forget. He scored more than a hundred first-class centuries and ended his career with a batting average of 55. Thanks to his technique and temperament, his Test average was one run better still.

The statistics only matter because they prove that his recovery was complete. The achievement would have been a triumph of character had he done no more than *try* to confound adversity. But he not only tried. He persevered, although the old and the wise told him that he must accept that his career was finished. At twenty-two, he'd been acknowledged – along with Headley, Bradman and Hammond – to be one of the four greatest batsmen in the world. At twenty-five, he was a man without a trade or prospects. He was entitled to despair. He challenged, and conquered, adversity.

Heroism is a word that sports journalism debases by applying it to cup defeats of premiership teams by non-league opponents and to outsiders being whipped to victory in classic races. But it can be properly applied to one cricket legend. When I was a boy, I would not have believed it, but the 364 against the Australians was not Len Hutton's greatest triumph. Twenty-five years ago, I was driven to Headingley by a real hero.

Guardian 4 September 2008

Animal Writes

In the month which followed the 'Battle of Cable Street' – the hand-to-hand combat between Oswald Mosley's Black Shirts and the anti-fascists who were determined to keep them out of London's East End – the British Communist Party enjoyed the most popular period of its not very successful existence. The British Union of Fascists, on the other hand, only recruited one new member – an elderly lady who was wholly non-political but objected to the way in which Mosley's opponents treated the police horses. When I first read that story, my heart filled with pride. The English are a nation of animal lovers – a view which, I recalled, had always been denounced by my mother.

Her complaint was not that the expression is a cliché – although she prided herself on being a stern grammarian. It was her firm conviction that the English are a brutal race who hide their barbarism behind a sentimental façade. She was particularly concerned about the way in which they – or we – treat their – or our – dogs. Indeed she rarely saw one without assuming and announcing (usually in a very loud voice) that it was beaten, starved or neglected. Elderly gentlemen, out walking with obese Labradors, would be instructed to 'give him a good meal'. Ladies who allowed their terriers to shimmy towards her in a gesture of greeting would be asked, in accusing tones, why their dog or bitch cowered away as if expecting a thrashing. It was her mission to save lost dogs. Bessie, who lived with us for five years, was abducted from a family who were intimidated by my mother's threatening declaration, 'She needs a good home.'

I dare not have said it in her lifetime but my mother was wrong. For every brute who beats his dog there are a thousand families who love and cherish their best friends. And although dogs are my obsession, I have no doubt that other animals are, in an overwhelming majority of cases, loved and respected. The refuges I visited, in search of England – cats, donkeys, greyhounds – are signs of care, not neglect and ill-treatment. I remain astonished that insensitivity allows a majority of my friends and neighbours to eat pigs, sheep and bullock. But I have no doubt that most of those who do – including the farmers who rear them for slaughter – feel nothing but kindness towards their bacon, chops and steak while it is still on the hoof.

That is, of course, true in both the town and country. One of the regular claims, made in a certain sort of newspaper, is that the campaign against fox hunting was organised in metropolitan drawing rooms by men and women who had never smelt hay and would be offended by the thought of 'muck-spreading'. That is not my experience. The village in which I spend the best part of my life is in the middle of fox-hunting, grouse-shooting, fly-fishing Derbyshire. But most of my neighbours can distinguish between killing predators out of necessity and pursuing wild animals to the death for sport.

Perhaps I am wrong to imply that the English have a special concern for animals. Perhaps the other races feel the same. But in Tansley church – described in another part of this collection – I was told that only the effigies of English knights rest their armoured feet on dogs. And I regard that as proof of our ancient virtue. My mother would denounce it as a form of cruelty.

Goose Encounter at New Street

Believe it or not, Clive Jenkins was the star of the *Monty Python* sketch that brought down the curtain on the first half of the recent Amnesty International Charity Gala. He played the 'mystery guest' on an imaginary television quiz show in which bound and blindfolded contestants won handsome prizes if they guessed the identity of a visiting celebrity who kicked, punched and generally knocked hell out of them.

Apparently, Clive performed superbly. Carping critics may say that his triumph was no more than the outcome of shrewd type-casting. But when I saw pictures of Mr Jenkins putting his polished and pointed Chelsea boot in I could only feel regret that I had refused an invitation to do the same on an earlier night.

I had no sense of guilt. The Gala was a sell-out, with or without my trivial participation. I had no feeling of lost opportunity. I learned many years ago that politicians who do ridiculous things in public with the hope of appearing warm and lovable never look warm and lovable but only ridiculous. But as I looked at the pictures of the willingly pinioned victims awaiting with obvious pleasure the collision of Mr Jenkins's pointed toecap with the tender parts of their anatomy, I was overcome with a single simple conviction: into each life some farce must fall. And how much better if it can be exorcised on stage in aid of a good cause rather than in real life on, say – to take a single humiliating example – New Street Station, Birmingham.

I have alighted on New Street's concrete platform (remembering 'to take my hand baggage with me') at least once each week since the lovely red brick of Snow Hill was pounded into the ground to make a smooth surface for a car park. And my problem has never been leaving luggage behind but bringing too much with me.

During the transient days of ministerial office I travelled between London and Birmingham loaded down like a nineteenth-century Kowloon coolie. I could only manage it at all if every bag and parcel was suspended from me with the precision of a Guggenheim mobile.

My right elbow I kept close to my side, bent in an exact right-angle so that my forearm stuck out precisely parallel to the ground. A suit-bag over my shoulder and hooked to my right hand pulled my forearm upwards. But a ministerial red box clutched tightly in the same fist pulled my arm down and kept the Euclidian aberration in perfect balance. In my other hand I carried a suitcase, the weight of which kept my left arm

336

rigidly and vertically by my side, ensuring that the briefcase of constituency correspondence squashed between it and my rib-cage could not escape. My ticket I trapped between thumb and suitcase handle.

It was quite impossible to lift it to the level of the ticket-collector's outstretched palm. But most NUR members were kind enough to reach down and take it from me, and all preferred the thumbtrap technique to the alternative – carrying the ticket in my mouth and either blowing it to them as I passed their box or offering it from between my lips like a bird returning to the nest with a worm for its fledgling.

I tried to reconcile myself to the weight, inconvenience and risibility of my complicated load by thinking of the whole procedure as a health-giving combination of Canadian Air Force callisthenics and Tibetan yoga. But I could never complete the exercise with the degree of casual nonchalance that ought to typify the behaviour of a man with a Harvard suit-bag. Frankly, I had to concentrate very hard to move at all. No doubt it was the effort of moving forward that prevented me from noticing the packing-case that was rattling and shaking at the other end of the platform.

It was when the shaking turned to a shudder and the planks that made up its front and sides collapsed that I first became aware of the goose. But by the time it stepped out of the debris my attention was fully engaged. My first, distant thought was that there was a man inside. As a child of the twentieth century, I suspected a publicity stunt. As a child of Yorkshire, I wondered if geese travelled more cheaply than people and if this was an elaborate way of defrauding the railway. Then it drew near and I realised it was the work of God, not man: a goose's goose, the sort of goose that sensible swans would like to be.

The goose walked towards me, perfectly goose-shaped, like a four-foot pear covered in feathers. It was a well-adjusted goose that walked calmly and with self-possession in regular paces, not high-stepping idiotically like a German soldier. It looked neither to left nor right, but moved with enviable certainty towards the first-class waiting room.

I have always thought of the goose as a benign bird that lays golden eggs, flies up suburban sitting-room walls and saves the Capitol. A small boy, attempting to smash a chocolate machine, must have been to the wrong pantomimes, subscribed to a more sophisticated school of interior decoration and lacked a classical education. He was terrified by the goose and ran screaming to his mother, colliding in his flight with a massive tin tumbrel used by British Rail to carry Red Star parcels from train to post office. By unhappy chance his impact released its brake. The juggernaut began to roll slowly towards me, down the platform incline. It quickly gained pace.

By this time my hands were totally atrophied, approaching the stage when failure of blood supply produces either gangrene or frostbite, or both. But I did not lose my nerve. Lifting my left foot I diverted the rogue wheelbarrow into a pile of mail sacks where it no doubt remained for several days. But my pleasure in the passage of

338

athletic, indeed balletic, self-defence was dimmed by my failure to keep hold of my ticket. It spun from my right hand and landed on the line between train and platform.

But I was, after all, in Birmingham, the city I had represented in Parliament for well over a decade. If I could not talk my way through the barrier here... So I advanced to the ticket-collector and boldly announced, 'I am Roy Hattersley.' His reply – 'Well done' – was less than encouraging, but I pressed on. 'I have no ticket,' I confessed. The subsequent long silence destroyed my remaining confidence. I rushed in to fill the verbal vacuum.

'London train ... platform six ... weighed down with luggage ... packing-case shaking ... split open ... great big goose ... three feet tall ... grey ... four feet tall ... perfectly amiable ... five feet tall ... little boy ... very frightened ... screamed and shouted ... crashed into trolley ... released brake ... at least forty miles an hour ... nasty accident ... stopped with foot ... look at mark on shoe ... ticket fell on line. Recovering it would be both dangerous and illegal.'

The ticket-collector was a reasonable and compassionate man. In any case, the queue building up behind me had begun to turn ugly. 'OK, Squire,' he said. 'On your way this time. But if it happens again you'll have to pay.'

Listener 20 September 1979

Me and My Dogs

Dinah was an unintentional cross between a black Labrador and some sort of terrier. She was mine between my fifteenth birthday and the Tuesday on which I left home. Thereafter she became part of the ever-present past that I could comfortingly recreate whenever I returned to Sheffield. I have, of course, had other casual canine acquaintances but Dinah was the one permanent relationship.

Before I was born, my mother and father brought with them, from Mansfield, an expert rat-catcher called Mick. Wire-haired, white, with a black patch over one eye and an ear permanently cocked for sounds in the undergrowth, Mick appears in many box Brownie snapshots taken by my father to immortalise his intended, not her dog. I still think of him as part of an age of short dresses, pleated skirts and cloche hats. Like the 1920s he came to a bad end.

There were two interpretations of Mick's attempts to kill me. His defenders said that he mistook me for one of the sleepy rodents whose necks he specialised in snapping with a single nip – a vole or something of the sort. His detractors attributed his intended infanticide to pure jealousy, the refusal to allow any other living thing to be patted or stroked. Whatever the reason, about three weeks after I began to compete with him for attention, he was apprehended with teeth bared and about to spring. It was agreed that one of us had to go. Having seen the faded sepia photographs of Mick and my mother sitting on Nottingham stiles and fences, I never dared ask how difficult the choice had been.

After Mick we turned to mongrels in the belief that, like the working classes, what they lacked in breeding they made up in temperament. One called Teddy (after the bear of the same name) enjoyed a brief brown existence before it died of some wasting illness. The decline, death and disposal of our furry liability proved such a trauma that, after burying it in the garden like Tess of the D'Urbervilles' horse, we decided that in future we would confine ourselves to rabbits.

Not that captive rabbits lie lightly on the consciences of suburban sentimentalists. Peter, a giant black-and-white improvement on any of the pink-eyed monsters that Dürer ever painted, kept us in emotional turbulence for seven years. The first cause of concern was his claws, which grew into curved white talons of which a Manchu mandarin would have been proud. The second was the home-made hutch which we always feared could not withstand the stigmas of a Yorkshire winter. At the slightest sign of snow or rain we nailed an extra piece of lino to the roof. The result was a hutch capable of withstanding aerial bombardment and a rabbit shell-shocked from a holocaust of hammering that preceded every wet and windy weather forecast.

But at least in winter Peter was declared to be in hibernation and the decision that all he wanted was food and sleep at least absolved us from blame about his lack of exercise. In the summer we exercised our guilt on Wednesdays and Sundays by unwinding a roll of wire netting and setting up a temporary corral on the piece of grass that was sometimes a cricket pitch, sometimes a parade ground but was never lush enough to be a lawn.

Once coerced out of his hutch, Peter made great twitching leaps from side to side of his compound. Although we never associated the twitches with the psychosis of confinement, we did fear that the signs of joy on two days a week were indications of misery on the other five.

Peter died in advanced old age. He was pronounced dead by the butcher, whose previous opinions about his health we had accepted with a mixture of relief and cynicism. We wanted to believe that a sleek coat and clear eyes were a sign of contented good health. But we took the anthropomorphic view of domestic animals and the butcher, being a part-time farmer, thought of them as stock, not family. So we doubted his ability to understand a rabbit's inner emotions.

For some years after Peter's passing, we directed all our surplus affection towards wild cats and stray dogs. The cats really were wild, the issue of vagabonds who had deserted the boiled fish of domesticity for the starlings and field-mice of the nearby churchyard. The dogs were almost always found before they were lost. They belonged to distant neighbours who allowed them to wander from lamppost to lamppost. We always assumed such dogs were in need of our care and protection.

The distant neighbours never seemed to mind.

So Bessy, a Cairn terrier from up the road, spent more time with us than at home. We tried to keep her fringe out of her eyes and we untangled the coat that naturally matted around the twigs and burrs she picked up from other people's gardens. Whisky – so called because he came from Scotland rather than because of any resemblance to the pure-bred exquisites who advertise that substance – actually lived next door. Had his owners not decided to move to a flat from which animals were prohibited, we would almost certainly have been prosecuted for abduction. When it was suggested that Whisky might be 'put down', we stepped in. He went for rest and recuperation to elderly aunts in Worksop where, to my chagrin, he stayed – despite the indignity of initially being called Frisky, a name thought more suitable for the pet of two maiden ladies.

But all that was no more than preparation for Dinah. I do not recall why, after ten years of only making friends with dogs, we decided once more to have one in the family. All I remember is a freezing December journey across Sheffield, a change from tram to bus in Pond Street and the farm of Mr Russell, farmer and part-time rabbit pathologist. Some weeks earlier one of Mr Russell's Labradors had escaped at quite the wrong time and formed a disastrous liaison with a notorious terrier which, to add insult to insatiability, 'didn't even have a collar'. The issue lay half asleep in front of a cast-iron outhouse stove.

With gentle encouragement from Mr Russell, three of the puppies got up, yawned, stretched their back legs and stumbled across the brick floor, exuding conscious, bewildered charm as if they knew that 'a good home' went to the lucky winner. One took an incompetent bite in Mr Russell's direction and went back to sleep. Perversely, though not uncharacteristically, we decided that the dissident was our dog and Dinah was carried off between me and my blue gabardine school raincoat.

If she ever took a bite at another human being we never heard of it. She bit every other sort of animal, but not people. She even tried to bite a bumblebee. We saw her snap at it as it hovered above a marigold and shake her head as it began to buzz inside her mouth. Before we were out of the kitchen door, the biter had been stung and was racing into the forbidden territory beyond the front gate. It took us three days to find her. Eventually she was cornered and caught by the Neepsend gasworks and handed over to the RSPCA. My father reclaimed her and phoned home the message that which was lost is found and I stopped feeling guilty about going to the pictures on the previous night when I might have been out on the streets shouting 'Dinah' into disused shops and broken-down garages.

We loved her most simply because she was ours. But we loved her as well for her sheer irrational indomitability, the unreasonable hope and unjustified expectation that keep animals going in tough times. On holiday, in Filey or Mablethorpe, she spent her days leaping a yard into the air absolutely convinced that she was about to catch one of the seagulls that flew fifty feet over the beach.

The whole family lived in perpetual fear of attempted leaps across impassable gorges and improvident assaults upon Alsatians. But it was all worth it for the example that she set. Twenty years after Dinah was dead, on a sunny afternoon in Ipswich marketplace, a journalist asked me why I still believed that we could win the election. 'Pathological optimism,' I told him, with damaging accuracy. But I did not add that I had learned it from a dog called Dinah.

Listener 17 April 1980

'Fetch the shoebox, fetch the shovel'

Tortoises, although lacking a reputation for dash and daring, have a record of public relations success that must be the envy of all Madison Avenue. They are a zoological celebration of the dependable virtues, the victory of determination made wrinkled flesh. Racing tortoises have done more to undermine hares' morale than all the metaphors about March madness and split lips. But nobody worries about the damage done to the self-confidence of a sprinting rodent when it is outrun by a reptile whose name proclaims the deformity of its legs. All our sympathies are with the winner inside the carapace – the runner held back by a suit of prehistoric armour but carried forward by an indomitable spirit.

345

There may be a reference in fiction or fable that is not to the tortoise's advantage, but usually it is other people who come badly out of tortoise stories. Mr Evelyn Waugh used one in *Brideshead Revisited* to illustrate the apparently ineffable vulgarity of Rex Mottram, who made a present of 'a small tortoise with Julia's initials set in diamonds in the living shell'.

Tortoises have cunningly encouraged the association of their name with the Fabian Society, the violently reasonable and ostentatiously cerebral socialist sect, and their picture appears on the covers of old pamphlets. We know that, like Quintus Fabius Maximus, when they strike they will strike hard. If they too are called 'cunctator' it is because they have the wisdom to wait until the right moment. Anything that lives for a hundred years learns patience.

Even their distant aquatic brothers have a good press. The Galapagos turtle receives as much credit for unearthing the theory of evolution as does Charles Darwin. Mr Lewis Carroll's Mock Turtle is the most educated animal in nineteenth-century literature. 'Reeling and Writing to begin ... then the different branches of Arithmetic – Ambition, Distraction, Uglification and Derision... Mystery, ancient and modern, with Seaography: then Drawing, Stretching, and Fainting in Coils.'

All these tortoise memories came flooding into my mind a couple of weeks ago when I spent a disturbing morning talking with officials at the RSPCA and the Royal Society for the Protection of Birds. Hares I knew to be cruelly exploited, butchered at the Waterloo Cup to make a

Merseyside holiday in a contest just as mortal and unequal as the Roman games. But I never thought of tortoises needing protection until that day when I discovered the numbers in which they are imported into this country, their mortality rate in transit, the chance of the few escapees surviving the shop window and the prospects of those which actually find refuge in a suburban garden living through the following winter.

Until that day, I had always assumed that the victims of misplaced brief sentimentality which Philip Larkin saw 'on shallow straw, in shadeless glass, huddled by empty bowls' were soon-to-be abandoned puppies. The discovery that a single pet shop in my constituency had been prosecuted for the neglect of seven thousand tortoises and fined five pence per dead or distressed reptile made me realise that every small animal that can be caught or bred in captivity is in danger. 'Fetch the shoebox, fetch the shovel. Mam, we're playing funerals now' is a lament for dogs, cats, rabbits, white mice – anything that can be taken home on a bus and kept at the end of the garden in an orange box.

Unfortunately, although small, portable, placid creatures are particularly suitable for sale, bigger and more demanding animals are not wholly protected from the deprivations of captivity. I once believed that filmstars, strolling down Sunset Boulevard with cheetahs on chains, were exhibiting a moral failing that was as rare as it was deviant. I thought of it as an interesting example of how words change their meanings: the common people could never behave with such vulgarity. Exotic animals, ostentatiously kept and flamboyantly displayed, were, I hoped, an aberration of the rich.

According to statistics supplied to me by the RSPB, that cannot be so. Between 8 February and 10 December 1979 the classified columns of *Cage and Aviary Birds* offered for sale thirty-eight buzzards, fifty-one tawny owls and thirty-six sparrowhawks. The 'Wanted' section included twenty-six advertisements for eagles. The bird of prey both most in demand and most on offer was the kestrel. Barry Hines's *Kes* has made the possession of that particular predator a desirable symbol of status in the industrial North.

At least five thousand birds of prey are kept in captivity in Britain – two thousand of them by falconers who behave like Norman warlords and Tudor grandees and let fly in pursuit of the traditional defenceless victims. Falconry is a 'legitimate field sport' in Britain. A falconer needs a licence neither to keep nor to kill. Subject only to the suitably feudal requirement that he does it on his own property, anyone who is moved by such spectacles is entitled to set a falcon on a wood-pigeon or starling and call it a sport.

I know that it is the nature of birds of prey to live off creatures that do not have the wit to evade them, the speed to outstrip them or the strength to repulse them. The nicest dog I ever knew would certainly have baited any bear that came within range of her myopic vision. Even well-fed cats kill mice. But none of that is an excuse for human beings to organise war between the species. Encouraging animals to kill one another and enjoying the spectacle is the sort of barbarism that ought to have ended with the death of medieval England. It is no excuse to say that, up between the sky and the clouds, the chase and the kill assume an aesthetic, almost spiritual quality. That is the sort of rubbish that Ernest Hemingway wrote about bullfights. Nor is it any sort of defence to talk of living from the output of abattoirs and walking on the product of tanneries and knackers' yards. The objectionable feature of killing for sport is the enjoyment of the death.

Late one rainy West Country afternoon last spring, safe within the camouflage of a rural telephone box, I watched a starling methodically killing a succession of snails by beating their shells against the kiosk's concrete base. As the starling swallowed down the exposed green entrails and hopped back into the hedgerow to drag out a second and third course for the evening meal, I felt no obligation to break off my argument with the operator and rush to the rescue of the unwilling supper. This was how the starling lived; red in beak and claw, but protected by an innocence in which men cannot take refuge.

The eagle which dropped the tortoise on Aeschylus' head was no more guilty of murdering the reptile than the tortoise itself was responsible for Aeschylus' death. Eagles, at least Attic eagles, killed tortoises in much the same way and for absolutely the same purpose as my Somerset starling slaughtered snails – but from a greater height. It was Archimedes' misfortune to possess a bald head that looked like a round, smooth boulder, and the tortoise's bad luck to feel the eagle's talons clutching at his shell.

Thomas Macaulay was right: 'The Puritan hated bear-baiting, not because it gave pain to the bear, but because it gave pleasure to the spectators.' That is no criticism of the Puritans, their standards of value, or of the sort of England they would have created. It is simply a statement of the indisputable fact that people who find pleasure in the creation of pain diminish themselves. That is clearly true of the furtive figures found crouched around bloodied feathers at cock-fights. It is just as applicable to men and women who take part in more socially acceptable blood sports, explaining that the fox actually enjoys our country traditions. I fear it is also true of those innumerable families who casually buy and carelessly neglect millions of small birds and animals each year. Theirs are not sins of commission. But after a short summer of passing amusement they are engulfed in *accidie* – the sin of not bothering. Wise tortoises will probably argue that not bothering is the worst sin of all.

Listener 14 August 1980

Peace and a Carrot from the Queen

Palm Sunday at the Freshfield Donkey Centre, a couple of miles outside the village of Peak Forest on the road between Chesterfield and Stockport. Beethoven – silver-grey with a curly coat and

350

known to experts as a 'blue roan' – has just returned from leading a religious procession through the streets of Liverpool. He has specialised in Christian celebrations ever since he returned from Assisi, where he was blessed at the Shrine of St Francis.

Donkeys are only English by adoption. They are the natives of warm climates where they are often expected to carry burdens far too heavy for them to bear. But they have essentially English characteristics. Stubborn as well as patient, they bear hardship bravely. They choose their friends with care. At Freshfield, the donkeys decide for themselves who should be their lifetime companions in the double stalls. And, perhaps most typically English of all, they kick rarely but, when they do, they kick hard. A donkey sanctuary is a thoroughly English institution.

Beethoven typifies its work. In his time, he has stood silent and motionless throughout morning service in Manchester Cathedral. But he disappointed a group of nuns who visited his stall on Christmas Eve in the belief that, at midnight, he would kneel down. They did not understand the donkeys of Freshfield, whose religious speciality is not faith but good works.

The sanctuary welcomes into its twenty-nine acres the outcasts of the breed. Beethoven is stone-deaf – the result of having been constantly beaten about the head in the past. And his is far from the worst case history among the centre's sixty-seven residents. John Stirling, who runs Freshfield, speaks of new arrivals who – their hides covered in sores and riddled with maggots through neglect – are too weak to walk. Sky, named after the TV company that paid his fare from Cyprus, was abandoned at the top of the cliff down which his mother had been thrown.

Although most of Freshfield's donkeys have tragic histories, they live in a contentment which is more than easeful retirement. On Palm Sunday, the twenty geriatrics were out in the fields, happily taking the air until a cold wind persuaded them that they would be best back in the stables. In the next block, the younger generation looked fit and well and ready for the work which gives the sanctuary its extra purpose.

Freshfield was created almost by mistake. Michael Elliott, sometime head of drama at the BBC, bequeathed his two donkeys to his friend John Stirling, a television producer whose friendship with the stars made it possible to raise the cash the donkey sanctuary needs. The stable walls are lined with photographs of celebrity patrons – Judi Dench, John Mills, Martin Shaw and the casts of *Coronation Street* and *EastEnders*. One photograph shows the Queen meeting Tinker and Josh. The two donkeys had just completed a sponsored walk from Balmoral to Buckingham Palace. To Michael's astonishment, they were invited in. And the Queen, after asking permission, fed them carrots.

Showbiz money saved the donkeys. Michael Elliott and his wife Annie had the inspiration to employ the foundlings to help educate children from across the country. School parties make regular visits. But the really important work is done by the half-dozen 'special needs' children who 'live in' at Freshfield for a week at a time. Each one is given a donkey to look after – feed, muck out and exercise. 'They sleep with them if they want to,' says John. Only the special half-dozen are allowed to ride them. Freshfield does not regard its donkeys as beasts of burden.

Although donkeys came late into John Stirling's life, he has absolute confidence in their healing powers. When he feels anxious or agitated, he sits among them and listens to the sound of grass being munched. He knows each one by name, insists that he will be on similarly familiar terms when the numbers more than double in the summer and points out the different breeds with pride.

There is far more to donkeys than most of us realise. Take for example Oliver – a Sicilian 'miniature', thirty-two inches high, who arrived at the sanctuary with papers to prove that he was in no condition to make a nuisance of himself with the female residents. Before Stirling realised that Oliver was not only able but more than willing, he had sired twelve foals – seven as small as their father and five with mothers three times as high. 'Don't ask me how he managed it, but he did,' says Stirling.

Every donkey – grey (originating in India) and white (from Israel) – has one feature in common. A cross is clearly visible in the hair along their backs. That, the legend says, is the reward for the donkey's role in the first Palm Sunday. To most of us, they simply bring back memories of English holidays long before anyone but the very rich flew off to more exotic places. I hope that the donkeys I rode on the beaches at Morecambe and Bridlington long ago ended their days as happily as the residents of Freshfield do today.

Daily Mail 22 March 2005

Shepherds Suffering with Collie Wobbles

Ten miles west of Sheffield and not a factory chimney in sight. In a field overlooking the Hathersage Valley, Carol Mellin – elegantly modern from the sunglasses on top of her auburn hair to the bottoms of her tight blue jeans – is trying to persuade Maisie, her border collie, to edge four reluctant Swaledales into a pen. It is the Fox House Sheepdog Trials and Carol Mellin is a competitor.

Jim Copper – a farmer from Bacup who (with his dog Sid) came fourth in this year's international championship at Tullamore in Ireland – predicts that Carol Mellin will be the day's winner. But, at the last minute, one sheep cuts loose and bounds away. The whistle sounds and the permitted time is up. Carol and Maisie are out of the contest.

'More disappointed than frustrated', Carol Mellin is not sure how she should be described. She is a farmer's wife from Haworth in Brontë Country and, although sheepdog trials are her 'passion', shepherding is her job as well as her weekend enthusiasm. So 'shepherdess' – which

354

sounds like a porcelain figurine complete with crinoline and ribbon-decorated crook – cannot be right. She is as much part of the twenty-first century as sheepdog trials are part of England's history.

The rules on which the trials are based are so exacting that it is hard to believe that a 'run' can ever be completed successfully. Sheep are released at the distant end of a long field. The dog – almost always a border collie – is then required to guide them, at awkward angles, through three gates before securing them safely in a pen. Then the pen is opened and the dog must separate the sheep into two groups. And it must all be done in eight minutes.

The dogs – sometimes crouching menacingly but more often racing to outflank a wandering sheep – respond to the sound of a whistle. According to Trevor Jones, an octogenarian who has trained dogs since he was ten, there is only one way to teach obedience to a border collie. The secret is 'kindness and patience'. The shepherd must be 'always firm but never cross'.

Men and dogs, says Jones, combine to build each other's character: 'The shepherd must discipline himself to be patient.' One of the partners gives orders and the other obeys them, but they forge what is very nearly a relationship of equals. Obedience is reciprocated with respect. When asked how a novice would perform, Jim Copper's concern is only for the border collie. 'He would make a fool of the dog.'

But important though the training is, good sheepdogs are born, not made. Trainers merely develop a talent that has come with the genes. And sometimes it is the man, not his hard-working best friend, who needs the instruction. David Meaden, a smallholder from South Yorkshire, is happy to admit that Gruff, a recent acquisition, 'can already do it'. But Meaden is a spectator rather than a competitor at Fox House because he has yet to master the whistles to which his dog is accustomed.

It is the genes that make a good sheepdog so valuable. Earlier this year at Skipton, Floss was sold for 4100 guineas. Her new owner may recover some of the cost by selling her puppies. But there is no money to be made from sheepdog trials. The competitors take part for glory, silver cups and cash prizes which would not buy a month's supply of dog food.

Gordon Watt – this year's world champion and a judge at Fox House – brought home £3000 from Tullamore. It just about covers his annual expenses. Watt, like his father, is a professional shepherd. He works on a farm north of Sheffield. In some months, ten thousand sheep graze its land. York, his dog, is one of the tools of his trade. It is not a pet that lives in the luxury of its owner's house. Like other working dogs, its home is a kennel. But York and Watt have a special rela-tionship. Otherwise, they would not have become champions of the world.

It is a relationship which can be enjoyed as much by amateurs as by professionals. Between the bales of straw which pass for seats at Fox House, Lawrence Taylor and Janet Priestley stood side by side, unconscious of each other's presence as they concentrated on the runs. Janet Priestley is the wife of a farmer who, with Jess, tends the sheep on the Derby College Farm. Lawrence Taylor, a retired motor mechanic, owns a few sheep – but not enough to justify a dog. He decided to follow the sport for love.

The Fox House competitors – farmers' battered trilbies side by side with baseball caps – had only one thing in common, the pleasure they felt watching dogs at work. And their border collies showed every sign of feeling even greater joy. Sheepdog trials offer a nation of dog lovers the chance to see man and his best friend happy in their work together.

Daily Mail 19 July 2005

Farmer Tom Is a Breed We All Need

Mid-morning on the first day of the 175th Bakewell Show. Ladies in top hats are riding around the centre ring in ever-decreasing circles. Business on the trade stands is picking up. Stewards are fighting a losing battle to prevent children from climbing on the agricultural machinery which is on show. The band of the Yorkshire Volunteers has formed up in preparation for its lunchtime parade. Rural England is en fête.

The real business of agricultural shows is being conducted in the stockyard behind the aggressively modern Agricultural Business Centre. The pens are packed with pedigree cattle and anxious owners. Prizes in one of the imminent competitions can add immensely to the value of a bull, cow or heifer. But more than money is at stake. Farmers who compete at cattle shows are moved by the emotions which also inspire the proud mothers at beautiful baby contests.

Tom Cox, the thirty-year-old owner of the Bleaklow Herd of pedigree Charolais, is in a stall at the back of the stockyard grooming his entry in Class 145 – 'Heifer in-calf with first calf or with calf at foot'. She is called Bleaklow Ulla, weighs a ton and is due to give birth next January. Her quality was confirmed when she won first prize at the Leicester County show. But she lost to Westcarse Tanya, from Loughborough, at Derby. The two heifers are about to go head to head at Bakewell.

According to the show catalogue, the Charolais judging is due to begin at '10.45 a.m. prompt'. It begins at noon. Neither the cattle nor their owners show the slightest impatience. Show cattle have to be immaculate. Cox and Vic Holmes – a local authority motor mechanic who spends his annual holidays working with the Bleaklow Herd – have plenty to do. The intense grooming began on the previous day when Bleaklow Ulla – separated from the herd and kept overnight in the pasture behind the cow sheds with Bleaklow Vivienne for company – was worked on for most of the morning.

After a thorough wash down with coconut shampoo ('gentle formulation for all animals') Cox had trimmed her back and belly with electric shears of

358

which any metropolitan barber would have been proud. Holmes provided what amounted to a pedicure. Stroking his shaven head, he suggested that someone else backcomb her tail. As the two men worked, passing villagers wished them good luck. John Lomas, a neighbour who described himself as 'farming a commercial herd', was optimistic. 'It's not just the beast, it's the man as well that makes a champion.'

There was the clear implication that Tom Cox – the fourth generation in a Derbyshire farming family – is all the things that a young farmer should be. His father described Tom's passion more wryly. 'I'm trying to read the paper at breakfast and he's talking all the time about Charolais.' Bleaklow Ulla had to wait while shorthorns, Holsteins and Ayrshires were put through their paces. As she waited, Cox and Holmes performed a strange ritual. Charolais are milky white with naturally immaculate smooth hides. For competitions, their hair has to be frizzed up into little tufts with the aid of 'show soap' – a combination of household soap and glycerine. Tom Cox, being an enthusiast, scorns the commercial product and makes his own. When the Charolais judging began the bulls were first in the ring. Among them was Iceman Bollinger, an old gentleman of twelve with a belly and double chin. According to Hilary Taylor, its owner's wife, he was so used to competing that he could 'walk round on his own'. Cattle show judges have no respect for age. Iceman Bollinger was not placed.

Westcarse Tanya was led into the ring by Sarah Burton (her proud owner) followed by Ligmoor

Annie, her ten-week-old calf. Mrs Burton's husband led the calf and, in his vulnerable position behind Westcarse Tanya, narrowly avoided an avalanche of what is politely called manure. He discreetly removed a piece of toilet paper from the pocket of his white coat and carefully wiped the heifer's bottom.

It would have been easy to argue that the calf – which excited 'oohs' and 'aahs' from the crowd – made the difference. For Westcarse Tanya came first with Bleaklow Ulla second. But Tom Cox was not disposed to feel any emotion except justified pleasure. Asked if he would spend the night celebrating, he replied that he had to be back early next morning. Not to include Bleaklow Ulla in the final day's livestock parade would be discourteous.

These are uncertain times for British agriculture. And Tom Cox knows it. But a man who owned his first Charolais when he was fifteen is not likely to turn his back on farming. He represents a thoroughly modern view of cattle breeding combined with an old-fashioned commitment to the ancient values of the land. Men like him will survive even the European Common Agricultural Policy. And many more rosettes will adorn his Charolais.

Daily Mail 9 August 2005

Unnatural Behaviour

We are a canine village. Of course people out-number dogs. But I doubt if the ratio is much above three to one. Like the rest of the country we favour Labradors and Jack Russells – most of which (or 'whom' as their owners would say) are imaginatively called 'Jack'. There is the occasional scuffle when incompatibles meet. My Buster was actually attacked by three inoffensive-looking golden retrievers who belong to an even more inoffensive-looking middle-aged lady, whose woolly hat creates a false sense of security. For-tunately, in my attempt to fend them off, I slipped and, by landing on Buster, both protected him from harm and won the reputation of a man who is prepared to risk his life to save his dog – or, at least, crush him to death rather than have him savaged.

However, most of us are conspicuously respon-sible owners. This means that we never fail to 'pick up' – maximum fine £200. The only time, during my eleven years in the village, when excre-ment was found on a footpath, it was denounced in uncompromising terms in the parish magazine and there was a tacit agreement among dog-owners that the offending animal must have been a stray from outside our boundaries.

Our determination to keep the streets clean survived the Dowager Duchess of Devonshire's condemnation of faeces-collection as 'unnatural'. Speaking at the nearby Buxton Festival she expressed her horror at the discovery that Baslow, barely three miles away, has special boxes in which the plastic bags of ordure can be deposited. Open disagreement with the Dowager Duchess is not in the village's nature. That we have dared to defy her in this particular demonstrates what responsible owners we are. Consider, therefore, how we reacted when we read in the parish magazine that two miscreants had been observed menacing pregnant cows. The force of the complaint was increased by the fact that it came from our own farmer – a man who enjoys universal respect. He also reported that when he told a lady in Bakewell to stop her dog chasing ducklings she replied that it was 'doing no harm'.

One of my neighbours attributes the increase in anti-social behaviour to the Peak District National Park Authority's encouragement of the conversion of barns into holiday cottages. Whatever the reason, the situation has suddenly deteriorated. Now a pet sheep has been killed. Contradictory rumours accuse a variety of owners. As was the case with the Paris Commune of 1871, fear of being found guilty when innocent promotes the temptation to excuse oneself by denouncing others.

One story suggests that the dogs which harassed the cows jumped through the kitchen window when frightened by thunder. The implausibility of that happening does not prevent us all wanting the explanation to be true. We would like to find some sort of excuse, no matter how tenuous, for the uncharacteristic behaviour. Nobody has mentioned

Zoltan, Dracula's dog in the B-movie, who came back to life when struck by lightning. But one question still arises. How does a village which hates unpleasantness deal with the canine fundamentalists who, unless they are brought under control, will continue to terrorise local livestock?

Our farmer – a man of conspicuous good temper – has published what amounts to a friendly warning, or perhaps no more than wise advice, in the parish magazine. Strong action, he reminds recent arrivals, is usually taken against dogs which kill sheep. No one can imagine him firing the shot. But up in the hills someone certainly would. A dog-loving village would find it hard to reconcile itself to the knowledge that, somewhere in our midst, a border collie – no matter how great its crime – had faced summary execution.

We believe that there are no bad dogs, only bad owners. So most of us would think that the gun had been pointed at the wrong target. That is a blatantly sentimental view. But what else can be expected from men who drive dangerously, not because they are looking at girls but because they are ogling dogs?

My mother – who believed that every dog she did not own was ill-treated or neglected, and probably both – would have marched up to the front door of the negligent owner's house and announced that she was taking the offending dogs into protective custody. I do not have the nerve to follow her example. Anyway Buster would not like it. I suspect that he is less worried about the slaughter of the innocents than I am. He has grown so smug with the years that he neither identifies nor sympathises with other foundlings. No doubt, he is wondering why the border collies cannot be sensible like him and limit their murderous intentions to cats. In our village, the ratio of cats to people is about one to a hundred.

Spectator 26 August 2006

Bombs Away to Secure a Public Seal of Approval

Donna Nook – a beach on the North Lincolnshire coast and an RAF bombing range which holidaymakers are forbidden to enter when the red flag flies. White pyramids and orange drums mark the approach to targets along the line where sand meets sea. On the distant horizon, tankers follow each other south. And, on the wet, dark sand below the dunes, hundreds of female grey seals lie, almost motionless, waiting to give birth.

The seals' permanent colony is on a sandbank out at sea at a latitude a few degrees north of Skegness and Mablethorpe. Nobody is quite sure why they chose that location. Usually, because they are particularly vulnerable when they come ashore, they prefer rocky, inaccessible islands. But there, like millions of holidaymakers in that part of the world, they are attracted to the Lincolnshire coast for sole and crab. So, every November, they come inland and take up residence on the beach until their pups are born. Then, they conceive again and swim back out to sea.

The snowy white pups appear within a couple of days of their mothers' arrival on dry land. During the next two weeks, a strange transformation takes place. The mothers, who have lived off their blubber since they left the sandbank, visibly lose weight as the babies they suckle grow fat. Both parents and children are blissfully unaware that they are spending their most intimate moments in full view of the visitors who make the pilgrimage each November to the Lincolnshire Wildlife Trust's nature reserve.

By two o'clock on a cold Sunday afternoon, Peter Cox – an assistant warden at Donna Nook – had recorded well over eight hundred visitors to the reserve. By the end of the breeding season the total will be over ten thousand. Last Sunday they stood silent and fascinated behind the low fence which was built to protect the visitors, not the seals. As they lie on the beach, or make slow progress across the sand on flippers which were clearly designed for swimming, seals look the most harmless of animals. But they have sharp teeth and short tempers.

Six-year-old Ben Elwood – at Donna Nook with his mother, father and three-year-old brother during a family visit to his northern grandparents – was not deceived by the seals' gentle appearance. He had 'seen them fight'. Before the afternoon was over, a bout of snarling aggression proved him to be a reliable witness. A couple of dozen males hovered around the expectant and nursing mothers. Some of them are there to

365

protect the young. Others have less honourable intentions. When protector meets philanderer, the result is usually blood on the sand.

Just as the light was fading, there was a demonstration of how brutal seal life can be. A marauding male advanced to about twenty yards of a sleeping female. Then her protector rushed at him, as fast as his flapping flippers would allow – breaking into something like speed when he could make more speedy progress along a rivulet in the sand. As he rushed forward, he made a strange barking noise. The would-be molester decided that it was best to make a quick and undignified retreat.

In the shadow of a grass-covered sand dune, a mother suckled two young seals. Twins are rare, so there was great interest in the pair of babies – destined for little more than three weeks of maternal care before they are abandoned and left to find their own way to the sea. By then, they will have shed the white coats which make them the quarry of seal hunters and will be as grey as their mothers.

It is difficult to imagine how a human being could club such a small and helpless creature to death. Patricia Robinson, who had travelled up from Lincoln with her husband, spoke for most of the entranced spectators when she explained why she had made so many visits to Donna Nook in the breeding season. 'I love them,' she said, unable to look away from the pups. 'It's their big eyes.'

Peter Cox, who has worked at Donna Nook for more than ten years, thinks the special appeal of the reserve is the chance it provides to see nature as it really is. Birth, and (since 10 per cent of the baby seals never reach the sea) death, mother love, male aggression, and the peculiar dependence of the very young, are all on display. And grey seals have another attraction. They are simultaneously cuddly and exotic. That is an unbeatable combination.

What is more, despite the occasional fight, they seem a vulnerable breed which needs human protection. The way that they flap along the sand excites our sympathy. Clearly, they are only at home in the sea. But fate has required them to live part of their lives on land. 'I would like to take them all home' said Esme Burton from Spennymoor, Co. Durham, 'and look after them properly.' She can rest assured that, in one respect, the grey seals of Donna Nook are perfectly safe. The Royal Air Force, in its typically British way, is careful not to use the bombing range near the breeding ground until the grey seals have completed their annual visit.

Daily Mail 21 November 2006

Silent Night with Old Brock and His Family

A wooded hillside a couple of miles outside Crich – the village that is the home of the National Tramway Museum and the site of the tower that is a memorial to the Sherwood Foresters and the Worcestershire Regiment. It is six o'clock on a

Saturday night and the light is fading fast. In between the pine trees, a group of motionless figures sit in absolute silence. They are waiting to see badgers – England's oldest surviving mammals – come out of their setts for their evening exercise and meal.

Silence is essential. The watchers have been told to wear clothes that do not rustle and they have checked time after time to make sure that their mobile phones are switched off. They sit, uncomfortably, on rubber mats which were designed for the floor of motor cars and concentrate hard on not moving because of cramp, or coughing, or allowing their stomachs to rumble too loudly.

An owl screeches, a faraway fox howls and on the road above the ridge, a lorry rumbles past. None of those familiar noises is likely to make the badgers stay at home. The watchers stare into the darkness through 'image intensifiers', which provide a clear but mysteriously green-tinged picture of the route which it is expected the badgers will take. Normally, badger watchers refrain from using bait. But tonight a novice is in their ranks. So temptation – in the form of dried fruit and nuts left over from Christmas – has been spread around the hole which is the entrance to the sett.

There is no way of knowing how long the waiting has lasted. Moving an arm to look at a watch might make a noise. Everybody fears that no badger will appear tonight but nobody is prepared to admit it. Irene Brierton, a wildlife artist who chairs the local Badger Group, remains confident. She reconnoitred the area two nights earlier and, although it is early in the year for family excursions, two or three adult badgers wandered out into the cold of the hillside.

Ms Brierton makes no secret of her infatuation with Old Brock. She describes herself as 'absolutely hooked' and admits that 'on a moonlit night, going out to look for them is irresistible'. Three stuffed badgers, the victims of hit and run drivers, stand in the hall, on guard at her front door. She collects badger corpses – the victims of road accidents – from the side of the road and buries them. It is, she says, 'a necessary sign of respect'. Night after night, Ms Brierton is called out by police or public to rescue an injured survivor. With other members of the group she runs what amounts to a badger ambulance service.

She possesses a special carrying case which acts as a stretcher and what she calls 'a grasper', which secures a wounded badger without risking its benefactor being bitten. A local vet tends them free of charge. In her time, Ms Brierton has acted as nurse and physiotherapist. One injured badger was about to be put down when she insisted on nursing it back to health in a neighbour's barn. It was then carefully prepared for a return to life in the wild. 'Very important to put it back near the place where it lived,' she says.

Before the watchers had set out on their expedition, Ms Brierton had spoken of badgers with such affection and admiration that the thought of not seeing one was intolerable. So we perched on the hillside with a clear determination to wait for as long as it took. It took about forty minutes. Then the first badger loped into

369

sight and began to lap up the nuts and dried fruit with the relentless efficiency of a vacuum cleaner.

The two white stripes running down its head and along its muzzle shone in the ghostly green glow of the image intensifier. And, despite its broad shoulders, it moved with an enviable elegance. It was the benign badger who defended Toad in *The Wind in the Willows* – 'a kind-hearted gentleman as everybody knows'. Remember, he is an Englishman who has given his name to a hundred hamlets and a thousand country inns.

Then a second badger sauntered out of the sett. It took no notice of the first but made its own determined way along a line of Christmas leftovers. It may be that the watchers saw a third. After the first two had vanished as quickly as they had appeared, what seemed to be another badger glowed green in the image intensifier. Perhaps it was one of the original pair, returning to finish its meal. But it is hard to tell with badgers. They come and go with a silent mystery which adds to their magic.

They live in a silent underground world of their own and appear in the world of human beings when and if it suits them. Rabbits can be seen on hundreds of English hillsides. Grey squirrels abound. Hares rise up in the long grass before they sprint away. Foxes are sighted in towns as well as country. But badgers make humans work hard to see them. On the evidence of last Saturday night it is, for some reason that is hard to explain, well worth the effort.

Daily Mail 20 February 2007

Mongrels

Do not believe that the class war is over. Whether or not it is still fought out in human society it still rages on in the battle of the breeds. The canine kingdom is a deeply divided society and the divisions will become unpleasantly apparent at the next Crufts dog show. On one afternoon during the week of proprietary dog-food promotion, the crossbreeds will make a brief appearance in the prize ring. Then the Kennel Club will get down to the business in which it really believes – choosing the thoroughbred which it can call a champion.

Canis or *Homo sapiens*, I am on the side of the proletariat. I am a mongrel man. A mongrel I was born and it is a mongrel which I want to walk beside me across the hills of home. I am biased. Mongrels are the only dogs which I have ever owned. Bessy was a Scottish hybrid which my mother used to describe as 'mainly Cairn terrier'. Dinah, we explained to the neighbours, was 'almost Labrador'. Admittedly, when I was born, my mother owned a pure-bred fox terrier – Mick, the champion rat catcher of the North Derbyshire coalfield. Shortly after my birth, he was found – elegantly balanced on my pram – looking down at me with obviously murderous intent. It is because of Mick – who could not tell a month-old baby from a rat – that I developed the pro-

371

found conviction that thoroughbreds are stupid.

Perhaps my view on pedigree intellect is prejudiced. But there is no doubt that mongrels – or crossbreeds as my dog Buster prefers to be called – are likely to be more healthy than their more exalted contemporaries. In-breeding encourages genetic defects – as the haemophiliac Russian royal family will confirm. And the RSPCA has identified half a dozen congenital defects which are the result of attempts to produce a perfect specimen. It is barbarous to breed a dog with a brain too big for its skull – just to make it look right when it is walked around the competition ring. But the idea of breeding the perfect specimen is wrong in itself. Dogs should be loved as dogs, whatever their shape and size.

Dogs were made to be friends, not exhibits, status symbols or 'positional goods' which demonstrate their owner's aesthetic sensibilities, status, income or fastidious good taste. I am for mongrels because they proclaim the glory of just being dogs – not heads set at the right angles, legs of the proper length or ears suitably pricked. Mongrels are the essence of dog – dog as a virtue in itself. Of course, if you want me to be wholly serious on the subject, I readily agree that thoroughbreds possess those qualities too. But they are expected to have something more. I believe that being a dog is – or ought to be – enough.

My mother's last dog was called Sally. She was a bitch of such sublime ugliness that we were able to argue, with absolute conviction, that giving her a home was a moral duty. Sally had long hair at the front and was almost bald at the back and the two sections of her bifurcated anatomy came together in an absolutely straight line around her middle that made her look as though Doctor Frankenstein had sewn her together from two separate parts. But we calculated that she added five years to my mother's life – something else to look after, to admire and to love for being a dog.

Sally came from a rescue – an institution whose name was, in her case, justified by the brutal treatment which she had received before she found refuge. There are dogs to be 'rescued' all over Britain. Finding them a permanent home is often very difficult. It is callous madness to breed thoroughbreds for sale when there are literally thousands of dogs of every sort waiting to be loved. And not only madness. There is a special sort of vulgarity in only wanting a dog which has a particular shape or a special colour. When my dog Buster dies, we will certainly want to fill the hole he leaves in our lives. And if the Battersea, or our local, shelter has a pure-bred that it cannot place, no doubt we will gladly take it in. But the idea of saying 'only this type of dog is good enough for us' or 'only this breed will give us pleasure' would be an insult to dogs in general and Buster in particular. There are too many unwanted dogs in the world for real dog-lovers to pick and choose.

Take my word for it, a once unwanted dog can become a joy. We took Buster because the advertisement said 'hard to home and lacks social skills with animals and people' and it was close to Christmas and we had an uncomfortable feeling that he might be required to make room for one of those dogs which are bought as

373

presents and suddenly discarded. He was almost a year old. So training began late. And, at the start, he was wild. But he responded to love – to be honest, a combination of love and bribery. When he did well – which meant doing what he was told – he was rewarded. So doing well became a habit. Admittedly, while he was young and foolish, he killed a goose. But that was just another example of his essential dogginess – an aspect which we have mercifully subdued.

The result has been fifteen years of joy. No doubt, if he had been a real bull terrier, instead of only half, I would have loved him just as much. And had he been wholly Alsatian, rather than merely part, he would have given me just as much pleasure. Though, clearly, in any other manifestations he could not possibly have been more handsome, intelligent or faithful. But, as he is, I do not have to worry that his importance is his cost and his pedigree, or has won a cup. He is a dog. I could ask for no more.

The Times 17 September 2008

Hot Metal

Although I was born and brought up just within the boundaries of Sheffield, I have always been susceptible to the Arcadian delusion that, in the words of Rudyard Kipling, 'our England is a garden'. Much of it is – if the image is intended to create the impression of careful cultivation. But much of it is wonderfully wild. And part of it – a diminishing part, it is necessary ruefully to admit – is devoted to making things. Perhaps the claims – 'workshop of the world' and 'cradle of the industrial revolution' – were always an exaggeration. But steel was first smelted in Shropshire, spinning and weaving was first mechanised in Lancashire and every development of steel making – including the processes which have German names – was pioneered in my home town. The dark satanic mills are – or at least were – part of England too.

It is not easy to accord them their properly honoured place in the English pantheon. Blake and 'Jerusalem' take much of the blame. But William Cobbett and his 'backward glance' are the main culprits. The idea that before the factories came all England lived in rural tranquillity is buried deep in our national subconscious. It is why businessmen buy houses in the country which they rarely visit and what makes their employees rent allotments which they neglect. Virtue is in the soil. My childhood and adolescence were spent suspended between town and country in a village which the spread of semi-detached occupation was just about to swamp. Indeed we were washed in on the suburban tide. I could see the moors – a street and the alms-house away – from my bedroom window and my parents looked out from theirs on a view which stretched from Beely Woods, past the Batchelor's Peas factory to the Neepsend gasworks. It did not make me a neutral in the war between town and country. I was on the side of the gorse and heather. But I realised that man cannot live by rural dreams alone.

There was a moment – I admitted it fifty years ago and the admission follows – when I was suddenly infatuated by the romance of heavy industry. I was eight and was returning from a visit to my great aunts when I saw – in the steel stock-yard outside the railway station – ingots (really called blooms and billets) of still red-hot steel glowing in the half-light. My first job brought me into closer contact with forging, pressing and stamping and for a while – at a rough calculation, a month – the emotion glimmered again. Perhaps if I had actually worked a drop-hammer instead of merely calculating how much faster it could clank up and down, the brief glimmer might have become a permanent glow. But I wore a suit, not overalls, and that made me feel I was in business not industry. But at least I once had a glimpse of the England of hot metal.

A celebration of the real England – not the chocolate box and Christmas card caricature – requires proper homage to be paid to the places where, before the Clean Air Acts, smoke and dust brought prosperity. As Doctor Johnson said about never being a soldier and never going to sea, I would feel less of myself had I not once briefly been one of its inhabitants.

The Name on the Knife Blade

On the day that I was born my grandmother wept to think that she should have a grandchild who would never see a green field. An invalid, she had travelled by closed car from Nottingham and all she really knew of Sheffield was the walk, last made thirty years before, from the Victoria Station, through the Pond Street slums to the Edwardian shops on the Moor.

The Pond Street slums were demolished in 1930 during one of the earliest and most imaginative slum-clearance programmes in English history; the Edwardian shops were flattened by a ruder hand during two December nights in 1940; even the Victoria Station will soon be swept away. But one thing about Sheffield never changes. It is still the unknown city, the name on the knife blade and no more. The real people remain hidden behind a pall of now imaginary smoke. Most of Britain knows as little about Sheffield as my grandmother did.

History is to blame. It set Sheffield at the foot of the Pennines on the millstone grit which made its grindstones and near to the water that drove them. Coal confirmed its place at the heart of nineteenth-century England, but made it an

379

industrial city where people work, not a commercial city that people visit. In consequence, Sheffield has fewer hotels than most towns half its size and hardly any of the goodwill that replete salesmen and satisfied representatives carry home from Birmingham and Manchester.

But Sheffield has hills (more than Rome) and rivers (more than Venice), and although they are no longer the tools and the power of the city's trade, they have an abiding influence on the character of the place. Sheffield is divided by them into suburbs as distinct and separate as the cutlery processes in which they each once specialised. The people of Walkley, Woodseats, Firth Park and Wadsley still talk of 'going into Sheffield' as if it were some friendly but distant place. Sheffield is less a unified city than a federation of sovereign suburbs which owe guarded allegiance to the Labour local government that has ruled from the Gothic town hall for over thirty continuous years.

It is almost as long since one of the Sheffield football clubs won either the Cup or the League. Although the city has no time for any other winter game (Rugby League is unknown, Rugby Union has a precarious toe-hold on the southern Derbyshire boundary), only grandfathers can remember the last time a local team came home to a civic reception and was carried through the cheering crowds on a beribboned bus. Supporters of United and Wednesday eye each other warily across the city lest, by some freak of chance (merit being out of the question), 'the other side' wins the Cup or League first. The rivalry between them is of the fratricidal, not the fraternal, sort. As a boy, I genuinely believed in the man who never ate bacon because its red and white stripes reminded him of United – indeed, I supported and applauded his loyalty. But although I despised Bramall Lane in the winter, in the summer it was the only place I wanted to be. When Worcestershire beat Yorkshire for the first time in the history of the County Championship, I suffered every ball that was bowled.

Bramall Lane seemed to me the only flat cricket ground in Sheffield. I played my youthful strokes on pitches cut into hillsides where, on one side of the wicket, uppish shots hit the ground a yard above the batsman's head, and on the other, fielders waited for catches, eyes on a level with the batsman's boots. Gradients like that broke fielders' hearts, but they made the reputations of several architects. Most of the virgin land available for housing after the war had been rejected twenty years earlier as too steep for practical building. Yet houses have been cut into, hung from and stuck on to the steep slopes of Gleadless, Woodside, Stannington and Netherthorp. The maisonettes and the town houses, the point blocks and the flats have extended and elaborated the city skyline and provided a thousand new vantage points from which the city can be seen spreading out from the factory roofs of the East End to the Victorian suburb of Broomhill in the west.

Men who spend their lives working with hot and sharp metal acquire special virtues. Twenty years of bending and breaking steel will convince any man that no task is beyond him, given the tools and given the time. It will convince him too that caution as a virtue is second only to courage. When, as the bloom or billet goes back from the hammer to the furnace, one of its masters spits on it with unerring aim and precision, it is not a sign of contempt for the cooling steel. It is an admission that even now it possesses hard, hot strength. It is an indication that although he will shape it in the end, if he approaches it too rashly its value and his bonus (and possibly the hand or eye of one of his mates) will be destroyed as quickly as his spittle vanishes from the hot ingot.

So Sheffield men are both cautious and cocky, and they are sceptical too. They are especially sceptical about the proposition that outside Sheffield there are places with ideas or habits or neighbours as good as theirs. Because of this, they have preserved pieces of the nineteenth century unspoilt by improvement. The Whitsuntide processions of Sunday School queens and captains that sing in the public parks, the typically Sheffield suit, broad-shouldered, narrow-waisted and bell-bottomed, the pipeclayed steps and window-sills are part of an earlier, less sophisticated age. Sheffield has kept its trams longer than any other English city. It kept them for good practical reasons and parted from them with solemn and formal regret. 'The Last Tram' drove ceremoniously to the town hall to the tune of 'Auld Lang Syne' and, in the square where the unemployed rioted in 1926, the assembled corporation bade it a last sad farewell.

Sheffield is a booming city. Although the

craftsmanship of its cutlers will soon be swamped by the new techniques of European mass production, its engineers, its rollers, its turners, its coggers, its stampers and its pressers still exert a great influence on the life of the nation. But despite its new (and doomed) enthusiasm to take its place as capital of one of Britain's new regions, despite the success of the campaign to convince the nation that within five miles of the city hall is some of the most beautiful country in Britain, Sheffield will remain a city to itself.

Three years ago, a party of Russian visitors was astounded to hear the Lord Mayor explain that within the city boundary it is possible to shoot grouse, tickle trout and sail a yacht. Most Sheffielders prefer pleasures other than these, but they believe that all that they need can be found along the banks of the Sheaf, the Porter and the Don. Oscar Wilde believed that 'when good Americans die they go to Paris'. There is no doubt where the good Sheffielders go. They go to Sheffield.

Spectator 7 May 1965

Goodbye to All That

When I was twelve I was desperate for the ownership of the steel industry to pass into different hands – mine. I was not moved by the national interest, filled by a desire to stimulate production or fired by a determination to rationalise invest-

383

ment. I just wanted to own some of those big black chimneys and deep golden furnaces.

I compiled an envious list of the great names of Sheffield steel – Osborne, Doncaster, Vickers, Tozer, Firth, Peach and Tyzack. I knew the gaunt grey houses they had built in the smoke-free south-western suburbs. I could recite lists of their overlapping directorships and recount which grandfathers had played baccarat with Edward VII at Tranby Croft.

During the annual taxi-ride which completed my summer visit to Mablethorpe or Bridlington, I travelled from the station with my nose pressed against the window, intoxicated by the billets and blooms in the stockyard below the station approach and hypnotised by the red glow that hung over the Wicker and Shaksmoor. I was in thrall to the steel-masters, to their steel and to the huge corrugated-iron sheds in which they broke and bent it.

When I am old I shall certainly pretend that at twenty-one the finger of fate beckoned me home to Sheffield, and that replete with a new and shiny BSc (Econ) I determined to become, if not a captain of my native industry, at least a corporal. But it will be an old man's fantasy. I returned to home and steel simply because I was not sure of where else to go. My boyhood love affair with cogging and stamping had been eroded by youthful cynicism and overlaid by an all-consuming passion for politics.

Throughout my finals year I had toyed with the nation's great manufacturing companies hoping – irrationally and vainly – that an academic

384

miracle would free me from industry altogether. The miracle mirage faded, the Ford Motor Company lost patience and five weeks before finals and seven before my wedding day I was still potentially unemployed. Then it happened, the 'makers of high quality steel pressings, forging, extrusions and drop stamping; established 1781' came into my life. Undeterred by the unfavourable omen of appearing for interview at the Efficiency Department on the wrong day, I gave the managing director a short lecture on mobile lifting gear (having seen an advertising film the day before) and offered my services. The lecture apparently forgotten and the confusion of dates overlooked, incredibly I was offered the job and began to re-create the relationship that steel and I had once enjoyed. Having returned from the Trojan War I found my old love still waiting, weaving her endless tapestry of crankshafts, propeller blades, car valves and steel balls.

Sometimes it was easy to relive the old emotions. At six o'clock in the morning it was the most romantic place in the world. The furnaces glowed a friendly red instead of the fearful white that they shone later in the day. The hammer drivers struck speculative blows and there was so much rolling of sleeves and flexing of muscles that it was possible to forget the holes in the roof and the oil on the floor and believe that every day brought a new technical breakthrough.

But for the rest of the day it was simply purgatory. For one thing, nobody really believed in graduates. There was a grudging acknowledgement of their existence, but an outright rejection of the notion that they could be helpful. I was a concession to modernity and no one was going to waste time or money pretending anything else. In the early Fifties some firms wasted their graduates' talents by flinging them into management innocent of any experience of the way their industry worked, believing that they had nothing more to learn. It was not so with me. I was taught nothing, not because I already knew enough, but because I was adjudged industrially ineducable.

There was the occasional period of character building, usually a painful lesson in humility. One morning an Oxford historian and I poked about in a blocked-up drain with pieces of ineffectual wire. Most of the time I stood about watching other people work. Occasionally I held a stopwatch in my hand as part of an elaborate, but ill-fated, campaign to convince the workers that piecework rates were based on a more rational calculation than a shrewd guess at how little the management could get away with.

For long periods I did virtually nothing. I arrived each morning a little late but appreciably before other employees of my grade. The day began with tea made by an ex-submarine officer who, splendid in flat cap and long brown dust coat, then went off to fulfil his duties as heir apparent to the manager of the saw shop. I then read the previous day's *Express* and awaited instructions.

Sometimes they never came. Sometimes I did simple calculations with all the complicated precision of a totally unnecessary slide rule. Sometimes I looked at stock cards and sales records, seeking to understand them in order that they might be improved. If they are better now than they were ten years ago, no credit is due to me. The secrets of only a few were vouchsafed to me. The occasional improvements that I recommended were invariably turned down. Often I just talked to the 'lads', elderly employees past hope and retirement, who shuffled about sweeping floors and making tea if there were no graduate trainees about to do it. We shared the despair that comes from inactivity. The fearful prospect of becoming a 'lad' myself seemed at times to stare me in the face.

But it was not the sheer indestructible hopelessness of it all that finished me. I could stand the refusal to employ engineers because of their tendency to agitate about new machinery, and I could survive in offices kept down to a dingy overcrowded minimum to ensure that executives were encouraged to 'get out into the works'. It was the uncongeniality that was beyond endurance. I was in daily contact with people who really did believe that art galleries hung Picassos upside down and no one knew the difference, who really did suspect that all poets are homosexual and were certain that 'politics is a dirty business'.

And then came Suez. The moralists, who usually confined their wisdom to the proposition that all decent men and women are at home by half-past ten, found a new scope for their virtuous advice. One morning as I read *Unconditional Surrender* (carefully keeping it free from the bacon grease that ran out of the sandwich I was eating) a phone call told me of a job in adult education. I lost a hundred pounds a year but gained, for almost the first time, the approval of the management. 'You have made,' they said, 'a wise choice.'

I left with no regrets and little experience but two things remain. The first is the absolute conviction that something must be done about the steel industry. The second is the imperishable feeling that, as far as I am personally concerned, the steel-masters can keep it.

Spectator 17 December 1965

Of Miners and Men

Two Saturdays ago, while discussing variations in the quality of champagne, Mr Clement Freud, MP, constructed a metaphor to illustrate why listeners to *Breakaway* should not squander hard-earned wages on vintages that their uncultivated palates would not appreciate. The image with which he illustrated his point concerned Yorkshire miners. In Mr Freud's experience, such persons 'did not dream of eating caviar instead of chip butties'. In a Yorkshire phrase with which Mr Freud may not be familiar, 'What you never have you never miss.' So, having never tasted what I discovered is 'the roe of the sturgeon, pressed and salted, and eaten as a relish' *(The Shorter Oxford English Dictionary)*, miners are content with what I know to be fried potato sandwiches (personal experience).

It so happened that a few days earlier I had been the guest at a Barnsley dinner. Of the eighty people who sat down together in the school hall, sixty were miners, ex-miners or members of miners' families. There was not a chip butty in sight. Neither, I admit at once, was there any caviar. All that was on offer was roast beef and that special courtesy that middle-aged miners always display on formal ceremonial occasions.

Gentlemen stood up at the approach of ladies in a way which I suspect would be regarded as embarrassingly antique at the Playboy Club. We all responded to the Chairman's Chapel-learned Grace in subdued unison. Nobody started their soup until everybody was served. When the dinner was over, there was formal, restrained dancing and men who had spent most of their working lives cutting and shovelling coal performed complicated steps with careful agility.

Between the dinner and the dancing there were speeches – a political speech from me and mining speeches from everybody else. We sat, literally, above the seams of what was once Wharncliffe Woodhouse Colliery. That pit is now closed, but its memory haunted our dinner. As I drove to Barnsley I had passed the great grey and green hills that were slag-heaps when the mines were working. One had been carved into a gentle concave incline that, in a different climate, would have become a ski-slope. Another had been cut into careful steps. It could not have been landscaped with greater precision if the bulldozer had been driven by an archaeologist burrowing for the lost kingdom he believed to lie buried

389

underground. As the speeches got under way, I realised that the ancient civilisation was all around.

Wharncliffe Woodhouse Colliery is part of South Yorkshire mining folklore. It is a part of the past that makes mothers warn sons not to be miners. And it is an episode in mining history that makes fathers tell their sons that they are proud to have worked down the pits. Seventy-three men died at Wharncliffe Woodhouse during a single sorrowful night in 1936. On the day after the Wharncliffe Woodhouse explosion the school in the shadow of the winding-gear was closed. It became the mortuary in which the miners' bodies rested. The pupils, one by name Roy Mason, gave thankful prayers that the visitation had come at night when only the 'skeleton shift' was underground. If it had been a daytime disaster the death toll would have been ten times as great and almost all the school would have been fatherless.

Roy Mason, now Member of Parliament for Barnsley, and in his time the occupant of half a dozen ministerial posts, began work the following year at Wharncliffe Woodhouse, the pit down which his father and grandfather had worked before him. At the Barnsley dinner he talked about those desperate, though not despairing, days – the time when the collier's week was 'three days on and three days off'.

One day's work did not pay as well as three days' dole. So, forty years before the term became fashionable, Barnsley miners were caught in a 'poverty trap'. Or at least they would have been had not Wharncliffe Woodhouse developed the mysterious tendency to 'flush' each week towards the end of the third shift. On Thursday mornings, miners would hang about their cottages ready but reluctant to set off, waiting to hear the hooter signal that the pit was flooded again. They rarely waited in vain.

Whether the week lasted for three, four or six days, Roy Mason set out each morning, carrying the same 'snap' – six slices of bread and lard and a bottle of cold water. It was his staple midday diet for years. 'If ever I got pork dripping, I felt as if Christmas had come.' The Chairman of the dinner was uncertain as to whether his Member of Parliament regarded a regular six slices as a sign of social superiority or lard as a proof of unusual deprivation. The Chairman had been down the same pit at the same time and his lunch menu had been equally reliable – four slices of bread and jam and a bottle of cold tea. He was not sure where these epicurean revelations placed the two young miners on the Barnsley social register.

They told these tales of the 1930s with a gaiety which made all the more obvious the gloom of the Depression they described. There was nothing mawkish or sentimental about their stories. After forty years they still had no doubts about the iniquity of the system under which they had laboured. But with the exception of Walter Morel I have never known a miner who wallowed in the luxury of self-pity, and I suspect that D. H. Lawrence describes the psychology of Nottingham miners as imperfectly as he re-creates the habits of Nottinghamshire gamekeepers. And even Morel is cheerful in the face of the adversity that came from his mine rather than from his marriage.

On the day that I went to Barnsley, J. P. W. Mallalieu died and his death encouraged me to read again some of the beautiful essays he wrote for the *Spectator* in the late Forties and early Fifties. One described the Durham 'Big Meet', the Miners' Gala that, in the days when coal was king, used to fill Durham city with a procession of twenty-five thousand pitmen and their families. The procession had bands and pit banners and on the day that Bill Mallalieu was there, some of those banners were 'draped with black to show that a man had died in that pit during the year'. The essay ends with a threnody for the men who died, a commentary on their character and a marvellous memory of Bill Mallalieu's style and sensitivity:

Long ago, in 1880, 164 men died entombed in a Durham pit. When at last the rescue workers found the bodies, they found, written on a roof plank, the words 'The Lord has been with us. We are ready for Heaven. Bless the Lord. We have had a jolly prayer meeting. Every man is ready for glory. It is past two o'clock Thursday. Sign Ric Co.' Miners rub shoulders with death. They know how to face death. Last Saturday I saw that they will not let death spoil life.

That was written in celebration of a much grander occasion than my little Barnsley dinner. But it was written about the same race of men, even though they lived and died in a different coalfield.

392

Two Saturdays ago, when the presenter of *Breakaway* ended the programme with a graceful little apology for Mr Freud's nonsense, I took immense satisfaction from the thought that my friends in Barnsley would be listening. Not because their culinary reputation had been restored but because these days miners too take their holidays on the Costa Brava and fly to Paris on summer afternoons. It all seemed a long way from Old Oaks and Silkstone. Miners still die. But they remain determined that death will not spoil life.

Listener 27 March 1980

The Wind Blows Cold in Consett

Consett always looked better under a thick layer of recently fallen snow A light sprinkling was hardly noticed, for it quickly took on the colour of the cold grey grime that used to smear the streets of old industrial towns. And even a thorough covering of 'uncompacted lightness' was not enough to absorb and obscure the rust-red iron dust that the Consett steelworks once spewed out into the Durham sky. Patches of coral-pink snow may be all the rage in California at Christmas. At Consett in February they look like jelly stains on a tablecloth. High on those exposed hills, where coal, iron ore and limestone once met, they really needed 'full seven inches' for 'hiding differences and making unevenness even'.

In Consett, when the snow comes flying, the 'dazzling whiteness' lasts for less than half a day. But, while the miracle endures, the town is transformed. Men hurrying to early morning Mass would barely recognise the old bus station from which they travelled home the previous night, hardly able to hold a half-empty bottle. The wind that cuts cold across the square, even on summer afternoons, picked up jagged particles of ice from the roof of the Rex cinema and spat them into the faces of the frozen worshipper who, after the fall, hurried even more urgently towards the warm redemption in St Patrick's. But the sharper sting on the cheek and the larger tear in the eye was a small price to pay for the sudden uniform serenity that lasted for most of Sunday morning. Now everything has changed.

Last weekend it was snowing so hard that the road from Witton-le-Wear was barely passable. A bright, almost alpine, Friday morning turned into a gloomy tundra afternoon and then into a cloudless arctic night. On Saturday morning the snowploughs were out, racing through Tow Law with their blades slung so low that sparks flew from beneath the slush as steel scraped on tarmacadam. Castleside was encased in a dappled cloud made up of mist spotted with giant snowflakes. As we skidded east to Consett, the world seemed to end immediately the other side of the windscreen wipers. But I knew what should be out there, a mile nearer to Newcastle, the Tyne and the sea. Straight ahead was a huge steelworks surrounded by the houses necessary for its successful operation – a company town.

Originally, the houses had been arranged in 'company rows' along streets with names so severely practical that nobody doubted their purely utilitarian purpose. The man who built Front Street and Middle Street gave little thought to the joy their residents might find, at home, in between shifts. But Consett specialises in over-coming adversity. Once upon a time it was a coal, as well as a steel, town. In those days, the banners of over two hundred miners' lodges were paraded through Durham on Gala day. This year, there will be barely twenty. Only Sacriston, where men were still mining a seventeen-inch seam, survives to represent the Annfield Plain. Consett became a one-horse town – and last year the horse was shot.

Five days ago, sliding down the moorside 'bank' that joins Castleside to Consett, the view that I wanted to enjoy was denied to me by more than the fog alone. Beyond the council houses of the Grove I should have seen a sight as starkly spectacular as the sudden vision of Baalbek. Admittedly, the blast furnaces and the water coolers cannot compare in elegance with the Corinthian columns of Heliopolis. But, on a bright day, they are etched as clearly against the skyline; and, both in sunshine and shade, their stark silhouette was once dramatised by a pyrotechnic display that the Temple of the Sun never attempted. Steam, as well as smoke, was pumped, hissing, into the air. Great gas jets spouted giant golden flames. Rivers of molten lava streamed down the side of the tips where the waste was dumped. Red-hot billets and blooms were carried across the horizon on little locomotives. Suddenly there would be an eruption of white light, as a furnace was tapped of its liquid steel.

All that ended last year. The western gates of the steelworks are chained and padlocked. Nearer the town centre, lorries pass over the weighbridge only to carry out those parts of the silent factory that have been sold to speculators and sentimentalists. The boardroom table and company clock have been auctioned. The cooling towers are to come down. The men and women who once worked there have taken their redundancy pay and clocked off for the last time. A quarter of all Consett's working population is on the dole. Three men out of every ten are unemployed. A visitor, absent since the days of the new plate mill and the promises of everlasting prosperity, arrived in the Market Square expecting to find a ghost town, as cold and bare as the Klondike after the gold ran out.

At least, last weekend, we had Alaskan snow. There was four full inches crushed on to the pavement outside the Trade Union Club in John Street. Inside, the noticeboard provided information about the ISTC 'holding branch' – the trade union organisation for steelworkers with no steel to make or fashion. For men with time on their hands, the club offered a multitude of distractions. Catweazle ('as seen on television') would wrestle Sex Symbol Maurice. There would be an appearance of the Jarrow Lads, 'a hilarious comedy group'. 'Hilarious' is a favourite Consett word. It is the local alternative to 'bizarre' and 'ridiculous'. No doubt the perceptive local audience will enjoy the bizarre irony of Jarrow bringing good cheer to Consett.

One of the young men playing pool – a game that is rapidly replacing snooker – had been unemployed since Christmas. He was not a victim of the steelworks' closure but a casualty of the cutback at the Ever Ready Company. Ever Ready came to Consett, like Ransome, Hoffmann Pollard, as part of the brave new world of regional policy. Neither batteries nor ball bearings have provided the promised redemption. Men and women, who placed so much faith in the doctrine of new industries for old, stand in the dole queues alongside the redundant miners and the dispossessed steelworkers. The pool player remained indomitably impassive. There was no question of cancelling the wedding. His future wife was in work and, if they waited for him to follow suit, they might wait for ever.

That gloomy view was certainly confirmed by the notices in the Job Centre window. There were advertisements for bar staff – always in demand in Consett. A couple of companies wanted maintenance men – always in demand everywhere. The other situations vacant cards came in the 'hilarious' category. The demands of Yarmouth were particularly prominent. The young unemployed who survived the four-inch slush of the Durham winter could look forward to competing for the jobs of sports organiser or lifeguard/swimming instructor in the east Anglian holiday resort. Across the road, the fancy goods store had begun to feel the secondary effect of the local industrial collapse. For months they had only sold 'brass stuff' – the sort of enduring family present that justified 'dipping into the redundancy money'.

It will not be long before the redundancy money runs out. The provident have done their best to make sensible preparations for the future. A canny Leadgate pork butcher offers 'bulk buys' as his deep-frozen speciality and urges his customers to buy 'whole pork legs' against the coming of the rainy days. A few of the unwanted craftsmen have pooled their savings to create little companies of their own. Everyone is slightly bewildered about the future – overcome by a tragedy which was not of their making and which they have no power to resolve.

Last Saturday's snow could not quite obscure the changes that have come over Consett. The company cottages have been either 'improved' by new bathrooms and bigger kitchens or pulled down to make way for modern council houses. The old corrugated bus shelters in the Market Square are being replaced by an architect-designed terminus. Rossi's ice-cream parlour no longer displays the timeless certainty of heavy mahogany booths and thick glass counters, but has turned into a modern coffee bar. The Rex caught on fire and has closed down. The snow stays white all day. For there is no red dust and little new industrial grime. But the winds will blow cold in Consett even when summer comes.

Listener 5 March 1981

Bands and Banners

The pitmen of Northumberland will not, I think, resent my saying that Durham is, each year, the site and scene of the greatest miners' demonstration in Britain. It is the Durham Big Meeting – the Gala with a hard and emphasised first syllable. It has passed into folklore; its brass bands playing, its lodge banners held high against the wind, the Labour leaders on the balcony of the Royal County Hotel and the fashionable visitors from London and beyond standing in the street as the parade passes them by.

But last Saturday I went to Bedlington for the annual picnic of the Northumberland miners. I hope that in the comparative south of Durham they will forgive me for confessing that, after years of wanting to see and write about their immovable feast, I am delighted that my first chance of joining Miners in the Sun was at Bedlington a week ago.

I write of Miners in the Sun for a reason wholly unconnected with the climate. For it was a bright sharp day and, as I shivered inside my summer suit, Peter Heathfield of the National Union expressed bewilderment that an old campaigner like me had come to the picnic without a raincoat. He could not know that I was reliving (and transposing from Durham to Northumberland) an essay which J. P. W. Mallalieu wrote for the *Spectator* almost thirty years ago. He chose his title because of the sun which had 'come gloriously into the sky as seventy-six bands and banners and marchers began their return through old Elvet'. I went to Bedlington last Saturday without the slightest doubt that the sun would shine down on us as well.

The picnic in Bedlington is preceded by a march to Attlee Park where the speeches are made. The march is called a procession; not because miners are contemptuous of things military, as countless volunteer battalions of light infantry and fusiliers have proved in two world wars. It is a procession because, after its martial beginning in the village square outside the office of the Wansbeck district council, it turns into a sort of gentle Roman triumph.

The afternoon's spectators – together with the council chairman and the officers of the union – lead the way down the long winding hill to the picnic ground. There is no attempt to keep time or pace with the band which blows at their heels. And as they saunter their way into the afternoon, the people of Bedlington village come out into their carefully cultivated front gardens, lean on their freshly painted gates, and wave.

They do not wave like an audience applauding entertainers or as if they were the led acknowledging their leaders. They give the nice-to-see-you-wish-you-had-time-to-come-in-for-a-cup-of-tea waves of one friend to another. Old ladies wave from behind the not quite drawn curtains of old people's homes. Children are taught how to wave by their parents. Men outside the public houses put down their pints of Federation bitter, either to wave more effectively or to ensure that not a drop is spilt. And the marchers in the ragged column that calls itself a procession wave back. Even those who have never been to Bedlington before feel at home.

The band that led this year's procession came from Ashington Colliery. But at the picnic ground it was the musicians from Ellington who took pride of place. We all stood as they played what must have been a lament – not one of the tunes of glory that are half of the brass bands' repertoire but something that sounded as if it had been written in sadness or mourning.

It is, for me at least, impossible to hear such music without needing to blow my nose and remove particles of dust that have flown into my eye. I suppose that I am weeping for the past, the days when there were dozens of collieries in Northumberland, all of them with banners and bands and all of them with hope for the future.

These days there are only three thousand miners in Northumberland, barely a tenth of what there were a couple of decades ago. Some of the old banners have been preserved – laid up like regimental colours in a county cathedral. But the bands are in decline. The quality is as high as it always was. And the uniforms remain in-corrigibly Ruritanian. The problem is with the prizes, the W. Dunsmore Challenge Cup, the Dick Hoskins Memorial Trophy and the Wall Clock presented by Hirst Progressive Social Club. The ratio of prizes to bands is five to one.

But another north-eastern musical phenomenon flourishes in Northumberland. It is called the jazz band. The jazz bands of Bedlington which marched to the picnic ground while the chairman of Wansbeck and his guests were still at lunch are not the six-man combinations of trumpet, drums, clarinet, double-bass, banjo and trombones we associate with New Orleans and upstairs rooms in 1950s public houses. They are monstrous regiments of little girls in mauve and silver, purple and gold, scarlet and black uniforms which are even more Ruritanian than the tunics worn by their fathers and brothers behind the cornets and French horns. All of them wear immense shakos, towering bearskins with gleaming patent leather peaks and lurex cockades.

Each miniskirted battalion is led by a pair of majorettes – one a teenager who twirls her baton and flings it spinning through the air with an amazingly self-confident dexterity, the other a tot of three or four who can barely carry her wand of office. The jazz bands play a sophisticated version of the comb and paper. But there is one aspect of their existence for which they must be forgiven everything. They are marshalled by proud fathers who strike out alongside them like drill sergeants. At first, the spectator feels that the men should have no place in the essentially girlish ritual. Then comes the understanding: they look after each other in Northumberland.

Thirty years ago in Durham, J. P. W. Mallalieu was struck by the joy of life which was expressed by communities which from time to time faced disaster and brutal death. At Bedlington last week, none of the banners was draped in black

402

and the pleasure of the picnic was unremarkably enjoyed. It was a different characteristic which showed through the cold afternoon. Miners are a family – these days a dwindling family, but a family nevertheless.

Guardian 28 June 1986

Bellmen Still Going Like the Clappers

The Whitechapel Road in London, at the end of the Romans' long march from the sea to the capital. Now it is a conglomeration of fast-food cafés, cut-price tailors and television rental shops. But, on the opposite corner of Fieldgate Street from the East London Mosque, one building stands out as a survivor from Old England. It is the Whitechapel Bell Foundry. The company started making bells in 1582, and it has been making them ever since. Inside the front door, a little exhibition of the bellmaker's craft is snugly at home in what can only be called Dickensian surroundings. The centrepiece of the display is Big Ben – cast by the company in 1858 and hung in the tower of the Houses of Parliament which has expropriated its name. Big Ben weighs 13 tons, 10 cwt, 3 qt, 15 lb – almost twice as much as the Liberty Bell which rang out freedom over the North American colonies. The Liberty Bell was also cast in Whitechapel.

There are bells everywhere in No. 32 Whitechapel Road – big bells and small bells, old bells and new bells, bells to be rung by hand and bells which strike the hours on clocks, tower bells which peal from church steeples and turret bells which toll above gatehouses to warn of approaching dignitaries and advancing enemies, bells about to be delivered to customers, and bells waiting to be recast.

Recasting is really breaking up old bells and melting down the old bell metal (23 per cent tin and 77 per cent copper) to start all over again. In the Whitechapel yard, the ancient bells of St Martin on Ludgate Hill, a City of London church, lie waiting for the parish council to decide their fate. Should they be abandoned or recast to ring again? Fortunately, for both the Whitechapel Bell Company and the glory of the English Sunday morning, brand-new bells are constantly cast in the foundry.

The casting – hot metal poured into loam-filled moulds – is only the beginning of the process. Bells have to be tuned. Five strategic cuts are made in the metal by a craftsman with a perfect ear for the vibrating note. 'There is,' said Nigel Taylor – the tower bell section leader – 'no college for bell-tuning.' But times are changing. These days his sophisticated eardrum is some-times assisted by an 'electronic read-out'. Nigel Taylor – twenty-nine years in the Whitechapel Bell Foundry – rang bells before he made them. And he rings them still, every Sunday morning. So does Peter Trick, the Whitechapel engineer and blacksmith. His parents were Sunday School teachers. The only way to avoid sitting in their class was learning how to ring the changes. Katharine – wife of Allen Hughes, the fourth generation of master bell-makers in Whitechapel Road – came into the firm and foundry by a similar route. While she was a student at the Guildhall School of Music, she took a holiday job in the foundry because she was a hand-bell ringer. Making bells is a vocation, not a job.

There is a bell in Westland Ashby which was cast in 1582, and it has rung out, loud and clear, every day since then. But that is something of an exception. But Whitechapel does far more than ring out the old and replace them with new. More bells ring out every day – many of them bought by customers who walk into the foundry and specify their needs and wants. A one-ton tower bell with a 4 ft diameter at the lip can be made and installed for £25,000. When they offer to make and install, the Hugheses really mean it. They cast two or three sets of tower bells every three weeks – always on Friday to give the metal time to cool. Whitechapel wheelwrights construct the wheels on which the bells turn and White-chapel engineers put together the frames from which they swing. A frame for Hursley in Hampshire stands assembled in the workshop. It is about to be taken apart so that it can be carried up the church steeple to the bell chamber, where it is put together again.

The big bells – bells that ring out rejoicing or doom – are what made the Whitechapel Foundry famous. But the Hugheses do not underestimate the delight of small bells made to ring by hand or cry out the time from clocks. Stephen McEwan, head of the department which produces the delicate end of the trade, was polishing a bell no bigger than a snail's shell. He moved to bells from bagpipes in Glasgow and has, somehow, caught the enthusiasm that goes with peals and chimes.

Bells are an indispensable part of English history. They rang to celebrate victory in two world wars, and they would have rung to warn of invasion by Napoleon and Hitler had either tyrant dared to land upon our shores. They now toll for our dead, ring out for weddings and call us to worship. There is not a poet in the English language who has not written in praise of bells. Most of the objects of their reverence were made in Whitechapel.

Daily Mail 23 May 2006

Remember the Children Killed for King Coal

Nabs Wood in the West Riding of Yorkshire. Even on a cold and windy morning near the turn of the year, the birds sing and a little stream – which runs through the valley by the side of the road – gurgles merrily.

The scene has not always been so peaceful. On the far bank of the stream, at the end of the plank bridge, a strange memorial has been built into the rising ground. Two small stone figures seem to be crawling out of dark and narrow tunnels. A plaque, attached to the rough stone wall between the statues, explains who they are and why they are there. In 1838, twenty-six children died in the coal mine beneath that spot.

A notice on the wall of the Red Lion in Silkstone – the public house in which the inquest was held – fills in the details of the disaster. Torrential rain prevented the children from leaving the pit by the main mineshaft. So they attempted to escape by the 'drift' that ran into Nabs Wood. But the stream that normally gurgled so merrily was in flood. They were all drowned.

The disaster at the Huskar coal mine was not the last or even the greatest of the tragedies to strike the area. Fifty years later, 361 men died in the great fire at the Oaks Colliery near Barnsley. Some were killed immediately by an explosion. Others – there being no hospital within twenty miles – were carried home to die slowly of their burns. The day after the fireball struck, the rescue bell rang – suggesting that someone was still alive at the coal face. A party of volunteers was lowered down the shaft to see if there was anyone left to save. A second explosion killed them all.

The story of coal – an essential part of England's history – is punctuated with accounts of heroism in the face of tragedy. But some disasters occupy a special place in local memories. And the twenty-six children, all dead in half an hour, are still mourned in the villages they called home.

Joseph Hewlings, serving in the chemist's shop at Silkstone, gave me directions to Nabs Wood and Peter Garbutt, one of his customers,

407

accompanied me to make sure I did not lose my way. As I looked for the footpath across the stream, Elsie Wragg, who was walking past, asked if I had 'come to see the children' – her pat description of the monument.

The oldest killed was seventeen and the youngest seven. The boys were employed to push coal tubs between the pit face to the bottom of the shaft. The girls were mostly 'trappers', who pulled the strings which opened and shut the ventilation blinds and pumped the bellows that kept the fetid air moving. They were the sons and daughters of miners and worked in the pit knowing that, if they were not struck down by some calamity, they would (like their fathers) die of one of the various diseases which they called 'the dust'. Their lives were short, nasty and brutish. The risks they took and the fate they met was accepted as the natural order of things and the will of Providence.

A monument erected in Silkstone churchyard as a communal gravestone makes that clear. It describes its purpose as 'perpetrating the remembrance of an Awful visitation of the Almighty' and leaves no doubt that the 'Act of God' was accepted with humble resignation. 'On that eventful day, the Lord set forth His Thunder, Lightning, Hail and Rain, carrying devastation before them by a sudden irruption of water into the Coal pit of C. P. Clark Esq.' It goes on to say 'the 26 human beings whose names are recorded here were suddenly summon'd to appear before their Maker'.

The reluctance to describe them as killed was not the result of misplaced sensitivity. The men who erected the monument wanted the message to be a promise of redemption and resurrection. 'Reader remember. Every neglected call of God will appear against thee on the day of judgment.' The inscription ends with an injunction from the Gospel according to St Matthew: 'Therefore, be ye also ready.'

It is unlikely that many of the victims of the flash flood had accepted that advice by the time of their death. George Birkenshaw was ten, his brother seven. Propriety and male superiority had to be respected even in death. So the memorial explains: 'The mortal remains of the females are deposited in graves at the foot of the males' graves.' Among them is Elizabeth Clarkson, aged eleven. She lies at the feet of her brother James, aged sixteen.

Outside the Red Lion, Malcolm Moore, a retired factory inspector, added his own epitaph. The Huskar Pit disaster was, he said, one of the tragedies that brought about the Factory Acts. But, he added: 'It is important to remember, there are still accidents – particularly in coal mines.'

In Silkstone and the surrounding villages they haven't forgotten the twenty-six children who died in the Huskar Pit. On the cold and windy morning I visited, two wreaths of flowers lay in front of the memorial in Nabs Wood.

Daily Mail 30 January 2007

The Colossus of Roads

The gorge through which the Bristol Avon runs to the sea. For most of its length, trees cling to the cliffs which tower above the river. But there are places at which the naked stone reveals the almost vertical sides of the deep ravine. Travellers without a head for heights should tread warily. But not even the most severe attack of vertigo could spoil a trip to the place where one of the wonders of Victorian England joins together what, in some primeval time, nature ripped apart. The Clifton Suspension Bridge leads from Bristol to nothing in particular. But it is both a miracle of English engineering and a conscious tribute to an English engineer of genius. It is an example of the spirit, as well as the talent, that made the country great. And it is beautiful.

Mike Rowland, an ex-police inspector who reveals the mysteries of the bridge to trippers, tourists and school parties, says that the first reaction to the sight of the roadway, suspended in space on its mighty chains, is always 'Wow!' David Moth and his wife Margaret – on holiday from Portsmouth – proved him right. At first they were lost for words. Then David said, 'Breathtaking' and Margaret added, 'And to think that it was built all those years ago.' There was a pause before, in almost unison, they both said 'Elegant' – a remarkable way to describe fifteen hundred tons of steel and wood hanging in mid-air. Yet elegant is exactly the right word. Clifton Suspension Bridge is elegant in concept, elegant in design and elegant in construction.

It owes its construction to a whim. In 1744 William Vick, a Bristol wine merchant, left £1000 in his will to be invested until it grew into a sum sufficient to finance a crossing of the Avon at a point which joined a wood, on the Somerset side, to fields on the outskirts of the city. It was over eighty years before either the investment or interest had grown large enough for the work to begin. Then, in 1829, Thomas Telford – 'The Colossus of Roads' – was asked to judge a competition for a bridge which was high enough above the gorge to permit the passage of tall-masted sailing ships. He rejected all the entries as unsuitable and said that he would do the job himself. Only the City Fathers liked his design. After a public outcry, the commission was given to a virtually unknown engineer, whose principal qualification seemed to be that his father had helped to complete a tunnel under the Thames. His name was Isambard Kingdom Brunel.

His design had the virtue of simplicity. The bridge was to be hung across the river from chains which, after passing through the top of giant towers, were secured on the rock on either side of the gorge. The towers were said to be in the fashionable 'Egyptian Style', which meant that they had roughly the shape of a doorway from the passageway inside a pyramid into a pharaoh's tomb. Visitors require convincing that 'chain' is the right word to describe the great arcs

411

of iron which curve down from the sky and are attached to the 'flying road' by iron rods. Each link is a twenty-five-foot-long steel ingot.

Perhaps it was the size of the enterprise, as well as the daring design, which made the Bristol Council lose its nerve. Whatever the reason, for a quarter of a century the work was left half finished and the towers stood, at each side of the gorge, without the bridge between them. 'They must have looked like two memorials to something,' said Grace Winthrop, a student from Liverpool. In fact it was as a memorial that the bridge was completed. When Brunel died, engineers who had been inspired by his genius raised the money to finish the first example of his unique talent. His Hungerford Bridge was about to be replaced by a rigid structure over which the railway could run. So the chains were brought halfway across England and hung across the Clifton Gorge.

The result is a bridge which has become more than an easy crossing from Bristol to Somerset. It is an icon which excites all sorts of passions. According to Mike Rowland, courting couples visit it late at night to achieve a status which he discreetly describes as 'similar to joining the mile-high club'. It has a deadly attraction for suicides. And because it is such a spectacular landmark etched against the sky, protesters of every sort risk their lives by perching precariously outside the guardrail that runs along its length or climbing the huge towers from which it hangs. Clinging to such a landmark, they are bound to be noticed. It became such a favourite with

412

bungee-jumpers that now – no matter how deserving the charity or how experienced the jumper – they are never allowed. But the emotion which it arouses most often is awe and wonder.

John and Grace Millward – exiles from Bristol who live in London – had brought Sean, their eleven-year-old son, to see the bridge for the first time. They paused at the old tollbooths on the city side of the gorge. And, looking at the cars driving through space across the Avon, Sean said 'Wow!'

Daily Mail 28 August 2007

Where It All Began

As they came round the bend in the river, the canoes became gradually more visible as they emerged through the unseasonable haze of mist and rain. The boys at the front of the flotilla struggled to keep on course and the men at the back paddled backwards and forwards to make sure that no stragglers were left behind. Both the sheep and the shepherds were concentrating so hard on mastering the currents that they seemed not even to notice that their journey took them under the arch of what was – and, in its way, still is – one of the wonders of the modern world. The River Severn flows to the sea beneath the Iron Bridge at Coalbrookdale.

In eighteenth-century England, bridges were built across the Severn from Clifton, near the sea,

413

to the river's source beyond the blue remembered hills of Shropshire. But the bridge across the deep gorge that divided Madeley Wood from Broseley was different from the others. It was the first iron bridge in the world. Its ribs, rails and arches were cast in the nearby works of Abraham Darby III, the grandson of the man who, by smelting ore with coke instead of charcoal, had found a way of making iron in bulk. His discovery marked man's leap forward into the age of machinery and mass production. The industrial revolution began in Coalbrookdale. And the bridge is everlasting proof that it was 'Made in England'.

Of course, the men who paid for the bridge wanted nothing more than another shortcut on the long and winding road from England to Wales and a toll house that would collect the crossing fee – two shillings from every carriage drawn by six horses and a half-penny from every man, woman, child, calf, pig, sheep or lamb. The bridge builders would have been perfectly happy with stone and wood. But Thomas Farnolls Pritchard, a Shrewsbury architect, had dreamed for years of designing a bridge of iron and Darby grasped the opportunity to prove what iron could do. The notice on the north bank is clear. The bridge is a 'sampler' – bait to catch engineers from all over the world. And the visitors are still coming to Coalbrookdale. Oscar Dempsey – a builder from Chicago – was in Coalbrookdale 'to see the bridge I learned about in college'. His next stop was the remains of the foundries in which the bridge was made and the blast furnaces that smelted the iron.

It took 378 tons of cast iron to make the bridge. And a Shropshire blast furnace could produce no more than twenty-five tons a week. But Darby had seven blast furnaces blazing before the plans for a new river crossing were approved by parliament and while the money was being raised to make the dream a reality, he built two more. They became part of a unique industrial community which thrived between the trees. Two great pottery factories – built where the Severn and Shropshire Canal met – made Coalport China famous. Bricks, tiles and clay drainage pipes were baked in Coalbrookdale kilns. Houses were built on the hillside for the men who made the valley famous – cottages for the workers, now mostly pulled down, on the edge of the river and grand villas for the masters high above the smoke and dust. The masters' houses still cling to the gorge's southern slope – each one a gravity-defying miracle.

The sale of Coalbrookdale iron was promoted in the style of many more recent advertising campaigns. The pictures showed only the best of the product. The painting of the bridge which Darby commissioned had, as its background, an industrial landscape of furnaces and forges. But only one plume of smoke drifts up into the clear blue sky. The iron bridge was meant to be beautiful. Thomas Farnolls Pritchard – who died before his work was finished – designed it so that, when it was reflected in the Severn, reality and image came together to make a perfect circle. Lucy Ashworth from Cambridge, staring into the dark water, bitterly disappointed that the sun was not bright enough to perform the trick, complained that, 'These days no businessman bothers about the countryside.' She was thinking of the five cooling towers of Ironbridge Power Station which dominate the skyline on the road to the west.

In fact the cooling towers are just another chapter in the Coalbrookdale story. Abraham Darby did not care a jot for the damage that his iron works did to the Shropshire hills. He exploited the beauty of Pritchard's iron bridge as a way of selling his product. In his day, according to a London visitor, 'Coalbrookdale wants nothing but Cerberus to give you an idea of the heathen hell.' And some of the workers found that an apt description of lives that counted for very little. One newspaper account of a woman's hideous death – caught in the wheels of the machine that she was working – described her injuries but did not bother to mention her name. Time and decay have mellowed Coalbrookdale. But visitors should remember that, when it belched fire and smoke, it ignited the explosion of enterprise which made England great. Everything we made in iron and steel – from nails to battleships – owed its existence to Coalbrookdale.

Daily Mail 5 August 2008

Envoy

Yorkshire – and Proud of It

It really is about time that we Yorkshiremen came out of the closet. I know that such an ambiguous assertion will cause disquiet in Hull, distress in Huddersfield and dismay in Halifax. So, before despair spreads right across the three Ridings, let me make clear that I intend no insult to the venerable and venerated traditions of the Champion County. Not for a second do I suggest that we should abandon the time-honoured habit of disappearing down the yard with the Sunday paper only to reappear when the public houses open. I speak not in the admirably literal patois of my homeland, but in the metaphorical jargon of the United States. My plea is for Yorkshiremen to stop being embarrassed about coming from Yorkshire. No longer should we feel inferior to men from Rutland, stand self-effacingly aside for sons of the Soke of Peterborough, speak more softly in the presence of islanders from Wight or lapse into total tongue-tied silence at the sound of an Essex accent. We ought to be ourselves; openly loyal to the white rose, brazenly the children of the broad acres, triumphantly tyke.

The victims of continuous social persecution react in different ways against their tormentors. Sometimes they pretend not to be part of the oppressed minority at all and assume the habits of the tyrannical majority in the hope that their apostasy will lead to half-hearted acceptance. To our eternal credit, Yorkshiremen rarely attempt to curry Southern favour by pretending to be cynical, effete, calculating, mercenary, decadent and craven. There may be a man who was born in Doncaster or Rotherham who pretends to be the product of Surbiton or Slough, but I – thank God – have never met him. Rather is the reverse the case. One man of particular distinction (whose name I only keep secret because he is the Deputy Leader of the Labour Party) is generally thought to be qualified (at least by birth) to open the batting with Geoffrey Boycott. Yet he was born in Kidbrooke, Kent. No blame attaches to him for either his original location or his subsequent mis-identification. He is a son of Yorkshire as Lloyd George was a son of Wales. The Welsh Wizard, schoolboy humorists will recall, was born in Manchester but first saw the light of day in Llanystumdwy some months later. The significance of the more recent radical's adoption of the West Riding lies in the fact that it is impossible to imagine a man born in Keighley allowing anyone to think that he came from Kidbrooke.

My mother (Yorkshire, alas, only by recent adoption fifty years ago) told in my presence the story of a nineteenth-century French ambassador to the Court of St James who, on arrival in London, was given a single piece of advice by his departing predecessor. 'Never ask a man if he comes from Yorkshire. If he does, he will tell you without being asked. If he does not, why humiliate him?' I suspect that my mother invented the anecdote. But whether it was just another Hattersley aphorism or Sydney Smith at his very best, the story illustrates the other way in which oppressed people defend themselves. They hide behind a caricature of the characteristics that the oppressors victimise. They exaggerate the attributes that the intolerant excoriate. In the lounge bar of a Kingston bypass roadhouse, an exiled Yorkshireman thinks that he must act as if he were a combination of Michael Parkinson, Brian Clough and J. B. Priestley – with his whippet tied up outside the door and the marks of the muffler still on his neck.

'A Yorkshireman in the South,' wrote George Orwell, 'will always take care to let you know that he regards you as an inferior... The Northerner has grit, he is grim, dour, plucky, warm-hearted and democratic. The Southerner is snobbish, effeminate and lazy.' Quite so. But we go on about it at such length out of a sense of insecurity. We play the part that life expects of us. Sometimes the result is intentionally and hilariously funny. Sometimes it is not. The great city of my birth has recently produced a little booklet that beautifully demonstrates how attempts to be more typical of Yorkshire than George Hudson and Harvey Smith can flop as badly as a lieder recital at a working men's club. It contains arch little sentences like: 'A Sheffielder, as the natives are known [sic], does not readily understand that visitors have not received the education that he has.' *Sheffieldish, A Beginner's Phrasebook* is the worst thing to come out of Sheffield since Charlie Peace.

Certainly, *Sheffieldish* touches on the central characteristic of the Yorkshire personality –

421

'being very proud ... he easily feels snubbed'. But, on most of its pages, it does not even do well the limited job which it has set itself. It translates 'naden' as if it was a literal corruption of 'now then' rather than an injunction with threatening overtones. It does not include amongst its phonetically expressed examples of our exclusive dialect the most famous of all Sheffield questions and answers: 'Who wa' shi wee?' and 'Shi wa' bi her sen.' Both the inquiry and the response are clear enough to me. But cockneys, overhearing that snatch of conversation on the top deck of a Walkley-bound tramcar, have been known to take it for Mandarin Chinese. If *Sheffieldish* is really to provide help to the millions of fun-loving tourists who flood into the city each spring, its commission is a grievous fault hardly excused by the explanation that, in the city of steel, 'how' is pronounced 'ow'. Worse still are the inadequate definitions of 'mardy' and 'nesh' that appear in its pages. For that there is no excuse. Every aspect of both words is explored in *Goodbye to Yorkshire*, that standard work on the county's life and literature that Gollancz published a few years ago. Unfortunately, the author's name escapes me for the moment.

But the failures of scholarship are not *Sheffieldish*'s most grievous fault. The worst thing about it is the coy way in which it perpetuates the worst aspects of the Cult of the North. The whole exercise is, of course, highly ironic, but the wink and the nudge are so obvious and the tongue bulges so visibly in the cheek that the little book creates in Northern breasts the emotion that

Northerners enjoy the least – embarrassment. The crime is compounded by proof that the way we speak in Sheffield can be described in a fashion that provides both amusement and enlightenment. *Sheffield Dialect* by Abel Bywater was published in 1877. It begins with an introduction Cobbett might have written for *Verbal Rides:* 'Having obtained a tolerable knowledge of the various dialects of the counties of Stafford, Lancaster and Derby, I determined to finish my excursion by taking a tour through Yorkshire.' It then records, with the help of a carefully constructed glossary, a series of conversations between famous local figures of the time, ranging from Freethinker to Luke the Barber, about well-known issues of the moment, such as 'tooth-drawing by steam' and the 'process of making a penknife'. Of course, coming from Sheffield, it has a didactic intention. Its real object is to improve and uplift.

Mr Bywater ends his little Pennine Primer with a series of 'Scraps' which contain a perfect Sheffield answer to 'a challenge to fight a duel':

O've two objections to this duel affair, one is, o'm afread o shud hurt yo, an t'tuther is, o'm afread yo shoud hurt me. O dooan't see wot good it ad do me to put a bullet throo yore bodda, for o cudn't boil it as o cud a rabbit or a turkey, an o'm not a cannobal, o cahnt heit it. Then wot's youse a shottin a thing at o can make no yuse on. Nah, if yo wantn to try yer pistols, shooit at a tree abaht mo soize, and if yo hitn it send me word, and then o'll say at if o'd been there yo'd happen a hitn me.

Since duels were not common in Sheffield during the late years of the nineteenth century, we must assume that the 'curious answer' was a parable concerning common sense and discretion. Those are the qualities for which South Yorkshire is rightly famous. And, what is more, they are portrayed in Mr Bywater's little lexicon in a way which would have caused no embarrassment to the advertisers who supported him – R.W. Brookes, Purveyor of Wedding Breakfasts, Reverend Alfred Gatty, DD, author of *Sheffield Past and Present*, and Widdison's Patent Medicine Warehouse. Reticence is also a Yorkshire virtue – the authors and publishers of *Sheffieldish, A Beginner's Phrasebook* please note.

Listener 16 April 1981

COPYRIGHT

Articles

Goodbye to All That: copyright © Roy Hattersley
1965

The Name on the Knife Blade: copyright © Roy
Hattersley 1965

Ministering Angles: copyright © Roy Hattersley
1971

Blackheath: copyright © Roy Hattersley 1979

Carnival in Sparkbrook: copyright © Roy
Hattersley 1979

Make Cowards of Us All: copyright © Roy
Hattersley 1979

Never Walk Alone: copyright © Roy Hattersley
1979

Turbans, Bangles and Beards: copyright © Roy
Hattersley 1979

Afternoon at Home: copyright © Roy Hattersley
1980

'Fetch the shoebox, fetch the shovel': copyright
© Roy Hattersley 1980

Me and My Dogs: copyright © Roy Hattersley
1980

Of Miners and Men: copyright © Roy Hattersley
1980

Official Rose: copyright © Roy Hattersley 1980

Skegness in Winter: copyright © Roy Hattersley
1980

Books

The publishers hope that this book has given you enjoyable reading. Large Print Books are especially designed to be as easy to see and hold as possible. If you wish a complete list of our books please ask at your local library or write directly to:

Magna Large Print Books
Magna House, Long Preston,
Skipton, North Yorkshire.
BD23 4ND

This Large Print Book for the partially sighted, who cannot read normal print, is published under the auspices of

THE ULVERSCROFT FOUNDATION